PRAISE FOR *FIRST, BRUSH YOUR T*

Lisa Espinoza has crafted a poignant and heartfelt homage. *First, Brush Your Teeth* is brilliantly written and sure to make you embrace life to its fullest.

~Martin Dugard
#1 New York Times best-selling author of
Taking Paris

In person and on the page, Lisa Espinoza's words are authentic, selfless, and unafraid. I have read many grief books since my son died, and I was often left feeling robbed, as if they had neatly tied a bow onto something that was without shape. *First, Brush Your Teeth* is a brave approach to grief and an invitation to anyone who has looked in the mirror and seen the face of suffering. To open these pages is to begin an incredible journey with Lisa. She does not hold back, not in her experience, the reality of the loss, or the wrestling with her faith. Lisa's words will lead you into the raw, along the rises of respite, through the darkness, inside the comical, beyond the unbearable, into an incredible space where hope and heartache live and thrive. This memoir in real time will resonate with you, challenge you, encourage you, and empower you.

Lisa, you have honored Chandler beautifully. On behalf of all of us at "the round table of grief," we thank you for your courage and honesty. You have laid down a pathway for each of us to grieve, process, remember, and celebrate.

~Monica Kalua Cline, Jojo's mom
CEO & Founder
Live Like JoJo Foundation

Mixing heartache, humor, and gratitude, Espinoza grants us an authentic view of life in the midst of shattering grief. She shares, with vulnerability and transparency, her painful path of learning how to inhabit the newly stinging reality of each day. Both practical and profound, *First, Brush Your Teeth* provides comfort, companionship, and hope to those staggering through the aftermath of loss. This book is a beautifully moving labor of love.

~Karen J. Hummel, PhD
Professor of Psychology
Vanguard University

A miracle from the inside—this is what Lisa details in *First, Brush Your Teeth*. We are invited into the sacred space of Lisa's soul—through her sharing of hope, sadness, anger, confusion, humor, victories, memories, support of friends and family, and deep, thoughtful reflections on life. It is a story that includes an abundance of paradox—loss with gain, hope with depression, peace with chaos, sadness with joy, memories with emptiness and aloneness with companionship. Lisa's vulnerable real-time process of loss while still having life is a model of healthy grieving—a miracle at work with all of its messiness and always with a sense of God's presence.

This courageous sharing becomes an opportunity for us to heal our own gaps and wounds of our souls. These gaps and wounds are not limited to loss of loved ones but can come from addictions, abuse, losses, relationship issues, depression and all traumas. If you are willing to read and share in this emotional and challenging journey, you just may find your messy miracle of healing along the way.

~Rev. Randy Powell, MS, MFT
Executive Director and Founder
Journeys Counseling Ministry

Grief can take your breath away, at times leaving you with unbearable sorrow. In *First, Brush Your Teeth*, Lisa walks us through this sorrow with raw honesty and gives us insight into a mother's unconditional love for her precious son. This book helps us navigate the grief process, giving us permission to be vulnerable, to accept our varying levels of grief from day to day, and to embrace the reality that the grief process is unique for everyone.

~Tracy Lewis, Phillip's mom
CEO & Founder
PADLS Pals

What a beautiful heart Lisa Espinoza displays in this searingly intimate portrait of a grief observed! Sharing her diary from the year following the bicycle accident that extinguished the life of her son Chandler, she embraces the reader as a trusted companion on a spiritual and emotional journey of profound loss, the struggle for acceptance, and the triumph of God's love made real in the tangible intimacies of family and many (some unexpected) friends. In the process, she discovers an impossibly deep well of gratitude and joy in the enduring love between a mother and son.

~Rev. Stephen Bauman, PhD
Senior Minister
Christ Church New York City

The loss of one's beautiful child is unthinkable. The journey through "what-if" and "why" and "what the hell?" is strewn with hope, agony, dreams, love, and deep pain. And in the case of Lisa Espinoza, who lost her beloved son Chandler, the road to healing is paved with an honest, deep, abiding faith, grounded in the truth that somehow, God comes through for us.

For people who have loved and lost a child, for anyone who has experienced deep grief at the death of a beloved, *First, Brush Your Teeth* may just be the book that will sustain you as you grieve. Lisa's honest, day-in, day-out reflections during her time of profound loss and healing speak to the realities of the roller coaster ride that is the grieving process. Her honesty in sharing the goodness of community that came alongside her and her family, as well as the raw and very real pain of those fist-shaking moments at God, may help readers who wonder if life, laughter, faith, love, and hope are possible after so great a loss.

~Karen Maurer, MDiv
Assoc. Vicar
St. John's Episcopal Church

I had the wonderful experience of completing a journey with Chandler Espinoza in "Mother India" as he called it. India finds what you need when you need it. Chandler was amazing in his ability to give back to Mother India through his compassion and spirit. Lisa has captured his wonderful life and passion and woven it into words that will help heal those with hearts that need mending.

Chandler took India by storm from treks in the foothills of the Himalayas, to camel safaris in the deserts, to the ocean of Goa, to observing teachings by the Dalai Lama, and I was fortunate enough to be part of the adventure! It is this spirit, compassion, and essence that shines through in Lisa's rendering of Chandler's legacy. With *First, Brush Your Teeth*, Lisa delivers a message of love, healing, and hope. A must-read!

~Bob Ney
Former Member of Congress
Political Analyst for Talk Radio
Friend of Chandler Espinoza

First, Brush Your Teeth

FIRST, BRUSH YOUR TEETH

Grief and Hope in Real Time

LISA ESPINOZA

WordCrafts Press

First, Brush Your Teeth
Copyright © 2022
Lisa Espinoza

ISBN: 978-1-952474-76-7

Cover design by David Warren.

Published by WordCrafts Press
Cody, Wyoming 82414
www.wordcrafts.net

Until we're able to be crucified and forgive the people while they scourge us, I don't think any of us truly understand unconditional love.

~Chandler Espinoza
The India Diaries

Posted on Instagram

One of the most vivid memories I will ever have is of Mom holding my tiny hand while I sat shotgun for the first time. It was during the last couple years I was still at home with her and not off to kindergarten. Dad was working and the brothers were at school. In those days, every step I took—every breath I took was by her side. Part of me is still stuck in that 5-year-old body whose eyes could barely see over the dashboard. Before I knew what it meant to consummate a marriage, I truly believed I would grow up to marry my mom. Almost every single day I told her I would. I'm pretty sure I even proposed to her with a few Ring Pops on occasion. You know that song "I Like It, I Love It" by Tim McGraw? Anytime that song came on, Mom would change the lyrics: *I don't know what it is about my Chan Man's lovin'/but I like it/I love it/I want some more of it.* When everyone has come and gone, she will still be there to make me feel like I'm the best guy on the planet.
#HappyMothersDay
#NoYouCannotDateMyMom
~May 10, 2015, by Chandler Espinoza

How We Got Here

My son Chandler wanted to be a writer. I never imagined we would be writing a book together. Not like this.

After Chandler's accident on December 15, 2018, at the urging of a friend, I started writing a blog to keep folks updated on Chandler's condition. I quickly realized that my regular updates had become a way for me to process the events and emotions of each day.

After Chandler passed...now, see...it's been two years as I write this, and my fingers still hesitate over the keys before typing the word. After Chandler passed on January 1, 2019, I knew I had to keep writing. I had to write for Chandler, as a way to honor his life and his desire to be a writer. I had to write for myself, as a tangible means of continuing to process the loss of my son. And I had to write for others on this same path of grief who were telling me my words were helping them through their own journeys of loss.

I determined to write a blog post every single day for a year, my first year without Chandler. I don't do anything consistently every day except brush my teeth and go to the bathroom. This was a monumental commitment.

So began my blog *First, Brush Your Teeth—Finding a New Normal After Losing Chandler*. Anyone who has lost a loved one knows the first days and weeks are disorienting. *I don't want to get out of bed. And if I do get out of bed, what for? What's next?* I thought if I would just drag myself out of bed and brush my teeth, I might make it downstairs. And if I made it downstairs, I would maybe get a bite to eat. And if I ate something, I could possibly feel up to getting dressed. But first, just brush your teeth.

Every day I knew Chandler was with me, cheering me on, inspiring me through his life and in his death. I knew he was proud of me for writing, especially on days when it was the last thing I felt like doing. Because that's what writers do. Me and Chandler.

Sometime toward the end of 2019, I came to realize that my heart's desire was to see this collection of blog posts published in book form. I wanted to share with the world a glimpse into the Chandler-ness I was privileged to experience for 25 years. I could never tell his entire story. It was too big—one of epic adventure, of living in the present moment. He would have had so much to share as a writer. Even though he's gone, I'm grateful we have done this together. And I believe the honest sharing of my own grief journey in real time can help others.

One of my greatest sources of comfort and strength since losing Chandler has been the companionship of others who have experienced similar loss. Sometimes that companionship has been face to face, but often it has been a common fellowship shared on the pages of a book. I had no use for pat answers or reasons why all this was going to work out for the good. I wanted to know I wasn't crazy to feel some of the things I felt, that others had felt the same, and that maybe a morning would come when I would wake up and not be consumed and obsessed and overwhelmed with the reality that Chandler wasn't there. I wanted to know what this might look like in a month or six months or a year. Would it be this difficult every day for the rest of my life?

First, Brush Your Teeth is my day-to-day raw grief process in real time, not a retrospective account of how I remember feeling or reflections on how I got through it. What you read on these pages is exactly what it was on any given day. I have added reflections and notes throughout where I thought they might be helpful.

When I posted my blog each day, I always added a picture. Often it was a picture of our family, of Chandler, or of whatever experience I had written about. We have included those pictures that are necessary to the meaning of the blog posts.

Rather than including all 365+ blog posts here, less than half of that number have been thoughtfully selected for this manuscript. The remaining blog posts can be found on my website:

www.lisaespinoza.com.

My desire is that *First, Brush Your Teeth—Grief and Hope in Real Time* will serve as a trusted companion in your journey of loss and grief. As you read these pages, I pray that your tears will flow freely when they need to. That you will find words for the difficult feelings and ideas that have been buried, without expression. That you will find freedom to laugh, and live, and be joyful even as you so deeply miss your loved one. That you will be inspired to hope.

People You Will Meet on These Pages

When I decided to process losing Chandler through a daily blog post, I had no idea someday the words I was writing would become a book. I didn't give much thought to explaining who the people were that I mentioned or providing context that would have been part of a normal book project. So I thought it might be helpful to introduce you to some of the people you will meet in the pages to come.

- Chip Espinoza—Love of my life, married since May 21, 1983.
- Chase Espinoza—The oldest of our kids, born September 10, 1987.
- Karen Espinoza—Chase's wife since September 30, 2016.
- Chance Espinoza—Our middle son, born June 27, 1991.
- Chandler Espinoza—Our youngest son, born July 2, 1993.
- Charli Espinoza—Our youngest child, our daughter, born August 6, 2001.
- Cholene Espinoza—Chip's younger sister (aka Aunt Cho/ pronounced "show")
- Ellen Ratner—Cholene's spouse since December 4, 2004.

THE DAY EVERYTHING CHANGED

December 15, 2018, was a warm, sunny Southern California day. Not at all like frosty scenes in the Christmas cards that begin arriving in the mail about that time each year.

I sat in the bedroom in my comfy armchair texting Chip and the kids, finalizing plans for that evening's family outing to look at Christmas lights.

I heard someone running down the stairs right outside my room and, not knowing which Espinoza kid it might be, hollered out, "Hey, can you go see Christmas lights with us tonight?" Chandler yelled back, "I gotta get to work."

OK, love you.

Love you, Mom.

I finished up my shopping list for our Secret Santa gift exchange at work and headed for TJ Maxx. Just as I expected, my go-to store had everything the person whose name I had drawn listed as "favorites." As I pushed the cart toward the checkout line, at about 4:30, my phone rang. I didn't recognize the number, but as parents always do, I answered it just in case it had something to do with one of my kids.

Hello, is this Chandler Espinoza's mother?

Yes. Who is this?

I'm from Mission Hospital. Your son has been hit by a car.

Is he OK?

Can you be here as soon as possible?

Yes, I'm on my way.

Chandler had been a defy-er of gravity since toddlerhood when he broke his collarbone jumping out of the toybox. Once he was old enough to engage in his exploits out of mom range, I'd gotten calls informing me Chandler had broken a cervical vertebrae, been bitten by a rattlesnake, bruised ribs, and needed stitches. He always turned out just fine. He was invincible.

For a split second, I thought, *This is like all the other times, I'm sure. I'll just go ahead and pay for this stuff real quick.*

Then the words I'd just heard started to sink in.

I shoved the cart away from me and heard myself say, "Oh, my God, my son's been hit by a car."

On the way to the hospital, I called some people to ask them to pray. Chip called me from New Mexico where he was visiting his step-dad who was suffering from dementia.

I said, "It can't be too bad—Chandler must have been able to tell them his pass code or our phone numbers or they couldn't have called us."

Chip had learned more than I had from the hospital.

"Lis, it's bad."

December 15, 2018. That's the day everything changed.

REFLECTION

As I begin the process of reading through my one year of daily writings in preparation for the publication of this book, my eyes land first on the CaringBridge posts of December 2018. As I read each update, one thing in particular flies off the page and jabs me in the heart. It is all in present tense. Chandler is here. He is still here. It is a different world...the one before.

December 2018

December 20, 2018 – New Surgery Date

Chandler is still stable, and they are keeping him well sedated so that he doesn't get agitated and try to move—a big NO-NO until his spine is stabilized. So spine stabilization surgery was originally set for Monday. We now have a new neurosurgeon who has changed the surgery to tomorrow (Friday) at 3 p.m. I will spare you the details of the drama surrounding our original neurosurgeon breaking up with us. Suffice it to say, there may have been a few utterances of the F-word involved. I won't say by whom.

Please pray that all of Chandler's numbers stay good and stable so that surgery can take place as planned. Pray that his intracranial pressure, blood pressure, heart rate, and all his other bodily processes remain stable during surgery so that we have the best possible outcome. Pray for Chandler to be calm and to sense deep peace and the Lord's presence.

I don't want to physically put on paper the medical prognosis we've been given. I'm not in denial. I just prefer to wait and see the outcome of the surgery and the next few days. There is medical reality, and I will accept what comes when it comes. There is also the reality of miracles. I'm praying for eyes to see and appreciate the big and small miracles every day.

Thank you for praying with us for miracles.

December 22, 2018 – Who Is Chandler?

If you are reading this, it means you care for Chandler, even though maybe you've never even met Chandler. So I wanted to take a minute to give you just a snapshot of my amazing son.

First, I will let you know that road rash, broken bones, and stitches are nothing new to Chandler. At less than three years old, he jumped out of the toy box and broke his collarbone. A few years later, he rode off a skateboard ramp and sustained a concussion and stitches under his chin. Once when I was making mac n' cheese, I said to him, "Chandler, don't touch the stove." Such perfect bright red concentric circles on the palm of his little curious hand. When he was about 9 years old, he wanted to see how red he could get his butt, so he put it on the glass door of the fireplace. The doctor said he'd never

really seen anything like that before. One time I heard chatter from his room and walked in to find him on top of the roof preparing to jump off on his new pogo stick. All this time, I thought he obeyed me when I said, "No, Chandler, you cannot jump off the roof." This week his brother informed me that he did ultimately jump off the roof. Chandler's response when the pogo stick broke— "It didn't work." He has sustained a cracked cervical vertebrae body surfing at the wedge, bruised ribs from doing tricks on his BMX bike, a bite from a baby rattler that he says looked like a stick. I'm not sure why he wouldn't have put it down after he discovered it wasn't a stick, but there you go. His frequent comment to his brother Chance when he runs to the bathroom to clean up his routine road rash is, "Don't tell mom." I could go on and on, and that's just the injuries I've been privy to. His brothers and friends spare me from the frightening details of many of his exploits.

Chandler engages life with his body, mind, and spirit. He is loyal, funny, a great dancer, athletic, a deep thinker, adventurous, protective, generous, and never meets a stranger.

I knew he had a lot of friends, but I never understood the impact Chandler had on those friends and what he meant to them until this week. Chandler makes everyone feel special. I have a whole new perspective on my son now.

If you know him well, you know he answers to Chandler Man, Chan Man, Chili Dog, Chan—and probably several others I'm not aware of. For some people, one simple name just can't capture it all.

My boy has the sweetest heart. I have to tell you that he asked me to marry him when he was about four. It didn't work out because I was already married to his dad. When he was five or so and working out big-time theological concepts in his little mind, he said, "Mom, I don't think people mean it when they say they have Jesus in their heart, cuz Jesus has us in His heart." Jesus has Chandler in His heart and in His hands.

December 23, 2018—Spine Stabilization/Sunday Update

We are grateful that our old neurosurgeon broke up with us, because our new neurosurgeon ROCKS! Take a look at his handiwork.* On top of doing great work in the O.R., he possesses emotional and interpersonal intelligence. Imagine that. Dr. Liauw communicated more with us in two days than our ex did in almost a week. He even texted as he was about to start surgery and when he was about to close up. Dr. Liauw is one more demonstration of God's great care for Chandler and for us.

Today's update is brought to you by the letter A (the grade we assign to everyone on Chandler's care team) and the number 40 (the number we like to see on Chandler's monitor because it means he is resting comfortably). Got some great news today—Chandler's movements are deliberate, not just reflexive. His heart rate went up to about 117 when I kissed him on the face and talked to him. Chip won points when he said the same thing happens to him.

I will share pictures of Chandler when he entered the E.R. last Saturday night, but not until I have an "after" picture showing my son awake, aware, and flashing his irresistible dimples. It is amazing the difference between a week ago and tonight. He no longer has one nurse 24/7. He is only on 40% oxygen. He is in a regular bed, not a spine stabilization bed. (Again, pictures will come in the days ahead.) He is moving his arms.

So what's coming this week? Well, Santa Claus for one thing. But also, docs will begin pulling sedation slowly and looking at trying to remove the ventilator (breathing tube). He did say that he's not worried about Chandler not responding currently to commands because he is so heavily sedated. The sedation is to help with pain due to the injuries themselves and to the recent surgeries, and when they tried to pull it today, Chandler's blood pressure went up. I think my blood pressure would go up also if I had been hit by a car, had back surgery, had numerous tubes stuck in my body and head, had foot and leg surgery, and then had someone trying to pull my pain and sleep meds.

It is not easy seeing my boy like this. He is a strong, vibrant young man. In the moments when sedation is lighter, I can see the pain, anxiety, confusion, and fear in his face. I can't tell you how it rips at my soul. Those moments will be part of this journey. Your prayers and encouragement will help sustain me through those moments.

*I had originally posted a picture of the x-ray showing the spinal fusion repair. Since Chandler did not leave the hospital, we have chosen to keep all pictures of him during those 18 days private. We want Chandler to be remembered fully alive.

December 24, 2018 – Tragedy, Theology, and Christmas

Many times throughout my life, I have had to grapple with my belief system—what do I believe to be true about God? A.W. Tozer said, "What comes into our minds when we think about God is the most important thing about us." Growing up in a pretty conservative tradition (i.e. "You have to stand behind the piano to sing a solo tonight at church because you wore pants"), I have believed God was ready to swat me at the slightest wrong move. I have believed God loved me to the extent that I could earn His love by being good. I have believed that the primary motivation for accepting Christ was to avoid hell. I have believed that if I just prayed hard enough with the right words and enough faith, my mom wouldn't die of lung cancer.

Today if you ask me about my theology...TODAY...I would say that the thing I most embrace is the theology of incarnation—God with us. This Christmas I grasp this reality more than ever. I just rubbed on some rose-scented hand lotion from my new friends at Beach Kids Therapy Center. I just read through CaringBridge and Facebook posts expressing care and concern for Chandler and for us. I just ate a scrumptious cookie baked for me by Julie Cumming. I could fill pages listing the many tangible blessings that have come to us since our lives changed last Saturday. Each text, post, gift, visit, prayer, phone call, and hug is a clear demonstration to us of JESUS WITH SKIN ON. That is the incarnational message of Christmas.

We are not in this alone. We know that God is WITH us. God is WITH Chandler. God is WITH you and your family this Christmas. That's the whole point, and it makes all the difference.

For me, I have arrived at the conviction that it is less important to believe the correct set of facts than it is to accept and embrace the simple reality that God longs to be WITH us. In celebration and in tragedy. This Christmas, the Espinoza family is utterly dependent on this truth—Immanuel, God is with us.

December 25, 2018–Christmas Day

Today was the best and the worst.

Chip and I went to see Chandler at the hospital this morning, then we came home to "do" Christmas with the fam. Chase and Karen brought posole, and Chip made beans, so we had a New Mexican Christmas lunch of chile rojo, chile verde, posole, and beans. Then we opened gifts—not quite the usual experience because most of our shopping and wrapping would have normally taken place in the last 10 days. After we had all exchanged gifts, I realized we hadn't given Chance his gift from Chip and me. I had to wander around the house asking myself, "If I were Chance's present, where would I be?" until I remembered where I had put it a month ago. I grabbed the gift out of the office and then threw it in an empty box before presenting it to Chance. We were all just so grateful for each other and to be together today. Gifts were really an afterthought. The unspoken sentiment was that the gift we all want this Christmas is Chandler home and fully recovered.

After the gift exchange, Chip and I fell asleep on the couch while Chase and Karen made homemade sopapillas with habanero honey and whipped butter. They also made cookies and "good" coffee to take to the wonderful people taking care of patients at Mission Hospital this Christmas day.

The best—our family. I could not ask for more. We are imperfect like every other family, but we love one another, and we LIKE one another. It is so easy to be together. We are honest, we cuss, we hug, we cry, and we leave room for each other to process however we need to process. It sounds incredibly strange to say this, but this has been one of the most meaningful Christmases ever.

The worst—seeing your son afraid, in pain, and confused. On the up side, he now has only 8 tubes attached to his body, and they have reduced his sedation medication. On the down side, they have been unable to get him to respond to any commands, and when they try to further reduce the sedation, he becomes agitated and restless. They suspect that he is not responding to commands because of the sedation, but less sedation means more agitation and restlessness, a Catch 22.

So here's where I'm going to tell you how I honestly feel. When I see my son's eyes open wide, staring at the ceiling of his room, his arms pulling at the restraints, desperately trying to spit out his breathing tube and speak, everything in me screams, "This is TOO much!" My heart feels crushed. But I have to find the strength to stand there and hold his hand and tell him he is doing so well. Or I leave the room and cry and come back in to try again. That's just what we do when shitty things happen. We don't crawl in a hole and hide.

Of course, all the while I'm praying for God's peace, His presence, His healing, His strength. And I will continue to do so. He is WITH us. I know that. But prayer and faith and God's presence are not magic. This still hurts like hell.

That's where all of you come in.

God showed up big time for us this Christmas through people visiting Chandler at the hospital, through texts and calls, through a homemade Christmas turkey dinner last night from a family who doesn't even know us, through cookies and goodies that showed up today in Chandler's room while we were home "doing" Christmas, through hugs from friends who were there when Chandler's heart rate went through the roof and I lost it (thank you Dan and Linda). I know Jesus is with us, with me, through this. But sometimes you really do need Jesus with skin on. You have all been that for us.

Please pray that tomorrow as Chandler transitions (they call it a "bridge") from being fully sedated to being more awake he would have less restlessness, agitation, and pain and be much calmer. Pray that they will be able to get a good baseline on his cognitive function. Pray for wisdom on behalf of the doctors as they decide when/if to move him from a breathing tube to a tracheotomy. PLEASE pray for God's supernatural peace to keep our hearts as we watch our boy struggle. It is the worst.

December 26, 2018—Chandler and Grandpa Bill—Two Tough Dudes
Every day is so good and so bad. Friends visited again today, our family was all together for dinner, Chandler is breathing on his own and was a bit less agitated today, Charli's friends just stopped by with Harmony milk tea with boba for us. So good.

Chandler is having trouble following simple commands. Genetically speaking, he probably gets some of that from me. Neurologically speaking, they need to watch closely the next couple of days to get a baseline of his cognitive functioning. I'm going to call this part bad. I don't like it. I want my son to smile at me with his brown eyes. I want him back. Now.

So why the pic of Grandpa Bill and Chandler? I just love this picture. Daddy and Chandler are so much alike. My dad was strong as an ox, even up until he died at 94 two years ago. I thought of my dad the past couple of days each time Chandler would squeeze my hand with a strength that seemed incongruent with his circumstance. In his younger days, my dad's pride and joy was a large tattoo that covered his left forearm, the exact nature of which I won't reveal in this forum. He got it during his time in the merchant marines during WW II. (When he married my mom years later, he went through the pain of getting it covered with a respectable American eagle).

When he was in India a few years ago, Chandler got a tattoo that covered his entire right side, armpit to waist. A tattoo artist worked with Chandler to design the tattoo which was a fractal (google it) of the Rolling Stones tongue and lip logo. Chandler is like Matthew

McConaughey—he will find a way to remove his shirt about every hour. So the tattoo gets lots of air time. My dad loved to visit his friends, check in on them, and make sure they were OK. I never knew until the past 10 days that this is exactly Chandler's M.O.

My dad was an amateur boxer in the Conservation Corp back in the day. His last fist fight (not in a ring) happened after I was born. My mom told him NO MORE fights. Chandler will not hesitate to assert himself, if you know what I mean, but it's usually because someone is picking on his friend or on someone who can't defend himself.

My dad loved adventure, travel, and being outdoors. Chandler is always up for a hike up Saddleback Mountain, a trip to a music festival (where he sleeps outdoors), or a ride at the skate park.

My dad loved to dance. He was a dancing fool—Texas two-step, waltz, jitterbug. Chandler has become a crazy dancer. One of my best memories is of dancing for hours with Chandler at a friend's wedding a couple of years ago. I was so proud to be with the most handsome guy on the floor. And he wasn't the least bit embarrassed by my Saturday Night Fever-esque moves.

Chandler and my daddy shared a special bond. I think Daddy understood Chandler. So while he worried about Chandler and would shake his head at some of Chandler's exploits, he probably felt responsible for passing on his own DNA.

After a tough day, I just wanted to write about two of the toughest men I've ever known.

December 28, 2018—Today's Update—MRI News

The MRI results from yesterday confirmed what the doctors had suspected. Once Chandler failed to respond to basic commands after the sedation was pulled to a large extent, the suspicion was DAI—diffuse axonal injury. The MRI confirmed severe DAI. While this is not good news on any planet, it was an answer to prayer. We needed definitive information to consider in addition to Chandler's presenting clinical picture, the CT, his progress thus far, and the entire constellation of data from all the professionals who have been caring for him the past two weeks.

I will update as soon as there is more to tell.

For now, since I have the mic, I get to talk. We are living through the unimaginable, and many of you have said to us that you don't know how we have the strength to do this. Ironically, you are part of that strength. Each text, prayer, visit, tin of cookies, hug has given us strength to put one foot in front of the other. Our hearts feel as if they are being crushed, but we just keep going—because of the love of friends, family, and even new friends we made because of Chandler two weeks ago.

And we keep going because at the core of our being, we believe that there is a power greater than us that holds all things together. Our faith is the stability beneath a world that for us has been turned upside down. We just celebrated Christmas, and as I said in a previous post, we have experienced more than ever the reality of what it meant for Jesus to come to earth. He felt pain and experienced rejection. God feels our hurt. He cries with us. He is holding Chandler. That is where our hope and our strength lie. I pray that those of you who are deeply hurting with us will allow the peace and strength of Christ to hold your hearts. And know that whatever you believe, you have been an instrument in God's hand to help carry us through this.

December 30, 2018—Pizza, Kombucha, and a Coloring Book

Sometimes in the middle of really big things, God shows up in the little things to say, "I see you."

The third day in the hospital, I went to the patient refrigerator to grab my kombucha (delivered with love by my dear friends), and it was gone. I approached the attendee at the desk and, with tears in my eyes, said, "My kombucha is gone! Who would take my kombucha? I just wanted to sit down in Chandler's room and sip my kombucha. Who would do this?" The poor attendee probably thought I was cracking up because here my son is lying in a coma with a brain and spinal injury and the thing I'm going apeshit over is a bottle of kombucha. I composed myself and went about my new normal routine of standing beside Chandler's bed talking to him and holding his hand, walking to the waiting room, visiting with friends, and starting the cycle all over again. About an hour later, the attendee came to me and said, "I found your kombucha." I hugged her and said, "You're my kombucha savior!" You have no idea how much I sensed God's whisper to me in that moment—"I've got you."

Today a few of us weren't able to get away for a lunch break and were getting pretty hungry. Out of nowhere, three large pizzas were delivered from someone who knows Chandler from Board & Brew (where Chandler works) and whose loved one is now in the surgical ICU a couple of doors down. Family and friends broke bread in true communion over that pizza. God was there, and He sent us really good pizza. We pray this kind man's mother-in-law recovers and enjoys a healthy New Year.

Soon after taking up residence in our new living room at the surgical ICU waiting room, Charli left her *Alice in Wonderland* coloring book and crayons there so that not only could she color in it each day, but also other families there in the waiting room could color a page and take it with them. A few days ago, the coloring book was gone. Charli had colored pictures in that book for a year and a half and could tell you where she was when she colored each one. We had colored pictures together. It's a huge stress reliever. Today a friend came to visit and handed Charli a beautiful coloring book with crayons and markers. I said, "How sweet! Did you hear about Charli's coloring book being stolen?" She replied, "No, I just thought the people who didn't like doing puzzles would enjoy a coloring book." God shows up in the small things, in the moments that make up the hours.

Chandler was calm and peaceful today for the most part. Please pray that whatever comes tomorrow, we will have the courage, strength and peace of Christ to sustain us. I trust this will be the case.... He has never failed us yet.

December 31, 2018—New Year's Eve

This is what it looks like when Chandler Espinoza hits the 2013 presidential inauguration ball.

As I sit here on New Year's Eve contemplating what to share with all of you who have offered such kind words and prayers and encouragement, the word that comes to mind is gratitude.

I wish I could say a specific thank you to every person who has brought snacks, gifts, cards, meals, flowers, and I could go on and on. Right now I just don't have the bandwidth to put on my Miss Manners hat and send thank you cards, but I cannot express how much each and every token of care for Chandler and for us has meant during these past two and a half weeks.

I am grateful for our family. Just no words.

I am grateful for friends who have rallied around us in so many

ways. When you say, "What can I do to help?" we know you mean it. When you come and hang with us in our new living room at Mission Hospital, it soothes our soul. When you send us a reminder that you are thinking of us and praying for us, it blows some wind into our sails to move us forward through turbulent water.

I am grateful for the continuous stream of Chandler's friends who have stood at his bedside since December 15. We had no idea—no idea—the breadth and depth of influence our son has had thus far in his 25 years. We have always known he is a special young man, but you all have added the most vivid colors to our ever evolving portrait of the amazing man who is our son.

This weekend, a family that frequents Board & Brew came to the hospital. They told us last time they were at Board & Brew, their little girl colored a picture. Chandler took it and put it on the wall to show everyone her artwork. The other night, this sweet little girl handed us a beautiful picture she had colored especially for Chandler. It's on the wall in room 6 in surgical ICU right beside Chandler's bed.

I am grateful for every Chandler story and Chandler picture you have all blessed us with.

I am grateful for the hope, the strength, the peace, the presence of Christ. Sometimes I want to scream. Sometimes I am filled with fear. Sometimes I want to pull the covers over my head and stay there. But by the grace of God, I come back again and again to my center, my core, my foundation, and I am able to put one foot in front of the other. One minute at a time.

Reflection

Sitting at my kitchen table, the one especially designed years ago to fit our family of six, I begin to review the blog posts from January 2019 in order to choose the ones to include in the book. And I find myself no longer at my kitchen table. I am back in SICU Room 206 at Mission Hospital with all the smells and sounds and images of January 1, 2019. I don't want to relive it all. The day. The day after. All the days and weeks and months that followed. I choose to go there because I believe that in the reliving, I can come alongside you or your friend or your family member as they attempt to find some new sense of normal in the face of loss.

There is no post for January 1. Understandably. It was the worst day.

JANUARY 2019

Chandler is now defying gravity...and winning.

My son packed more into 25 years than most people do in a lifetime.

So many thoughts and emotions I want to share, and also some things I'm pissed off about, but my body, mind, and soul are spent. I will continue posting tomorrow when I can gather more energy.

Thank you for caring for us through this. It's not over. There's a long road ahead as we find our new normal without Chandler Man.

January 3, 2019 – New Year's Day

The pain is unbearable at times, and my heart feels crushed beneath the weight. Tears are close to the surface and erupt at predictable and unpredictable times. I am leaning into the truth I hold so closely—that Chandler is freer and even more fully alive now than ever (II Corinthians 5:8). He has met his Grandma Ruth, my mom, who died long before Chandler was born. He has been reunited with Great-Grandma Trinnie who was crazy about him. He has met Great-Grandpa Reggie and Grandpa Geepo, both of whom died before Chandler came along. He is reunited with Grandpa Bill, my daddy, with whom Chandler shared a similar unbounded spirit. There are so many who have welcomed him to a better place. Knowing Chandler, he has found the BMX park, and they are all gathered around cheering him on.

January 4, 2019 – Board and Brew and Brownies for Breakfast

Life lesson—when your son dies, you can have brownies for breakfast.

On Wednesday, we went to Board & Brew for the first time since the accident. I was fine until I got to the counter to order. I'm sure no one has ever gotten that choked up about the Baja Wrap.

Then I saw the poster of Chandler they had put up right after the accident—STAY STRONG! I lost it. The wonderful staff at B&B came and gave me hugs. I felt like Chandler was right there with us. Chandler's brother Chance stayed at B&B from 11:00 until about 7:00 that night listening to Chandler stories and absorbing the reality of the amazing impact his brother has made on the fabric of the Board & Brew community.

Brendan, Joey, and everyone from Board & Brew RSM (including the regulars) have been with us from the first minute the accident happened. They are an example of everything that is right about people in general and Millennials specifically. As crappy as this has been, they have provided so many bright spots along the way—water, food, gift cards, hugs, texts, prayers.

Our tribe has grown. And we are in this together.

January 6, 2019 – The High Price of Not Accepting What Is

On December 15, I was thrown into the arena where acceptance of reality wrestles with hope and faith for the seemingly impossible. I have been in this arena before.

When I was 18, we found out my mom had lung cancer. I clung to scriptures, prayed and fasted, and refused to believe she would succumb to this disease. The day Chip and I got married (May 21, 1983), my mom was in a wheelchair and on oxygen, but she was determined to be at our wedding. I was certain God was going to heal my mom and that she would be visiting us soon in Soldotna, Alaska, where Chip and I were set to begin serving as youth pastors in June. So we set off for Alaska a week after the wedding, knowing my phone conversations with my mom would soon include something like, "The doctors are amazed! The cancer is gone." One of my last conversations with my mom before I flew home to be with her went something like this, "Baby, I'm not going to do any more chemo. It just makes me too sick."

Because I did not accept the reality of my mom's illness and its inevitable outcome, I robbed myself of precious time I could have spent with her from the time Chip and I were married until she died on July 4. Had I accepted what was, I would have had time to fix her hair, listen to stories of her childhood, watch our favorite TV shows together…just be there with her and for her.

On December 15, I found myself beside my son's hospital bed wrestling with the reality the doctors and medical evidence were presenting and the hope for something drastically different. To some who had been following Chandler's story on CaringBridge, his passing may have seemed abrupt. I did not share every detail of his prognosis because I was holding in one hand a set of evidence that said this isn't going to turn out well and in the other a strong conviction that "faith is the evidence of things hoped for." I held out hope until the very end.

If you are struggling to accept a reality right now—maybe Chandler's passing or some other life circumstance—I encourage you to consider Reinhold Niebuhr's serenity prayer.

God, grant me the serenity to accept the things I cannot change, the courage to change the things I can, and the wisdom to know the difference.

January 7, 2019—How NOT to Grieve

People say, "There's really no wrong way to grieve," but I think there is, and I perfected it.

When my mom died, I processed my grief through the lens of age (at 18, I didn't have life experience, perspective, or wisdom under my belt), the lens of faith background and family of origin experience, and the operating system I was born with, what I would call my Enneagram type (arguably a Type 7). I don't like pain, and I prefer to skip it to get to the next positive feeling.

So I did all the wrong things. I did not cry from the time my mom passed away until we had arrived back in Alaska to resume our lives as youth pastors. I insisted on putting Mama's makeup on her in her casket because after all, it was just a body lying there—my mom was in heaven. I sang "Because He Lives" at her funeral. I needed to be strong for everyone, and I chose to focus on the fact that Mama was in a better place rather than on the fact that the person who had loved me more than anyone else on earth was no longer on this planet with me.

The pain all erupted when I tried to settle back into normal life. Chip was so patient with me. I hadn't allowed myself to feel the pain, so it all came out at once in nightmares, uncontrollable sobbing for hours, and other yucky ways. I was a huge mess.

So I guess I had a practice round. It is different losing your child, but pain is pain. I now know you can't skip it. Instead, I'm choosing to let myself cry, let myself be numb, let myself be "normal"—all in unpredictable patterns. What I won't do right now is let my mind go certain places that I know I am not yet ready to handle. And I won't let myself get stuck in crying and inertia. I cry and cry and then I get up and get something to eat or text a friend or do something to move forward with my day. I put one foot in front of the other when all I want to do is stay in bed. So far, this strategy is working.

There are many ways to grieve. One size does not fit all. But maybe you can learn from my mistakes what NOT to do when faced with loss.

January 8, 2019—God Moments, Gratitude, and Friends

In July, I saw this really cool yearly planner in TJ Maxx that I decided to buy and make my God Moments & Gratitude Journal (GMGJ). I write about the crappy feelings and stuff in a different journal, but I wanted one that just allowed me to recall and reflect on the ways that God had showed up each day. OMG, it literally JUST dawns on me as I type this that TJ Maxx is where I received the call that Chandler had been hit by a car on December 15!!! It is either serendipity or a sign that I spend way too much time in TJ Maxx.

Anyway, my last entry in my GMGJ was on December 14. Yesterday I started writing in it again—not because there was nothing to be grateful for from December 15 until January 7, but because my mind, body, and soul were engulfed in the process of walking through the most difficult time of my entire life. Yesterday I was able to pick up one of my previous pieces of normal, and I wrote in my GMGJ.

I knew today would be a hard one. I needed to go through Chandler's room and glean items that he would want displayed at his memorial service. It was difficult for two reasons: 1) I NEVER wanted to go in his room because it was a freaking mess, and clutter stresses me out, and 2) well, I think it's pretty obvious why I wouldn't want to go in his room at this point.

My friend Anita came, WITH STARBUCKS, and we opened the door to Chandler's room. We both gasped. Don't feel sorry for him. He was fully capable of cleaning his room. She said, "Let's just start in the corner and work our way around."

By the end of the afternoon, the transformation was unbelievable, and we had amassed several items we knew would represent him well at Sunday's memorial service. Chandler's friend Grant came and helped and also cleaned out Chandler's car, something I was not looking forward to at all.

Tonight my friends Stephanie and Christine helped me plan the details of Chandler's memorial service and took details off my plate so all I have to do is show up on Sunday. We ate food that had been delivered to us by other friends. We looked at pictures that have been sent by Chandler's friends (now part of our tribe). And throughout the day and night, I returned texts from friends who are constantly checking in.

Here's the takeaway—if you're going through shit and looking for God's hand in the middle of it, look no further than the person who says to you, "What can I do to help?" They mean it, and they are God's hand reaching out to you. Tell them what you need and allow them to be blessed just as they are blessing you.

January 9, 2019—Picking Up Chandler's Bike
Today was wonderful and shitty.

Started the day at HotWorx for cycle, row, and isometrics. Dropped by Board & Brew where they showed me the most awesome gift that they were planning for us (it will be at the memorial on Sunday). Went to lunch at Lola's in Ladera with friends. Shopped with said friends at HomeGoods for some new pillows for my couch—score! While I was gone, Chandler's friends Hunter and Chase came and took a jillion bottles and cans to recycle for me, AND they cleaned up a huge mess in the garage.

Then my friend Jenny drove me to the police station in Aliso Viejo to pick up Chandler's bike. I started to tear up at the front desk. "I'm Chandler Espinoza's mom. I'm here to pick up his bike."

A few minutes later, a door opened, and an officer rolled Chandler's pride and joy into the lobby along with a paper bag bearing the name Chandler Espinoza and dated December 15. My heart poured from my eyes. I stroked the bike seat, over and over. This was the last place Chandler touched when he was fully Chandler. I looked in the paper bag and saw his shoes and the Santa hat he was wearing to work. My sweet, playful boy who wanted to bring the Christmas spirit to work with him. I held the hat to my cheek. It smelled like Chandler.

The officer reluctantly told me the bike wouldn't roll well, so he picked it up and carried it to Jenny's van. Through my tears, I told the officer thank you. He hugged me and told me he was so sorry for what I was going through. God bless that young man for not being afraid to demonstrate compassion during a mother's worst nightmare.

Tonight several of Chandler's friends dropped by. We went up to Chandler's room. I loved hearing them reminisce about my son as they looked through his things—clothes that only Chandler could rock, golf clubs, skate deck, journal from India.

Tonight I find myself exhausted. I haven't "done" that much today. But it occurs to me that this rollercoaster is draining. And tomorrow—we do it again. And we will continue to ride. One day at a time. Sometimes one hour at a time. One Santa hat, one bike, one pair of shoes at a time.

January 11, 2019—The Path Ahead

Yesterday on a hike with my Adventure Sisters, it struck me that we were all gazing at the beautiful view in front of us. That is where I find myself daily—straining to see the beautiful view but often seeing an obscure path shrouded in darkness and mystery. I don't know what each day ahead will hold. That's where trust comes in. By the grace of God, I have waded and crawled through lots of crap in my life and found myself safely on the other side, and I have no reason to believe the strong hands of the Lord will fail me this time. I will cry. I will feel as if my heart can't beat again. I will be angry. I will be unpredictable in my emotions and reactions. But by the grace of God, I will choose to trust Him. In Christ, with Christ, and through Christ. My life, my stability, my strength, my hope. The path ahead is unclear to me, but it is not unclear for the one who leads me one step at a time (Jeremiah 29:11).

*Here in 2021, as I read this blog post written just a couple of days before Chandler's celebration of life service, my faith, my system of beliefs, is undergoing a process of deconstruction in a sense. Not destruction. Deconstruction. I don't know all the answers like I assumed I once did. Reading this blog post reminds me that despite all the questions and answers I may never get right, my bedrock is this—God loves me, and God is WITH me.

January 12—Tomorrow

It's almost here. I'm excited and afraid. I'm excited because so many people will be celebrating Chandler's life. I'm afraid because I have no idea what I will be feeling, thinking...how I will respond, react... how my mind, soul, and body will move through a day that I never imagined would come just 25 years after giving birth to this precious little dimpled boy.

I am leaning into the people who love us, who love Chandler. I am leaning hard into arms that I cannot see and trusting them to hold me.

In Christ, through Christ, with Christ.

Tomorrow, whether you are able to come to the memorial service or the reception or not, please take a moment to thank God for Chandler's life, for the impact he had on so many people. How blessed we were to have him on this planet for 25 years!

January 13, 2019—Chandler's Big Day

My heart is overflowing.

GRATEFUL. For 25 years with Chandler.

Tears, laughter, dancing, hugging. Lots of hugging. Lots of "there are no words" and lots of words. Healing words. Chandler's celebration of life was more than I ever could have imagined.

Our family was literally overwhelmed by the outpouring of love for Chandler and for us today.

OVERWHELMED.

I will post this week some final thoughts, thank yous, pictures, and a link to the memorial service video. At some point, we will make available a link to the service.

My heart is so full, and my eyes are so heavy. Good night.

January 14, 2019—The Day After

My plan for this post was to say my thank yous for yesterday's amazing celebration of Chandler's life.

But as I sit here, my heart is hurting, and if I'm going to be honest about this journey, that's what I need to share. I will extend my thank yous in tomorrow's post.

The reality of grief is that as I work my way through writing this, I will probably cycle through a few different emotions.

The last of our family from out of town left about 45 minutes ago, and it is quiet. As soon as I said goodbye and closed the front door, the tears began to fall. My heart literally hurt. Every cell in my body strained to hear Chandler unlock the front door, stroll into the kitchen, and grab whatever leftovers are in the refrigerator. I could always count on him to make sure no food was wasted, much to the chagrin of his dad who would always yell out, "Who ate the last of my ice cream?" We will also find out now who actually opens the second bag of tortilla chips before the first one is finished.

Reaching for tissues, I saw my phone and noticed texts from friends. I knew this was God caring for me right when I needed it. One of the texts was from a compassionate fellow mom who is in the club no mom ever wants to join. She was extending herself to me from her own pain. I asked her, "How long before this isn't the first thing I think of in the morning, the last thing I think of at night, and the thing that consumes every moment in between?" I knew what the answer would be. This is going to be a long one.

Then Charli and her sweet friend came downstairs to grab a snack in between doing homework, and I was so happy to hear their laughter. We even laughed about a conversation she'd had with Chandler not too long ago. My heart felt lighter.

I know that losing my mom is a different variety of pain than losing my child. But I still take courage in knowing that after some time, I would end the day and realize I hadn't been sick at my stomach, or cried, or wished my mom were there. Mother's Day would come, and I would no longer feel an overwhelming sense of loss and sadness. It doesn't seem possible right now, but I know from experience, time does help in the healing process.

Speaking of time, I don't like that it is a necessary element in the process of healing. I have to just feel this pain. There is no way around it. It is natural and normal and not something to be skipped over. In that sense, time does not feel like my friend. I hope and pray that time will be kind to me.

On writing...I hadn't wanted to start a CaringBridge site when all this went down. But my friends told me they thought it would be good for me and that I could help other people through it, so I did it. This has been a lifeline for me. Each and every time someone said that my words were an encouragement or an inspiration or that it helped them in any way, that was a point of redemption, evidence that God was already bringing good from such a painful circumstance. So I'm going to keep writing. CaringBridge is not quite the appropriate venue now, so I'm trying to figure out what is.

I told you I would run through the gamut of emotions during this post, and here I am, ready to open up the Grisham novel I had almost finished before December 15 and find out the ending.

January 16, 2019—Grief: The Great Teacher

This morning I was talking to my oldest son, Chase. I don't mean to brag, but he's freaking brilliant, and I love who he is. He and I were both sharing how we are changed because of this experience. He said, "Mom, I don't want to live beneath the pain and miss what it can bring." Those are courageous words to utter. He doesn't say stuff he doesn't mean, so I know he is committed to allowing this process to be his teacher, even though it means he will allow himself to be steeped in hurt, sadness, tears, helplessness, and a myriad of other emotions people don't typically stand in line for. I want to be that courageous.

Just a few minutes later, I read these words in a wonderful book given to me by my friend Gail called *Permission to Mourn*: "Grief

is not the enemy. Grief is the teacher. The powerful, blessed, gift-from-God teacher."

If grief is a teacher, I enrolled in class on December 15. I thought I was grieving the loss of my son's ability to walk and, to an unknown degree, impairment of his cognitive abilities. As the days wore on, the classes became more rigorous. And on January 1, I was promoted to grief's master class.

I can choose to skip class, skate through without paying attention, or submit myself to the difficult, sometimes excruciating, learning process. By the grace of God, with the help of friends, strengthened by my amazing family, I will allow this pain, this grief, to be my teacher.

I have been encouraged by others to continue writing, as the sharing of my journey has been helpful to them. I will be posting on CaringBridge a few more days, then I will be moving my journal (I guess you could call it a blog) to www.lisaespinoza.com.

My hope is that as I absorb the lessons my teacher offers in these next weeks and months, those who sit in on my class will be inspired, encouraged, and empowered.

January 18, 2019—First, Brush Your Teeth

Mornings are hard. Before December 15, each weekday my alarm would go off, and my feet would hit the floor. I would brush my teeth, shower, and get ready for work. It was automatic. I didn't have to think about it. After the accident, for two and a half weeks, I swung my feet off the bed each morning and got myself to the hospital to see my sweet baby boy.

On January 1, everything changed.

Each morning, I have to will myself to put one foot on the floor, then the next. I know if I can just brush my teeth, there is a good chance I will get dressed and do something...even if it's just to go downstairs and sit down on the couch.

My chest carries an invisible weight. My feet trudge slowly through wet concrete I cannot see. This is grief.

I know God is with me. I couldn't get through this without that assurance. But there are moments throughout the day when the only thing I want is a hug from Chandler.

So night comes, and I crawl into bed. I try my best to block flash-backs of painful images from the past month and pray for peaceful sleep. The next morning, I will myself to just get up...and brush my teeth.

January 19, 2019—God is With Me

This morning I catapulted myself out of bed so I could get Charli to school, came back home, curled up on the couch, and pretended it was the most natural thing in the world to go back to sleep as if the rest of the day did not await me. My body and mind wouldn't buy it. I cried and said, "Chandler, I miss you so much. Just let me know you are here.... Jesus you are with me. I know you are with me." Then a friend called and asked if she could take me to break-fast. I admitted I just didn't have the energy, so she offered to bring breakfast to me. We sat and talked.

God is with me.

A friend and her two sweet kids came by later with milk tea and boba and some delicious healthy cookies (YES, that's a thing!) for me and Charli. It was good to sit and chat with them.

God is with me.

I journaled a bit and worked on figuring out what my new blog site might look like. Then another friend brought dinner. She gave me pretty much divine insight about some decisions I need to make about next steps. And her soup and gluten-free brownies were freaking delicious!!!

God is with me.

Friends who know firsthand what we are going through came to help us do some work in Chandler's room. They also helped us take down some WAY outdated cornice boxes (what the heck are those??!!) from our living room. More importantly, we shared a bond that you don't wish on anyone. The walking through wet concrete, carrying an elephant on your chest feeling is familiar to them. We asked the, "How long before...?" questions and received honest answers.

God is with us.

Our friends said they had experienced a similar "reverse nesting" when their child had died years before. They had repainted, purged, remodeled, etc. I resonate with that.

It's not about moving past or moving forward. It's not about skipping what needs to be embraced. It's about creating space to grieve, to mourn, to be in the moment. Sometimes that means removing the old and welcoming the new. Or removing the old and letting the blank space remain until the time is right to bring in the new. Sometimes it's about letting the old remain until the time is right to bring in the new. That's the thing about loss and grief. You have to decide what is right for YOU and WHEN.

What I know as this day comes to an end is...from the time I got up this morning until now as I prepare for my head to hit the pillow, God has been with me.

January 20, 2019—So Much Love for Chandler

Today was amazing and difficult and gut-wrenching and awe-inspiring and such a gift. Started the day hiking with friends. The beauty of nature and company of friends was medicine for my soul.

A dear friend had arranged with Ghost Bikes for a bike to be placed at the site of Chandler's accident in his honor. It was to happen at 3:00 today, and I will be honest...I was afraid. Afraid to stand at the spot where my son was last himself. Afraid of where my mind might go. Afraid to accept the reality of what this location will represent—forever. I pass by this spot multiple times a week. I often take the long way around to avoid it. When I do pass through it, my heart skips a beat. Sometimes I am sick at my stomach.

So at about 3:30, a kind man from Ghost Bikes met us, and we began painting a BMX bike donated by another family who had lost a loved one in a biking accident. I stood back and surveyed the intersection. So many questions about what happened on December 15. I forced myself to return to THIS moment with the people who love Chandler and love our family and to be grateful.

We left the beautifully painted white bike, covered in flowers, and joined friends at Board & Brew for a beer and a bite to eat. It was good to be with our B&B tribe. A couple we'd never met came to tell us they'd just heard about Chandler and wanted us to know what a wonderful young man he was.

Later, back at home, I received this text from one of Chandler's best friends—"Chandler seems to be getting a lot of love even through the night" along with a photo. The bike had been draped in lights that illuminated the darkness. That's what Chandler did. He brought light to dark spaces. This is fitting for a young man whose name means "candle maker."

As I looked at this bike glowing in the dark, I could not help but think that this was Chandler's destiny—to make a positive impact on this planet for 25 years and, in his death, to touch even more lives than could ever be imagined.

My heart is so full. So, so full.

January 21, 2019—Dancing with Chandler

A week ago tonight, I was dancing my heart out with my kids, my husband, Aunt Val, wonderful friends old and new...and Chandler. He wouldn't have had it any other way.

This is a paradox, a dichotomy, a contradiction. How can my feet dance when it feels like an anchor is holding me down? How can I laugh when tears soak my soul?

I knew that Chandler was smiling on his celebration—all his friends and family joined together for a big party. Surrounded by all this love, my heart was overflowing. And having my kids on the dance floor with me...are you kidding!? It was the best ever and the worst ever.

This is life. It is good and bad, light and dark, high and low—tangled, interwoven, often even interdependent.

Thankfully, the contrasts aren't usually this stark. The dog pukes on the carpet just as you're running out the door to your daughter's dance recital. You get a job promotion the same week you get a slab leak—yuck! You love your new car, but you wish someone had not just dinged it in the parking lot with a shopping cart.

If you're new, I'm really sorry to break this to you. Part of learning to live life on life's terms (as the wise folks in Al-Anon say) is to accept reality as it is, not as we want it to be. It's not easy. It takes intention and practice. And grace. Lots of grace.

When we learn to accept what we perceive as both the good and the bad, to accept each moment as a gift, we are able to laugh through our tears, smile through our pain, and dance our way through mourning.

January 22, 2019—Magnificent Tattoo & Tough Moment at Work

I love the picture of Chandler proudly showing off the freshly-minted tattoo that covered the right side of his torso. Not because I necessarily love tattoos, but because my son was so over-the-moon proud of this tattoo that artist Spike designed with Chandler when he visited India four years ago. Since his preferred state was shirtless, it was probably a good idea to decorate the property.

I started back to work this week doing speech therapy. I was afraid—will I be able to focus; will I break down and cry; will I end the day saying, "I can't do this right now!" It has gone well...so much better than I had anticipated. God granted me a mellow first day back on Monday...no one ate their snot!!!

But this afternoon I had a momentary breakdown. Fifteen minutes before my first client, I got a text from Chase. That text was fine. But the one just before it punched me in the gut. It was a text Chase had sent me the day Chandler died. I was back in Surgical ICU Room 6. My heart began to pound out of my chest. Tears filled

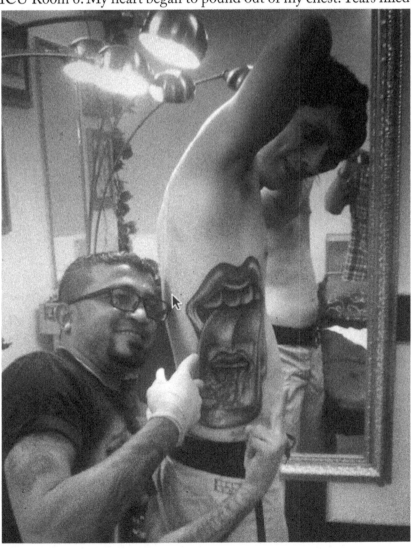

my eyes. I took some deep breaths and told myself, "You cannot do this right now." I texted a friend and asked her to pray that I could get it together before my speech client. I struggled to shift my attention to the therapy materials in front of me. It was a slow turn, but it happened.

I'm grateful for the prayer of my friend, the grace of God, and a sweet little boy who, at the end of our session, gave me the picture we colored and asked if I would put it on my desk.

January 23, 2019—Goodbye in Pieces

I went through the infamous reproducing shoe basket yesterday. Once the mound of shoes in the basket by the front door reaches about four feet high, my custom is to text Chance, Chandler, and Charli and tell them if their shoes remain unclaimed and not put away in their rooms, they get donated to Salvation Army the next week. I only texted two kids yesterday.

I kept two pairs of Chandler's shoes—the "Jesus" shoes and the hiking boots he wore in India.

Today I carried bags of Chandler's clothes downstairs and out to the porch for a Salvation Army pickup. I kept telling myself, "Chandler is not in his clothes. They won't bring him back to me." Still, I kept his Board & Brew t-shirts, his favorite Superman fleece sleep pants, some jackets, and other items that were special to me. I found a t-shirt that said, "I'd rather burn out than fade away."

It just didn't feel right. How can it be so simple and yet so very difficult to bag up clothes, bring them downstairs, and have them taken away as if they weren't a part of my son's life? Believe me, I had considered the alternative. What if I just kept everything so I could go through it from time to time, feel near to Chandler, and avoid the reality that he doesn't need any of those things any more? For me, for our family, it was OK to say goodbye a little more by letting go of Chandler's clothes. Even typing it now just seems so wrong.

So a few minutes before I was to leave for work this afternoon, I got a call from Salvation Army. The truck was full, and they had to reschedule for next week. Under normal circumstances, I would be ticked, get over it, and put the stuff away. Not today. I called

Chip, distraught. I said, "I can't do this again. It was hard enough putting everything out on the porch. I can't bear to take it back up to his room."

I put out the word on FB to see what the closest donation drop-off centers are to RSM. Within minutes, kind people were offering to pick up his stuff, and a friend texted to say she and her husband were on the way with their truck. I cannot tell you how relieved I was.

When I got home from work, I walked to the front door and was not forced to pass by the bags of memories—t-shirts he wore to skate in and bike in, golf shirts he wore to play a sport he loved, dress pants he wore to weddings and special occasions, jeans I saw him wear when going out with friends, shoes he danced, hiked, biked, and skated in. So many memories. But the clothes are not Chandler. They can't bring him back.

Today—another piece of goodbye.

January 24, 2019—No Love—No Grief, No Tears

The pictures I choose to post with each of my blog posts don't match most of the time. They are random and mostly of Chandler because that particular picture makes me happy at that particular moment.

Random.

One moment I'm laughing with a friend on the phone about some goofy thing, and ten minutes later, I'm curled up in a ball on the couch sobbing. Monday I get through the day with a few tears and some moments of sadness. Tuesday there are moments I can barely move, and the depth of sadness defies description. Wednesday I have a day that seems almost normal except for the constant heaviness in my chest. It physically hurts. Thursday, Friday, Saturday, and so on are a crap shoot.

I remind myself to be thankful for this twisting-my-heart-out grief. Without love, there is no grief, no tears. Today my eyes are heavy from pouring so many tears. It has to hurt this much because I loved him so much. It makes sense. It's normal. So why do I, why do we, find ourselves surprised at all the deep contours of grief?

These past weeks, I've read a lot of definitions of grief. For me, grief is love that longs to "be with" again. Tonight I watched Chandler's memorial video again and cried out, "I just want to be with him!"

How can there be more tears? But there are.

Much love. Much grief. Many tears.

January 25, 2019—What Do I Say?

Harsh reality struck again today in the middle of a conversation that before January 1 would have been entirely unremarkable. I was chatting with a mom at work before her child's speech session, and I offhandedly made the comment, "I totally understand. I've got four kids."

Wait. Do I need to back up and say, "Well, I did have four kids until January 1," or "I have three kids on earth and one waiting for me in heaven (if I wanted to make things really awkward)."

Which leads me to things people say to others who have experienced a loss. I'm not going to list a bunch of stupid things people have said to me, because up to now (thankfully), most everything has been welcomed, appropriate, sensitive, and not stupid. I think that's because I know what it's like to want so badly to say the right thing, the thing that will bring comfort and help alleviate someone's pain. I'm pretty much tolerant and appreciative of most every effort

as long as the person is authentic and not motivated by a desire to be the person who said the perfect thing.

Even though I lost my mom at a young age, it didn't teach me the right things to say in every situation to every person. Grief takes on limitless shapes and forms based on so many factors. I don't know how it feels to lose a baby. I don't know how it feels to lose a spouse. I know how it feels to lose a dad and a mom and a child. But my relationships and my circumstances are different than anyone else's.

That said, personally, I don't mind when people say, "I understand—I lost my child," or "Yep, I get it. I lost my mom." There is a level of understanding that no one can have unless they have experienced that type of loss. But the nuances are as varied as there are people who have ever died. No grief process is EXACTLY like another.

I do have to share a priceless response someone offered Charli. She was asked by an acquaintance, "How's your brother?" She shared that he had passed away. "Screw that!" he proclaimed. "That happened to George Bush!"

So back to, "I have four kids." I refuse to be the grief Nazi, so I won't tell anyone exactly the right thing to say in any particular circumstance. Actually, I don't know how I will feel from day to day—I reserve the right to become the grief Nazi at any given point in time. For now, I choose to say, "I've got four kids."

January 26, 2019 – Where Is Chandler?

Today a friend asked me where Chandler was buried. I told her he is being cremated. Then I thought—*Wait, HE is not being cremated. HE is not in there any more.*

My son inhabited a body—the body that I gave birth to. That I held and nursed and rocked. That I picked up and bandaged. That I hugged and kissed. That I drove to skate parks and BMX jumps and school dances. That I baptized in my tears as it lay broken and still.

I ache to touch his skin, to smell his scent, to hear his voice. It was just a body. But it was my son's body. It was the container for his precious spirit, the strong, resilient container that allowed him to leap, flip, ride, swim, dive, dance, hug, write, create.

The moment Chandler took his last breath, he no longer had any use for that body. He was, in an instant, completely free of the

constraints of gravity and physics that he consistently tested while he was Chandler with skin on.

It is too much for my mind to comprehend that my son is no longer in the body that held him, that I was privileged to hold, for 25 years. I keep watching for signs that he's around. I believe he is. I just can't see him anymore, and that's just about the worst thing I can imagine right now.

January 28, 2019 — Too Many Steps

I haven't had a spinach smoothie since December 14. It requires too many steps.

I love spinach smoothies. They were my go-to breakfast on my way to work for years. Frozen spinach, chia seeds, peanut butter, almond milk, coconut oil, maca powder, frozen banana, frozen blueberries, protein powder, and sometimes if I was living large, a heaping table-spoon of cacao. I don't have the energy to do that right now.

Today I was reading a book called *The Worst Loss*, and it said, "The simplest tasks leave you fatigued. Chronic fatigue and exhaustion become constants…. You hear yourself sighing. Breathing hurts." The author read my mind.

So I'm trying to be gracious to myself and forego things that require too many steps. For now.

Maybe you are feeling the same. It's OK to skip some steps. For now.

January 29, 2019 — One Step at a Time

Hello, spinach smoothie. It took me four times longer than usual, and I almost cussed out loud when I couldn't find the peanut butter. But I finally found it tucked behind the tomato sauce, hit the start button on my Vitamix, and enjoyed my first homemade spinach smoothie since December 14. A step (or in this case ten) at a time.

Grief is not busy work. What used to be automatic takes immense energy.

There is no formula to follow that guarantees safe and speedy exit from this tunnel. I can't check off some things on a list today and know that I'm one day or month or year closer to feeling normal, whatever the heck that will come to mean. This is hard work that engages the very ligaments and fibers of your being, your gut, crevices in your mind you didn't know existed.

From *The Worst Loss*—"You are hard at work. Your mind is actively, intensely engaged in the hardest work that human beings must ever do: coming to terms with loss."

I ask myself, "Am I feeling what I'm supposed to feel? Am I crying enough? Too much? Should I be with people more? Less? Should I read more books on grief or just sit on the couch and be still?"

Because I did everything wrong the first time around when my mom died, I am trying to lean into this process and be healthy about it. I know I have to feel the pain. But there's a balance.

If I just look at pictures of Chandler all day, sit in his room, read through his journal, watch his memorial video, I am afraid I will become paralyzed by the pain of losing him. I can't take it in all at once.

A friend will come and sit with me while I read his journal and the memorial service sign-in book. But not yet. We will eventually make his room into a bonus room. But not yet. I may take an entire day to just soak in the reality of never being able to hug my boy again. But not yet.

I have to take it a step at a time.

January 30, 2019–Before and After

Before and after. That's how my life is divided now.

Before and after December 15. That's when everything changed... my world shattered and the pieces hung, suspended in air.

Before and after January 1. That's when the pieces came crashing down.

Today I went shopping with a friend for some things to freshen up the house—pillows, rugs, and such. As I do much of the time now, I found myself referring to "before all this happened" or "after Chandler was in the hospital."

Tonight I texted my friend about a pillow color to match a beautiful rose-colored candle. I explained that the candle is special because it was given to me "after Chandler died." As soon as I typed and sent those words, my brain was assaulted. No, you can't type that! You can never take it back! Is it even real?!!!

I got home and placed some of my special things together in a new little reading nook by the stairs.

Cozy rose-colored blanket—after December 15. Fragrant rose-colored candle, "Blessed" pillow and wool "grief" heart pillow—after January 1.

Friends, and even people who don't know us, have given us so many beautiful tokens of support and love. Each time I look at one of them, my brain categorizes automatically. I don't even think about it. We received that after Chandler got hit. We received that after Chandler died. I wonder if there will come a time when typing those words does not stop me in my tracks?

FEBRUARY 2019

February 1, 2019 – Today's Gifts

Grace and strength to get up, brush my teeth, get dressed, and go to work.

One of my sweet kiddoes at the clinic crawled into my lap and used his words to ask for bubbles.

Kept warm at work with a cozy neck warmer given to me by one of my Adventure Sisters—a HUGE blessing because being cold is on my top 3 list of things I HATE.

Met for coffee with a friend who lost her daughter last year. We both agree that we hate belonging to this club. We also agree that we believe more deeply than ever—God is real and He is WITH US.

Enjoyed a delicious dinner prepared with love by a long-time friend who has been with me throughout this ordeal. We sat and talked about everything—Chandler, the loss of her dad, decorating, relationships, raising kids, and what's next.

The best gift of this day—thanks to Brendan, Chandler's best friend—seeing a video of my gravity-defying son do his thing on the beach. My heart.

Chandler, I miss you so much. Your flips on the beach remind me to embrace the moment. To enjoy the gifts right in front of me. To breathe deep and take it all in.

February 2, 2019 – So Many Lives in 18 Days

I really do need to put the pictures on my phone in albums. Then

I can have some illusion of control over when I come face to face with the realities of December 15—January 1.

Today I was scrolling through looking at pictures of my home decorating projects when my eyes landed on a picture of Chandler in his special bed that kept him immobile and automatically turned every 20 minutes. I wasn't expecting to see that today, at least not with my physical eyes.

So many different lives during those 18 days.

Dear God, will I ever see my son alive again? Will he make it out of surgery? What will they tell us when they come through those doors?

He's alive, but it's touch-and-go for the next 72 hours. He will never walk again, and he suffered a traumatic brain injury.

He's strong enough for spinal surgery and foot repair. Hope.

Surgeries went very well. Moving toward our new normal. We will convert our downstairs office to a bedroom and put ramps to the front door and living room. I will go with him to Craig Hospital or Casa Colina for intensive spinal rehab. We will do whatever we have to do to get him to his best life. I will probably get a call someday that he's been injured doing a backflip off something in his wheelchair.

He's not responding as they'd hoped. We'll just keep praying and trying. Chandler, show us something, anything, that lets us know you are here.

No more days with Chandler. No hope for flips in a wheelchair. No more lives to live in Mission Hospital SICU Room 6.

February 4, 2019—One More Day Away

You would think with each passing day, something would get easier. You would think.

But with every passing day, I am one day further from the last time I heard his voice, felt his strong hug, told him, "I love you, son," for him to reply, "Love you, Mom." Sometimes that distance, just that one day's difference, takes my breath away.

The emptiness where Chandler used to be is deep and dark. It feels like I'm falling down a well with no idea if there is a bottom that will stop the fall.

It has to be this way. It can't sink into each of my trillions of cells and all the hidden crevices of my soul all at once, this new reality. I would be unable to think, to breathe, to continue.

So this is what grief does. It follows you every day, every hour, every minute, reminding you that things must be different. You can't include him on your family group text. He won't respond. You can't expect him to open the front door and run up the stairs. Not anymore. You can't ask him to move his car so you can back out. He won't be driving it.

Every day, there is something. Everything is a "first," and I wonder when it will all stop punching me in the gut, stopping me in my tracks, and making me dam up my tears for a more appropriate time.

One more day away from Chandler. You could say, "Well, that's one more day closer to seeing him again in heaven!" Maybe tomorrow that will work, but today it doesn't make me feel better. I can't fathom how far heaven is. But I know how far it feels from Chandler with skin on today.

February 6, 2019 – The Plaque

In August, one of Charli's friends made a plaque for Charli's birthday. In Katelyn's beautiful cursive lettering, it said, "Be joyful always; pray continually; give thanks in all circumstances. I Thessalonians 5:16-18."

We loved it, so instead of letting Charli put it in her room, we hung it in the kitchen.

Just after Chandler's accident, I walked into the kitchen to see a piece of paper taped to the plaque. Chip had written, "In this circumstance, I give thanks for..." followed by a list that included me (he got so many points for that), our kids, and the love and support of friends and family.

This was faith in action. Even in the worst of the worst circumstances, one of my husband's first responses was to embrace this scripture and live it out. It penetrated so deep into his soul that he shared this scripture and what it meant to us throughout this unforeseen journey at Chandler's celebration-of-life service.

I was so inspired by my husband, I decided to write my own list. Turns out, we were grateful for many of the same things. Those two pieces of paper remained taped to the plaque until a couple of weeks ago.

I took down the plaque because I decided to make a cozy little reading nook by the stairs, and this was the perfect sentiment to define that space and give it meaning. As I took it down to move it, I realized there was writing on the back that I hadn't noticed before.

As I read the words written to my daughter back in August, I was brought to tears by God's tender care for us.

"I hope this sign gives you faith and trust in everything you do, even when the worst of the worst times come, know God is right beside you and that He has plans to give you hope, not failure."

In its new spot by the stairs, you can't miss the plaque as you enter our family room. Dear Jesus, let me never, ever miss it.

*This plaque still hangs in our hallway. It is a permanent fixture in our home, a visible reminder that God sees and cares. I am in awe of how specifically God communicated to Charli through the words of her friend just months before "the worst of the worst." Our lists of things for which we were thankful are packed away with other meaningful mementos from that time.

February 7, 2019 — Washing Dishes With Chandler

Washing dishes hasn't historically made my heart skip a beat. It does now. Sometimes.

Whenever I would see a clean white dish on the drainer, I knew Chandler had been there. Sometimes he would bring about 50 pounds of dishes down from his room, caked in petrified food. He would run a sink full of steaming, soapy water and assure me, "Mom, I will wash these. Don't do it. I'm letting them soak." Sometimes I couldn't stand to see all those dishes in the sink, and I would wash them before the day was over. But if I didn't, he always kept his word.

Today I heard from a friend that whenever Chandler was at a party, he would stay afterward and help the parents clean up. I've heard that from a few parents.

This week I saw a clean white dish on the drainer. Chandler? Please be here. Please come home.

I look to the left and see the little decoupage pot he made me for Mother's Day at Living Word Lutheran School in 6th grade. I've kept it by the sink ever since he made it. Through the years, that little pot has held a lot of different plants—basil, thyme, mint, kalanchoe—I could go on. This is testament to the fact that I kill most everything I attempt to keep alive. I apologize to the kind person who sent us the pretty purple flowers that now appear to be dwindling in Chandler's little pot. I'm trying. I really am.

What won't die are my memories of Chandler. Every time I look at that little hand-made treasure. Every time I see a clean white dish on the drainer, the rest of my family channeling their inner Chandler. My heart will skip a beat. Washing dishes.

February 8, 2019—How He Loves

As I was going through some old computer files, I ran across a video of Charli singing "How He Loves" in the Mission Hills Christian School talent show in March of 2011. We were going through some pretty tough times as a family. Her brother Chance was there with her on stage playing guitar, and they did it—together.

I clicked on the video and began to cry. Here we are again, going through the toughest time ever. And we are doing it—together.

In this past week, God has shown His great love and care for me in such personal and practical ways. He sees me.

I used to read heady theological works and study Hebrew root words to help me interpret the Bible. Right now, the only theological truth I'm interested in is this—God is real…He is with me…. and He loves me.

Oh, how He loves.

February 10, 2019—Charli to Chandler

(Shared by Chandler's little sister Charli at his celebration-of-life service, January 13, 2019.)

You know, if you were to search "origin of the name 'Chandler'" on Google, you might finally understand Chandler's infatuation with fire. You would find that "chandler" was a Middle English term for someone that made and/or sold candles. The Middle Ages was not the brightest of times, neither figuratively nor literally. In fact, the early Middle Ages is sometimes referred to as the "Dark Ages." While people did not generally thrive in darkness, candles did. Thanks to chandlers, workers and families in the Middle Ages could function for more than 10 hours a day. They could take safer steps at night. They could see. And just like these chandlers, our

Chandler gave us the chance to thrive in the darkness, allowed us to persist through uncertainty and adversity, protected us from the consequences of our own missteps, revealed our blind spots, and directed our focus from the past to the potential progress directly in front of us. He opened our eyes.

Light does not discriminate. Light gives hope to a dark room and makes a bright room brighter. Light does not judge. No matter

how dark our rooms got, Chandler was not afraid to light them up. Chandler's light—that is, his love, his influence, his investment—was unconditional. How fitting that his name should reflect his purpose.

But even with this understanding of how Chandler made us feel, I've noticed family and friends pondering, "Did I even know Chandler?"

Did we know Chandler?

Unfortunately, etymology won't help us here. The word "know" is neither applicable nor appropriate to describe the way that we were connected with Chandler. One could not know Chandler as one knew someone else. He loved to defy the laws of physics with his BMX, diving, surfing, and other extreme sport endeavors. He loved to defy the laws of fashion when he would go clubbing in mixed patterns and women's shoes. He loved to defy the laws of society by refusing to exclude anybody. It only makes sense that he would love to defy the laws of language. "Know" is a box, and we can't put Chandler into a box. There is no umbrella word like "know" for our relationships with Chandler, for each one was unique.

With so many interests, so many friends, and so much zest for life, we cannot bind Chandler to "know."

If you learn something new about Chandler today, which seems inevitable by the looks of this populous and diverse crowd, don't feel as though you didn't know him. You did. And you do. You just don't know how to describe it. Because his effect surpasses human reason and time.

Now, for my letter to you, Chandler,

As I have sat here, writing this into the late hours of the night, I have found myself peeking at the front door. Somehow, I expect you to come inside, stroll through the kitchen, peruse the refrigerator, and then ask me what I want from Taco Bell, or the occasional, last-resort Jack in the Box. You know me; I'm all about logic, reason, rationale, and concepts of the sort—so much so that I used a thesaurus for the words succeeding "logic." This being so, I know in my brain that this memory-induced vision of you is only a coping mechanism—so why entertain it? But that's just it. You made us question our previously held beliefs, priorities, values, judgments, insecurities, and outlooks. Thank you for that.

Thank you for showing me what it is to be adventurous. Thank you for showing me what it is to love unconditionally. Thank you for teaching me that I have to paint color onto this grey and white world; but that I also have to be willing to switch out one of my colors for someone else's.

Thank you for your late-night talks, your rants, and your life updates. Thank you for playing soccer and basketball at the park with me one last time five weeks ago.

Your life came full circle. I think that your injuries at the end were a summation of all the injuries that you had acquired or experienced throughout the years, and they came to you on the bike that you made. It sucks that you had to go so early, but you did so much more than many people accomplish in a lifetime. You affected more people than anyone I've ever met. And the end of it all began when you were doing what you loved, riding to a place that you loved, on the bike that you loved. Thank you for fighting to the end through pain and suffering, undoubtedly to allow your loved ones to say good bye.

You defied the laws of science and of reason.

And so, you defy time.

Every light flicker

Every sunrise

Every open flame

Is a reminder—no, a remainder—of you, the candlemaker.

February 11, 2019–Finally, Groceries

Even the simplest of routine activities is marked by before and after. "I haven't done this, seen this, heard this since before…"

Saturday I went to the real grocery store for the first time since December 15. I say "real" because I did pop into Trader Joe's a couple of times—that's manageable. But walking down long aisles in a cold, poorly lit store surrounded by more options than my mind has the bandwidth to entertain—I just haven't had it in me. Add to that, I've been battling a sinus infection. So I did what I always do when I want to make any task more pleasant. I invited Charli to go with me.

I pass the dairy section and do not get milk. Chandler was the only member of our family who would drink it.

I used to run through the list of my at-home kids in my head as I would scan the shelves. "Chance, Chandler, Charli…would any of them like this?" And I knew if I got too much of something, or something no one else would eat, Chandler would eat it. He was like a human garbage disposal, not picky at all.

That list is a killer. I try so hard to amend it before I accidentally punch myself in the gut. It happens often. I'm about to send a group text about an upcoming family dinner, or I'm scanning the list, oldest to youngest, of where each of my kids are at any random moment (that's what we do as moms). It goes like this: Chase, Chance, Chan

I catch myself. I hate it. I hate it so much. Sometimes tears. Sometimes I skip to Charli, the last name on the list, and keep shopping.

How long before everything I do is no longer marked by the date that is seared in my brain? How long before my list no longer punches me in the gut?

Charli and I fill our cart, pay, and schlep everything to the car. Neither of us needs to say anything. We both know.

It will be a long time.

February 13, 2019—Laundry Hamper, Front Porch Light, and Leftovers

First, I have to say that I'm grateful for today. I woke up with energy, made my spinach smoothie, went to work and, in between actually working, received the sweetest hugs from two of the littlest people at Mission Hills Christian School. Oh, they make my heart happy. Hugs from the grown-ups weren't too shabby either. (*In mid-February, I returned to my role as Admissions Director at Mission Hills Christian School. It was exactly where I needed to be.)

Then there's Chandler.

In the sweetest of moments, he is there. In the most difficult moments, he is there. And I want him to BE there. REALLY BE there.

I can honestly say that, even though I am devoted to my kids and love them more than life itself, I don't think of each of them every single minute of every single day. But it's different now with

Chandler. Every minute. Every day. Not necessarily in words or pictures, but in a presence, a sense, a missing, a longing, an all-encompassing ache. I've been told that will ease up at some point. Hard to imagine, but maybe.

For some reason, our family has always had an issue with laundry hampers. Years ago, I transferred laundry responsibilities to each of my four kids. It makes sense. I only wear one set of clothes. If they're old enough to use a washing machine, why should I be responsible for washing, drying, folding, and putting away four extra sets of clothes? But since this transference of power, an oddity has occurred. Laundry hampers disappear. Sometimes they re-emerge. Sometimes they don't. Sometimes they appear in the laundry room full. Sometimes they appear empty. When there appears to be a shortage of hampers, I buy another. I've probably purchased five hampers in the past two years. Then they ALL show up at once in the laundry room, and no one claims them.

I decided if I put names on them, all would be resolved. So each kid has a hamper with their name written in black Sharpie.

This week, I discovered SIX empty hampers in the laundry room. Six! I'm so confused. But the bigger issue—as I picked up each hamper to try and discern its owner, I discovered that one of them belongs to a member of our family who won't be washing his clothes anymore.

A couple of nights ago, the front porch light was on, and I went to turn it off. Why? Because I knew that it would shine into Chandler's room upstairs and keep him awake.

There was leftover steak in the refrigerator. I wasn't worried. Chandler eats everything.

It's the little things. Laundry hampers, the porch light, leftovers.

*As of this writing, only one of my kids lives at home, and yet we still have a hamper situation. And...we still use Chandler's hamper.

February 14, 2019—WWHC?

What Would Honor Chandler? I find myself asking that a lot these days. It helps me in those moments when I'm tempted to shrink from my life, from who I am, from seizing a moment of pure joy.

Here's what I know. Chandler would not want me to become dormant or inert. That would not honor him. Certainly he would want me to miss him. But in my missing him, he would not want me to miss my life.

We shared a love for dancing. I'm going to keep dancing. He was proud that I could do push-ups. I'm going to keep doing push-ups. We both loved adventure. I'm going to continue embracing new experiences and learning new things. He lived in the moment. I'm going to keep reminding myself not to dwell in the past or become so preoccupied with "what's next" that I miss now. He loved to be on the golf course. I'm going to get back to learning the game he loved. I hate that it was pouring down rain a couple of weeks before his accident—we were planning to go to the driving range together so he could give me some tips, but it was closed.

When Chandler was little, no path from point A to point B was direct. Between point A and point B were ladybugs to catch, ledges to climb, flowers to sniff, dogs to pet, hills to roll down. Life was not waiting for us upon our arrival at point B. Life was begging to be lived at point A, point B, and all points in between. I loved Chandler's vantage point—notice everything, and enjoy the journey.

Tomorrow I'll share about another specific way I'm honoring Chandler.

February 15, 2019–WWHC? Part 2

In yesterday's blog post, I said that I was going to share today another way that I am answering the question—WWHC (What Would Honor Chandler)?

After January 1….

Sometimes I don't want to type the words. I just type the date instead.

After January 1, I was talking with one of Chandler's friends from Board & Brew who told me that Chandler had recently engaged in a conversation with an accomplished author who frequents Board & Brew. The conversation was about writing. I had to know more. Thanks to my great friends at Board & Brew and the kindness of this author, I was able to connect with him.

Chandler had asked this individual about what it takes to become a writer. My son wanted to be a writer. This gracious man told me that he was impressed with Chandler's sincerity—that he was serious about the conversation and the pursuit.

In my former life (aka before a full-time job), I was a writer and editor. My husband is an author. Chandler's aunts and grandma are authors. Chandler could have asked any of us for advice. I love that he wanted to do it, as the song in his celebration-of-life video says, HIS way.

Charli recently found one of Chandler's old essays from high school and said, "Mom, this is really good." She's a tough writing critic, so it had to be excellent. Chandler did not lack for intellect or the ability to write well. What tripped him up were those irritating due dates. Charli couldn't understand why he didn't get a higher grade. Then she saw the note on the page. Minus 20 points for being turned in late.

I always looked forward to reading anything he would write to me in my Mother's Day cards because it was full of Chandler-ness. He had a voice that, no doubt, would have made its way to the surface and found its audience.

Since a year or so ago, I've been thinking, praying, and talking with friends and family about my desire to get back to writing. I was putting it off because my plan was to start grad school in January 2019, and I knew I would be investing hours in academic writing on top of working.

Everything changed on December 15. New game. New rules.

When my friend strongly suggested I start writing on Caring-Bridge to keep people updated and share about this journey, I did so reluctantly. But, as I've said before, writing each day has become my lifeline. And hearing from you that it is in any way helping you in your everyday life…

Well, let's just say, I'd take my son back in a heartbeat and never write another word again. But since that deal's not on the table, I am abundantly grateful that my lifelong passion has now become an avenue for processing and healing that can help someone else. For me, it is a point of redemption that screams, "When the worst happens, it won't be wasted!"

Soon after my mom died of cancer, I watched a movie called *Beaches* about a woman who died of cancer. Not good timing on my part to watch that movie so soon. One of the songs in

Beaches was "Wind Beneath My Wings." Each time I heard that song, I thought about my mom and how much she loved me and believed in me.

WWHC? My baby boy who is gone—though my heart could never possibly be ready for that—my son who wanted to be a writer is blowing great gusts of wind beneath my wings. We will do this together.

February 17, 2019 – Thanks for Meals...Moving On

Tonight we enjoyed our Meal Train finale with dear friends we've known for decades who brought us a killer meal and stayed to hang out and eat with us.

I will be honest. It's a bit sad and scary to me that Meal Train is finished. Not because we don't have the capacity to go to the grocery store or feed ourselves. And please know I'm not making a veiled request for more Meal Train signups. Anyone who knows me knows I would speak right up and say, "Hey, can you guys please sign up for more meals?" What I'm saying is, this marks the end of something that started while Chandler was still alive, when there was still hope for his coming home. I want what that part of Meal Train represents to remain with us and continue.

On January 1, the meals stopped being delivered to a family who was at the hospital every day with their loved one and began being delivered to a family who was just trying to figure out how to get up the next morning. Every person who brought a meal blessed us in such a practical way, and we cannot express adequately our gratitude. But now it's finished. It's time to move on.

I was thinking yesterday as I lay in bed contemplating the idea of getting up and starting my day—I want to move on. Not past Chandler. I want to move on past the vivid, painful memories—the phone call, seeing him for the first time after the accident, the days in the hospital, his last hours. I was in a store this week when suddenly there was a scent in the air that was reminiscent of Chandler's hospital room. I was back there in an instant. It is all still so near, so raw, so tangible. It's still in my pores.

I want to move on. But I don't want to move on. I want to live in this moment. But I want to remember every moment with Chandler. Contradictions circle my mind, trying to work themselves out.

The best part of today was a wonderful meal with wonderful friends, the last meal in a season during which God has demonstrated His love for us through people bringing us food.

The blessing we would always pray before meals when I was growing up seems fitting here.

God is great. God is good. Let us thank Him for our food. Amen.

February 18, 2019—Another Punch in the Gut

First, I have to say that my wienie dog is special. He just licked wet paint off a coffee table I'm refinishing.

Second, this morning brought an inevitable punch in the gut I knew would come at some point. Just didn't expect it this soon.

I had a doctor's appointment. No big deal. I showed up and was escorted to the room with the genetic counselor to whom I was referred to investigate whether or not I may have a genetic marker for certain cancers. It's not anything alarming, just a proactive measure. BTW, doesn't appear to be any apparent reason for concern.

So she started interviewing me about family history. When I discovered she would be asking about each of my kids, I knew this was not going to go well. Chase... "He's 31 and in great health." Chance... "He's 27 and in great health." Chandler...

Trembling lip. Tears. Why do they have to make me say it? "He passed away January 1. He was 25. I never dreamed I would have to say this."

I've filled out countless medical intake forms for myself and my kids. Even for Chip once when he was sick as a dog and consented to let me accompany him to the doctor. I've never had a visceral response to the interrogation—verbal, digital, or written. Today was different.

New game. New rules.

I cried because that's what I had to do. It was the right thing in that moment. People need to know that my son—my amazing, athletic, passionate, strong, generous, kind son—isn't on this planet any more. But I HATE telling them. It makes it so very real.

Which takes me back to the reality that I—WE—cannot possibly process deep loss all at once. It comes in waves, in pieces, in moments of profound despair. But if we feel it, lean into it, then let ourselves move on and be in THIS moment with our lives NOW, we can engage in a healthy process of gradual assimilation. We take in what we can take in as it comes, but NO MORE. MORE is too much.

My heart hurts for EVERY parent who has lost a child. For every person who has lost a loved one really, but losing a child creates a very unique emptiness. As my sweet husband said, it's a feeling of being "lost." If you have lost a child, I am so very, very sorry. We are doing the best we can do, right?

There is something every day. Every day.

So for tomorrow, I'm putting in my room service request—"NO punches in the gut."

And yet, if they come, by the grace of God and the strong arms of friends and family holding me up, I will not fold and fall to the mat. I will move forward because…

WWHC?

February 20, 2019 – Stupid Question?

Since December 15, people have amazed me. Ninety-eight percent of the time, it's been in the most positive ways you can ever imagine. I am humbled by the love, generosity, support, shared tears, unselfishness, authenticity, and pure kindness of each and every person who has formed a circle of care around us—those who know us or knew Chandler and those who only know us indirectly.

People often ask, "How are you doing?" followed immediately by, "I know that's a stupid question." As far as I'm concerned, it's NEVER a stupid question as long as the person asking it actually wants to know how you're doing.

Stupid questions imply that there is only one obvious answer, and you should know it. There are a multitude of answers that could be offered on any given day or moment to the question, "How are you doing?" And it's not always obvious which answer may emerge.

In the case of someone who is trying to find a way to patch a gaping, jagged hole in the fiber of his or her being, the answer could be anything from, "I'm doing great today" to "I don't see a reason to go on" and anything in between.

Today was a really good day. I loved being at work. I loved stopping by HotWorx to do Pilates in 125-degree heat. My answer during most of those moments would have been, "I'm doing as OK as you can do in this circumstance."

But if you asked me when I got home and saw the AAA car insurance cancellation notice with Chandler's name on the envelope, I would have said, "Just shitty."

In general, I think I'm doing really well. Sometimes I wonder if a shoe is about to drop, and I won't be doing well. I am a bundle of contradictions. I'm happy and joyful and yet profoundly sad. I'm energetic and yet lethargic. I'm passionate and yet apathetic. I'm finding my way and yet lost.

Please know that I am making this up as I go along, this process of grieving the loss of my son Chandler. I've never done this before, and even if I had, these specific circumstances and constellation of details would be different than for any other loss. I don't know the right questions to ask or the right responses.

So when you ask, "How are you doing?" I will be as honest as I can. And I won't call your question stupid if you won't call my answer stupid. Deal?

February 21, 2019 – From Chance to Chandler...A Song

Chance wrote this song for Chandler and sang it at his celebration-of-life service on January 13. I will let you all know when his recorded version of the song is available.

I cried when I heard this song at Chandler's service. I cried from pain throbbing in every pore of my being. I cried for my son, broken-hearted, pouring out his soul for the brother he will never see again on this earth. I continue to cry.

Head First
Climbing to the top
You look out across the mob
You conquered gates and rose to heights twice your age

As you approach the edge
The congregation, with bated breath
Looked with wonder as they passed around your name…
And you step off of the ledge
Flying til you go again
Give or take the shirt
You were always head first
Ooh, head first
You leapt off every roof
If Babel stood, you'd have jumped that too
You always stood unafraid to jump or to speak the truth
When you climb up to the top
Of the pillow or a rock
You look through all our friends, our family, our parents
You know we love you man
And we know you love us back
From the time you touched the stove
And the toy box broken collarbone
When you climb up to the top
Of a cliff or plastic box
Give or take the shirt
You always went first
You, went first

February 23, 2019—Saturdays Are Hard

I've noticed a pattern. Saturdays are hard. I won't say they suck, because that would be an inaccurate generalization. Every moment doesn't suck. In fact, on average, most Saturday moments are good, sometimes better than good. Sometimes really great.

When I wake up on Saturdays, especially when it's sunny, I remember the plans we were making on December 15. I remember the family group text—"Who all can go to Sherman's Garden's tonight to see Christmas lights?" I remember calling out to Chandler as he ran downstairs Saturday afternoon, "Can you go with us to see Christmas lights tonight?" And hearing, "I'm on my way to work." Then, an hour and a half later, the phone call.

I remember Saturday afternoon and evening, late into the night, fading into Sunday...

Saturday held the first of everything. The first news of what had happened, the first operation to try and keep Chandler alive, the first prognosis of what was to come, the first time seeing my strong, vibrant son lying still, motionless. The first time seeing his brothers and sister enter a hospital room and live out the worst nightmare they ever could imagine.

As if Saturdays weren't difficult enough, today I was shopping in a large discount home furnishings store when Eric Clapton's "No Tears in Heaven" came on. My heart sped up. I began saying to myself, "Don't cry, don't cry. Breathe deep. Just shop. Act like this is a normal day. Cry later." When I got to my car, it was later, time to cry.

Also, this Saturday was very good. I talked with a dear friend for three hours over coffee where my son Chance works. With a friend and near my son. More than ever, both of those things matter deeply to me.

Tonight I cried with my husband, the only other person on this planet who knows what it's like to lose Chandler as his parent. He said, "It's OK to cry. It's OK to miss him."

Saturdays are hard. Also, Saturdays are really good.

February 25, 2019—Bonus Year

Today at work, I was talking with a mom about the kindergarten readiness assessment her daughter had just taken. It's common for young moms to worry about this assessment and whether their little ones are ready for kindergarten. I wanted to just put her mind at ease and bring some perspective. So I told her a Chandler story.

Chandler had just turned five years old, and I wanted to just get a professional opinion about his readiness for kindergarten. Since he was my third, by that time I had learned about what is referred to as the "bonus" year, an extra year in preschool to give little ones (especially those on the younger side) an opportunity for developmental growth. Who knew that just because a kid turned five and was smart didn't mean he was automatically ready for kindergarten?

Just a bit of relevant background here. When Chandler was little, I was doing a lot of ASL (sign language) interpreting, and he had learned a few signs from me.

So we show up for his assessment. I wait in the waiting room while he goes in to dazzle them with his dimples. I will admit, I moved closer to the door so I could eavesdrop. They had him do several things like hop on one foot, draw something on a piece of paper, and follow some simple directions. At one point, they asked him a question, I don't remember exactly what. After a brief silence, I heard his little lisp.

"I know thign language."

Really interesting information but completely unrelated to their question. Yep, Chandler got a bonus year.

I want a bonus year with Chandler. I want another year to see what crazy dance outfits he comes up with. Another year to have him around the table for holidays. Another year to celebrate his birthday before he goes off to meet all his friends who celebrate him like crazy as well. Another year to see him grow and begin exploring his voice as a writer. Another year to read his words to me on a Mother's Day card. Another year to feel his strong arms around me in a hug and to hear his voice say, "I love you, Mom."

My sweet boy. I want you back. I would give anything for a bonus year.

February 27, 2019—Kind of a Normal Day

I got so much accomplished today!

I went to HotWorx where I did yoga and cycle in 125-degree infrared heat, made myself a spinach smoothie, painted a coffee table while listening to 80s and 90s music, worked all day from home on Mission Hills stuff, and ended the day with dear friends over great food and drinks. In a few minutes, I will check my scoby (the growing blob of stuff that gives kombucha its magic powers) given to me by a friend who is trying to help support my booch habit.

From the outside looking in, it looks like a normal day. Well, maybe except for the scoby part.

There were a lot moments throughout this day when I felt kind of normal.

But there's always an underlying emptiness. Sometimes I acknowledge it, and it—this emptiness that seems to have its own life—allows me to continue painting or working or whatever I'm doing that makes me feel like I'm in a kind of normal life. Sometimes I skim over it like a rock skipping over a pond, because I fear that if I let it penetrate the surface, it will take me over, and I just want to enjoy a normal moment.

I was painting my table and dancing to "Fire" by the Ohio Players. And I thought, *But Chandler's not here.* I looked up on the shelf at one of my treasured possessions—a collage of Chandler pictures a friend made for me. I wondered what would happen if I just imagined Chandler there with me, enjoying the music and digging the new grey table. I remembered how we danced the night away a couple of years ago at a friend's wedding. It made me happy while I finished up my table. And also, it hurt like hell because I won't be dancing with him anymore. Not here.

I'm grateful for this day, this kind of normal day.

MARCH 2019

March 1. It was two months ago.

Sometimes as I'm going about my normal business—working, shopping, cleaning—it hits me. Last night, I was shopping for teal pillow shams online, and then out of the blue, I remembered.... Chandler died. There are only five of us now.

It doesn't seem possible. But the evidence tells me it is. He's not coming home. He's not texting or calling. I haven't seen him since January 1.

Chandler is not here anymore. I always know that, but I think it's still mostly hovering on the surface level. No, I'm not crazy. I know he won't be walking through the door after work and hanging out in the kitchen to discuss politics, hairstyles, fitness, work....

How do I say this? I know he's gone, but I am certain I don't know it in every cell, every pore, every fiber of my being. If I did, I don't think I could stand up. I don't know if I could take a breath.

I think this is by design. It comes as we can take it in. We just can't possibly take it all in at once. I don't know what that looks like in months, years, decades to come. I wonder if I will ever take it all in while I'm in skin?

A friend gave me a beautiful cross she'd made for me. I keep it in my office at work. She made various decorative ornaments to go on it that say things like "anxiety," "fear," "anger." The idea is that whatever heaviness you are carrying that day, you choose that ornament and hang it on the cross as a physical reminder and prayer to give that to the Lord, to lay it at the cross. Today I hung the ornaments that said "sadness" and "change." I knelt before the cross and the picture of Chandler and me and cried.

I'm still sad. And my entire reality remains drastically changed forever.

But I know I'm not in this alone.

As I take it in a little at a time, as much as I can, I'm grateful for family, friends, and all the tangible ways God continues to show up.

March 3, 2019—Prayers, Yoga, Boba, and Curry

This morning we went to the early service at church. It's always good to be there. But when it comes close to the time the congregation says Prayers for the People, my heart starts beating faster. I wonder if I will have this same reaction at the end of the year when the weekly mention of Chandler's name among those who have departed will cease? Or is it possible that my metabolism will acclimate to the sound of his name vibrating on my eardrum and my heart will beat with the same rhythm as if I were washing dishes or reading a book? It is doubtful.

After painting another table (somebody stop me!), Charli and I did some errands, and I went to a hot yoga class. Actually by "hot" yoga standards, it was pretty chilly—a crisp 95 degrees. Once again, WARM made me happy, and I was grateful for the opportunity to just be in the moment, becoming stronger and breathing deeply throughout every movement.

Sometimes I forget to breathe. I know that sounds stupid. Of course, I breathe. What I mean is, I forget to BREATHE. I find myself holding my breath or breathing with such shallowness, I know I'm cheating my body of the rich doses of oxygen it counts on for so many vital functions. Right now, an hour of movement with deep breathing as its foundation is one of my prescriptions for emotional and physical health.

After yoga, we treated ourselves to boba (little tapioca balls in milk tea). Charli and I are on a mission to try all boba places anywhere near us, whether we are at home or on the road for soccer. Such a simple pleasure. I treasure this time with her.

After boba, we went to Grocery Outlet, one of our favorite supermarkets that carries all kinds of fun stuff to try, including some unique healthy snacks, for a lot cheaper than regular grocery stores. Today we got Beet Puffs and Banana Walnut protein bars, among other things.

On the soup aisle, I spotted the Amy's soups we love, and I grabbed the Lentil soup. Next to it was another soup—something with red curry. I thought, *I should get that for Chandler.*

Ever since Chandler's trip to India a few years ago, he raved about how much he loved the food. So I would buy different types of Indian food for him when I was at the store. He loved anything flavored with curry. He always appreciated that I tried to bring him a taste of the food he loved so much. Not long ago, Chandler, Charli, and I went to Natraj, an Indian restaurant in our community. As we plowed through every single item on the buffet line, plus some seconds, we savored the rich flavors…and our time together.

Today was another reminder that bitter coexists with sweet, happiness with heaviness of heart.

March 4, 2019—Missing

I can't describe what it's like to have your family all together—but feeling like you're not all together.

Today's highlight—we went and looked at a couple of houses that Chase and Karen are considering buying. Believe it or not, they wanted our opinion! It's funny how you see these things through a mom lens, even after your kids are grown. Most of my comments about the two potential Espinoza homes went something like— "Those windows are kind of low if you have young kids around," "That opening is just the right size for a baby gate," "The patch of grass is perfect for a Little Tykes playhouse or swing."

My mind dipped back into the past. I want to relive the fun-filled days at the park, the beach, the pool with my three little guys, safe in my care. Then it leaped to the future. I want Chandler to see his big brother buy his first house, and I want him to be Uncle Chandler someday. I had to hoist myself back onto the ledge of today and tether myself there so I could truly BE in THIS moment.

After house shopping, we grabbed takeout and went home to enjoy dinner together. My favorite times ever…when we are all together.

But we're not. We're just not. We don't always talk about how

much we miss him, but we also don't pretend everything is as it should be, all in one piece.

We laugh so much. We talk about substantial topics and trivial minutiae. We love being together. We just are NOT ALL TOGETHER. And it hurts like hell.

I wonder a lot of things lately. And one of the things I wonder is—will Chandler's absence from among us always feel this deep, this dark, this achy, this boundless?

I wonder.

March 5, 2019—Dreaming, Avoiding, Appreciating

Last night I had my second dream about Chandler since he...

It is still just so damn hard to type the word.

In my first dream soon after January 1, Chandler was a little boy.

In last night's dream, Chandler was 25. Chip and I were somewhere out in public with him. We were walking around, casually chatting. Somehow, I knew that we were alive, and he wasn't. But he was whole, healthy, talkative, charismatic—he was Chandler. The best part...he kept hugging me. He was so full of life. I kept giving him kisses on his dimpled cheek.

Then I woke up.

I like it, I love it, I want some more of it.

I left home early this morning with my dream still on my mind. I made the choice to take the slightly longer route to work. The shorter route takes me past Chandler's bike memorial. It's surrounded by flowers and candles left by people showing their love for Chandler and for our family. Sometimes I just don't want to face the reality of what happened at that spot, so I take the long way.

Throughout the day, my heart was strengthened and encouraged by friends—through texts, calls, emails, and even a Voxer. I needed it. Beneath smiles, laughter, and business as usual, my heart was heavy, IS heavy. The missing is so hard. Memories of Chandler in the hospital, of seeing my kids' hearts break, of...everything. So hard.

This evening, I stopped by Beach Kids Therapy Center. The mom of one of the kids I did speech therapy for (I will call him Alan) had left something for me. I picked up the pretty pink bag and opened it up—a beautiful moonstone necklace and a precious handmade card from Alan. It melted my heart.

How many ways can I say, "I am so grateful"? As I look back over the hours since I woke up with Chandler on my mind, I see all those points of encouragement were God's fingerprints on my day, a day when He knew I would need extra hands carrying me.

Even when the dream doesn't come true, God is taking care of me…a day at a time.

March 6, 2019 – Hard Day Covered With God-prints

Man, today was hard. I didn't realize it was going to be so hard until I talked to Chip on the way to work—he's out of town today. The dam broke, tears flowed, and we both cried. For two fairly verbose individuals, sometimes our vocabulary shrinks to four words—"It's just so hard."

My mental auto-pilot took over and caused me to steer my car the short way to work. I passed Chandler's bike memorial. Just more tears.

I got to work, sat down at my desk, tears just barely wiped from my face, and my friend Gail popped her head in to say hi. I said, "I'm having a hard day." The dam broke again. Gail was with me when

we heard the first of the crappy news in the hospital the night of the accident. She's just real, and she lets me cuss. She hugged me and didn't offer any hyper-spiritual platitudes. I'm not going to say she cussed with me. I'm just going to say, she's awesome.

Also, have I said how grateful I am to be working where any time of day, I can hit a hard spot and have people surround me with hugs, love, prayer? Mission Hills Christian School is a very special place because the people are very special people.

Then another friend at work brought me a gift, a picture that depicts how she sees the Lord caring for me right now. That's for another blog post.

So now…the ring. I don't even have words. When a writer says that, it really means nothing. So here are the words.

A friend and mom whose precious little one goes to Mission Hills stopped by this morning with a "little something." When I opened the box and saw the WWHC (What Would Honor Chandler?) ring, just MORE tears. I told her, "The day I die, this ring will probably still be on my finger. I will treasure it always." As if that weren't enough, this friend texted me later the most life-giving, strengthening words.

After work, I sat with a lifelong friend and read through one of Chandler's sign-in books that was at Board & Brew after his celebration-of-life service. Just didn't want to tackle that alone. Added bonus, we met at Bodhi Leaf, so we got to see Chance and talk to him after he got off work.

More God-prints all over my day. He knew I needed them.

Tonight I talked with a friend who did some work moving a light fixture over in our downstairs bathroom. He told me, "The wires will only be live if you turn the switch on." I replied, "Well, the only person in our family who I'd be concerned about touching them just to check would be…." He and his wife simultaneously finished my sentence—"Chandler." I smiled.

March 7, 2019—Waves, WWHC, and a Bit of Chandler-ness

Today was easier than the last few days. There's a reason why the standard description of grief is, "It comes in waves." It makes sense.

You never leave the water, but some days, some hours, you find your-self simply floating on it, sensing some ripples here and there. Other times, the waves swell and subside—again, over a period of minutes or hours. And sometimes the tide is so strong, the waves so high, they push you down and drag you under, leaving you gasping for air.

I welcome the simplicity of ripples today.

I did hot yoga today, and every time my left hand came into view during the various poses of the class, I saw the letters on my ring—WWHC—and thought, *I am honoring Chandler by taking care of myself and staying strong. He would be proud.*

A bit of Chandler-ness to close today's blog post:

When the kids were younger, we used to spend a week or two in the Catskills in New York. So many fond memories there including themed dinner parties every night—Halloween, Olympics, Mardi Gras, and Aloha. Near the house where we stayed was a farm also owned by our family members. One of Chandler's favorite parts of our trip was visiting the farm. He especially loved the goats. Appar-ently, he wanted to play with them on their terms. Yep, he literally butted heads with the goats for fun and leisure. He also locked himself inside the electronic pen with a crazy turkey named Pavo who had a volatile temper. Don't ask me to explain. I just report the Chandler-ness.

March 9, 2019 – Giving Up for Lent

The religious season of Lent began on Wednesday. This is a time of preparation for the celebration of Easter marked by prayer and fasting in some form. It is customary for people who observe Lent to give up something as a sacrifice. In the past, some of the things I've given up have included chocolate, sugar, TV, wine, and social media.

Charli gave up junk food this year. So I probably shouldn't have kept asking her to try the amazing green chile peanut brittle Chip brought back from New Mexico yesterday.

I'm going to be honest about my struggle right now—I don't want to give up anything this year. On any given day, I'm afraid the very thing I've given up could be the thing that I've looked forward to or that will provide some semblance of comfort.

Yes, I know that my ultimate comfort is in the Lord. And probably if I gave up something that is important to me, I would draw closer to God during this season. I'm not trying to be selfish or rebellious or entitled. I just can't wrap my mind around giving something up for 40 days. I will fast during Lent, just not for 40 days. Right now, 40 days seems like forever to me.

I thought about giving up shopping—another thing I've given up in the past. But right now, one of my simple pleasures is finding the right pillow for the reading chair or the right paint color for the bathroom.

In the deepest recesses of my soul, maybe I feel like God took my son, so I don't want to give up anything for Him during Lent. I don't think that's the case, but I'm not above it.

I could give up something that I don't even care about—that would be easy. No steamed vegetables and liver. No pre-dawn five-mile runs. No binge-watching Baywatch.

Maybe during the next 36 days, it will come clear to me something I need to give up, to sacrifice. I pray for the ears to hear and the grace to carry it out.

I'm just going to keep doing my best—this moment, this hour, this day. I trust that in the Lord's grace and compassion, He will let me know if I need a course correction.

Maybe in a way, I'm giving up the need to do something to earn God's grace. Just a thought.

March 10, 2019—Adding, Not Subtracting

Today brought a new perspective on this Lent season. Yesterday I shared how I don't want to give up anything for Lent. I just don't. Not this year. At least not today. I don't want to subtract something, anything, that is marginally comforting or pleasurable for me right now. I just don't want to subtract.

Today a couple of friends suggested that rather than giving up or subtracting something, I add something. One friend shared with me some spiritual practices she has added to her daily or weekly routine in the past for Lent. She reminded me that the point of any spiritual practice during Lent is to orient myself in a way that allows me to draw closer to Christ.

She reminded me of Jesus' words in Matthew 11:28-30:

Come to me. Get away with me and you'll recover your life. I'll show you how to take a real rest. Walk with me and work with me—watch how I do it. Learn the unforced rhythms of grace. I won't lay anything heavy or ill-fitting on you. Keep company with me and you'll learn to live freely and lightly." (MSG)

I'm thinking I will try to get to the beach or the lake—someplace in nature—once a week during Lent. God speaks to me in nature. Daily, I'm going to shoot for reading my *Jesus Calling* devotional. Always a voracious learner and avid reader, I'm astounded by my need for simple and less right now.

This isn't like me. I'm usually pretty disciplined. When I decided to read the *Bible-in-a-Year,* I did it. When I decided to read the *One-Year Chronological Bible,* I did it. Now it's different. Maybe in this season it's less about discipline and more about surrender.

Back in my former life (before starting to work full time), I used to do a lot of speaking for moms' groups. One of the things I always said was, "There is a special grace for moms with little ones. The Lord knows the season you're in. He gave you these little ones, and He knows the time and energy it takes to care for them. Allow yourself the grace to experience God in the moments of your mothering… to engage in spiritual practices that fit with this crazy season of life."

I need to practice what I preach. God knows the season I'm in.

For today, adding, not subtracting. In the *unforced rhythms of grace.*

March 15, 2019 – Always on My Mind

I'm thinking of my sweet friend who is living through this day, the anniversary of her teenage daughter's death. I want to ask her how long before losing Chandler is not always on my mind. But today is not the day to ask. I'm praying for her. I know her heart is hurting.

Another friend observes the anniversary of her daughter's death on Sunday. I won't ask her this weekend how long before Chandler is not always on my mind. I know she is reliving all the pain.

Today we drove to a college soccer showcase. It's always such a joy to watch Charli play the game she loves. It's different now.

We love listening to the radio on these long drives. "The Dance" by Garth Brooks came on. Tears from me. "Drops of Jupiter" came on. Tears from Chip.

At one point, "She Thinks My Tractor's Sexy" by Kenny Chesney came on. Yes, we have eclectic taste in music. When Chandler was little, he would sing along to this song—"She really turns it wrong (his interpretation of 'it really turns her on')."

I took advantage of the drive time to call and make an appointment to get my car serviced next week. The guy on the other end of the phone said, "It looks like I have Chip in the system and Chandler." Should I say, "Well, you can remove him from the system. He won't be coming in anymore?" I didn't say anything except, "Yeah, I should be in the system. I just need my car serviced."

While Charli warmed up for soccer, I took a long 2.3-mile walk around the soccer complex. I tried to just be in the moment. Thank you, God, for the sunshine, for Charli's health and ability to play this game, for my ability to take a long walk, for my family.

But my mind seemed bent on revisiting December 15–January 1. Vivid moments of pain I wish I could forget.

Throughout dinner with other soccer families, I felt like I was there but not there. I kept thinking—*but my son isn't alive anymore. Everything is different.*

After dinner, Chip and I went for a walk. I told him that I'm not depressed, but I'm sad. Normally on a soccer weekend I would have a special energy and excitement. This weekend, I feel like there's a ceiling on how happy I can be.

It seems that every day, sometimes multiple times a day, something hits me between the eyes to remind me I don't have Chandler here anymore. And even when there's no overt reminder, it's still just beneath the surface.

He's always on my mind. Always.

March 18, 2019—Just Keep Brushing

After titling my blog *First, Brush Your Teeth,* my friend got me a framed black-and-white picture that simply says, "Brush your teeth." I see it every morning…a reminder that sometimes, often times, it's the simple actions that can help move me through my day.

Sitting beside the "Brush your teeth" picture is a curved, amber bottle of perfume. Chandler bought it for me for Christmas last year. It will be my forever treasure. And next to that bottle is Chandler's bottle of Blue Sugar cologne. He always wore it when he'd go out dancing. I nabbed it from his room and wore it to his celebration-of-life service, along with his Board & Brew t-shirt. I thought it only fitting that I smell like Chandler while dancing to one of his favorite DJs at Board & Brew after the service.

So, the simple actions…

First, brush your teeth. Then shower. Next, get dressed. Make a spinach smoothie. Take Charli to school. Decide whether it's a "short way to work" or a "long way to work" morning and start driving.

One small action usually leads to the next. Being still, feeling what I need to feel, giving myself space to just BE is one thing. Inertia is another. It's easy to feel like you just don't want to move when there's a two-ton weight on your shoulders. It's perfectly normal and even necessary sometimes to stop moving—completely. But I don't want to allow myself to be overtaken by prolonged periods of inertia. I'm fully aware, also, that what seems "prolonged" to me today could very well change with the passing days or weeks.

I really can't recall a single day since December 15 that I haven't experienced something positive—a moment of deep joy, an encouraging word, a reassuring hug, a sense that I'm being carried along by strong arms that I cannot see, a peace that seems out of place for the circumstance.

When I don't feel like moving, like brushing my teeth, I try to live into this reality—every day God is with me. So I will keep brushing my teeth. And He will just keep showing up. Every single day.

March 22, 2019 – Always Have My Heart

From the moment your child enters the world, your heart is never again your own. It goes where they go. It hurts when they hurt. It smiles when they're happy. It cries when they're sad.

I never babysat growing up. Didn't think I even wanted kids… mainly because the story around town was that it hurt to have them. I found out later—the story was true!

About four years after we got married, Chip and I had our first child, Chase. We had no clue what to do with him. It's a miracle any of us survived to tell about it. I had no idea how to even change a diaper, and the nurses selfishly refused to come home with me to help out for a while. Then came Chance, then Chandler, and finally Charli.

Until having kids, I didn't know my heart could live outside my body. It does. It resides with four of the most amazing human beings God ever came up with.

That's why my friend Jenny's gift to me yesterday touched me so deeply. The little card that came with it said, "You Will Always Have My Heart."

Oh, Chandler, my sweet boy, you have my heart. Today. Tomorrow. When I pass from this life. Always. It hurts a lot right now because I miss you. Because I hate what you went through. Because every family picture reminds me that the next family picture won't have you in it, and it's just not right. I have been told it will heal somewhat, with time. Whether it heals or doesn't heal this side of heaven, you always, always have my heart.

A reminder of what you would want for me, how I can honor you, Jenny also gave me a plaque that says—"Live." It was in a little basket with olive leaves. You remember the story from Sunday School, Chandler. The dove was sent out from the ark and came back with an olive leaf, a sign of life after the flood. It doesn't feel like there can be life after this flood. In fact, sometimes I feel like I'm in the middle of the flood and drowning. But I know I won't. I know there is life. Right now. And I know you want me, US, to live. Fully. In the moment. Passionately. WWHC.

Chandler, my sweet son…you always have my heart.

March 23, 2019—As Good As It Could Be

Today was a love/hate day.

I loved today.

It started off with a workout at HotWorx and a quick visit to drop something off at work. I love my peeps at Mission Hills. Every time I drive on campus, and every time I walk out of the office, I thank God for bringing me back, right where I need to be right now.

I ran to Lowe's to buy paint and got home just as my friend arrived to help me paint the downstairs bathroom. If I'm being honest (in the famous words of *American Idol's* Simon Cowell), she efficiently prepped and painted 80% while I struggled with my 20%. She singlehandedly hung a bathroom light fixture and helped me carry some old bedroom furniture from the hallway into Chandler's room and Charli's room. Best of all, we drank kombucha, talked, ate, and just enjoyed one another's company. She's one of the ones who knows. Really knows. What this is like. I hate that we know.

I hated today.

I went upstairs to put some things away in Chandler's room after my friend left. Part of today's efforts were aimed at getting it ready to be used as a guest room. We know the people who stay with us when they come to SoCal really love us because historically they have either slept on the couch downstairs or on Charli's fold-out futon.

Chandler's room feels undone, unfinished, without purpose now that Chandler isn't living his life and touching down there in between adventures. Chip and I thought maybe if we give that room a new purpose, it might help. Maybe that's total horse crap. We don't know. But we're going to try it. At least our guests won't have to sleep on a futon. Although I have to say, it's a pretty stinkin' comfortable futon.

In Chandler's room, I see the container of his belongings that were displayed at his celebration-of-life service. I pick up the Santa hat he was wearing on December 15 and smell it, hoping for even a hint of Chandler. I put something in his closet and my face brushes against his shirts.

I can't adequately describe the feeling. It's like you're falling into a dark well with no idea when or if you will hit bottom. Those are the moments when your mind and soul and body are most completely attuned to the reality of what you have lost. But you cannot remain in that state of vulnerability indefinitely or you will continue to sink lower and lower. Somehow, it's like a rope is lowered into the well, and you are able to grab it. You pull yourself up and out. You know it's not your last visit into the well. But you welcome climbing back out into the light for now.

WWHC? For me, finding the strength to climb out of the well is honoring to Chandler.

As I said good-bye to my friend after a long, really good day together, she said the perfect words, borne of experience:

"It was as good a day as it could be."

March 27, 2019—Too Close to Heaven

I wake up each morning with a sense that things aren't right. Sometimes it's a nebulous feeling that only becomes defined after I shake off the sleep and take a step or two out of bed. Then I remember exactly what isn't right.

This morning it became even clearer as I walked through the garage on my way to work and got a glimpse of Chandler's golf clubs. He won't be using them anymore, and that just doesn't seem right, or real.

Then I passed his bike memorial on Antonio Parkway where he was hit on December 15.

Not right. Real.

I had a dentist appointment today. What usually is a relaxing time for me (I know it's crazy!) lounging back in a chair with my eyes closed unable to do anything but lay there is now fraught with intrusive ruminations about what was happening the last time I was in that office on December 31. I had to go in to get an infected tooth pulled that morning and left the office in tears, unable to arrange payment, saying, "I have to get to the hospital to see my son." That day I was able to go see my son. I can't see him now.

Not right. Real.

This morning I had a conversation with a friend who also lost someone recently about how the grieving process has affected our regular spiritual practices. As we were talking, I began to make some sense out of my seeming inability or unwillingness to spend any lengthy amount of time in scripture or to listen to worship music or to have a regular devotional time. A couple of things came to me.

First, worship music touches the soul in a deep place, and I don't want to feel any more deeply than I already do. Not right now. I feel the same about any kind of emotional song that comes on the radio. I don't want to hear it right now.

Second, I don't want to get too close to heaven. They have Chandler. And I don't. If I get too close, I will be reminded that he is right there, but I can't touch him. And that hurts.

I pray, I journal, I read scripture a bit at a time, but none of it is disciplined or regular. Everything is random. Even the spiritual exercises I chose to do for Lent—not really happening. But my human process of trying to figure out a new normal after losing Chandler intersects with the boundless, incomprehensible grace of God. I'm OK. I know He is with me. I know He is carrying me.

Even when I'm not quite ready to be…too close to heaven.

March 28, 2019—Shout Out to Chandler's Friends

My heart aches for Chandler's friends. I know what it's like to lose my son. I don't know what it's like to lose the buddy I went to parties with and jumped off things with and surfed with and skated with and shared my deepest secrets and struggles with….

I just don't know.

I see the constant stream of faces coming in and out of the hospital from December 15 through January 1. Young faces and not so young. All friends of the young man I am privileged to call my son.

I remember their shock at seeing their strong, vibrant friend lying motionless in that bed. Their tears. Their words to Chandler—"You got this, Chan Man."

I remember so many hugs. Healing hugs, comforting hugs, hugs of desperation and fear. If one of my theories is true and Chandler was actually somehow privy to what was going on in that room, he was proud of how his friends came together for him, for one another, and for our family.

I remember being amazed at the depth of their responses, their commitment to coming to see him, and thinking, "Chandler has the best friends on the planet."

This is on my mind a lot, especially this week because one of Chandler's friends had a birthday. Chandler would have been right in the middle of the celebration. I know his friend felt the loss, the pain.

For Chandler, his friends were life itself.

I'm so grateful that you, his friends, loved him so much. You made his life rich. You joined him on adventures. You were his cheerleaders, his confidantes, his sounding boards, his dance partners. You invited him into your lives. That meant the world to him.

And it means the world to me.

April 2019

My friend gave me a "Brush your teeth" sign after I started my blog. I love it, but I wish it had been a sign that said *Welcome Home Chandler* posted over our door as he came back home after his recovery.

So today I reminded myself…get up, brush your teeth. Move.

I won't say that today was filled with meaningful activity. I spent most of the day doing returns of items that didn't work where I thought they would—wrong color, wrong size, just WRONG. And I bought new items in their place that I will likely return this week because they are the wrong size, wrong…well, you get it.

Some of my OCDness is being focused toward Chandler's room. We want it to be a comfortable, welcoming guest room. We also want to put some things on display that remind us of Chandler. But we don't want it to be a creepy shrine of sorts.

It's not easy to figure out the balance between too much and just enough. I think it is very unique to the person doing the grieving. Maybe for one person, walls covered with their deceased loved one's pictures may be just what they need. For now at least. Someone else may need to simplify and keep only a few special reminders of their loved one.

What I know for myself is that I cannot stay surrounded and immersed in all things Chandler all day every day. It may not seem like that because I wear Chandler's jewelry, have his picture on my living room shelf, display special gifts given to us after he died, and talk about him all the time.

What I mean is that on a regular basis, I have to make myself move outside of the all-consuming reality that my son is gone. I have to spend time in the "normal world" even as I am trying to figure out my new normal.

What does that mean in real time? It means I have lunch with a friend, even if maybe I'm not feeling like I want to go out. It means I go for a hike with my family or friends to allow all my senses to take in the majesty and beauty that God created for us to enjoy. It means I dance even though it doesn't make sense to dance right now.

My heart hurts knowing that so many people reading these words are missing their loved ones and would give anything to hug them one more time. I don't claim to know everything about what you should or shouldn't do—I'm trying to figure this out day by day. From my own experience, maybe if you feel like you don't want to get up tomorrow, just put your feet on the floor, walk to the sink, and first, brush your teeth. Then get dressed. Then go grab a cup of coffee and maybe a bite to eat. Maybe call a friend to see if they want to have lunch, or tackle a work or home project you've been meaning to get to. Put on your walking shoes and stroll the neighborhood for 20 minutes just focusing on your surroundings, not on the pain that is your constant companion.

Oh, my friend, it is not an easy road we travel. Loss is loss. We all experience it in one form or another. We have to feel what we feel, to embrace the process of grief. And we have to move outside the walls that grief can tend to build around us.

But first…

Brush your teeth.

April 3, 2019—Every Day Something

All I wanted was to grab a nice protein-packed snack and go about my evening. I pulled open the cheese/lunchmeat drawer and grabbed what looked like a tasty hunk of cheddar. Somehow this particular package of cheese had escaped my view for some time. I plopped it on the counter and saw on the packaging *Espinoza, Chandler. December 15.*

This was a special aged cheese someone had brought to the hospital for us. I had put it in the refrigerator on the SICU (Surgical Intensive Care Unit) floor where they allowed patient families to store things. After learning my lesson with the MIA kombucha*, I was not going to let this precious block of deliciousness escape my possession. So I went to the nurse's station and asked for a sticker... the ones they give you to identify your food in the fridge. After a specified number of days, your stash gets trashed. This Wisconsin delicacy was spared such a fate because our time at the hospital ended on January 1.

That was the day, the evening, we packed up everything. Actually, I didn't pack. I sat on the couch in the SICU waiting room—in shock, paralyzed, heavy, dazed, exhausted, reeling, speechless.

Someone among us remembered to recover our food and drink items from the patient refrigerator.

I would give anything to be back in that SICU unit with my kombucha and my Wisconsin cheese. When there was hope. Hope that my son would sit up and smile at me. Hug me. Say, "Hey, Mom," in all his Chandler-ness.

I would go to that refrigerator with an energy in my step to grab a drink or a snack knowing I needed to keep up my health and strength for the long road of recovery ahead. There would be spinal rehab, brain rehab, big changes in every area of our lives—but worth it all to have our son home and well.

When I grabbed this cheese, such a storm of emotions. The memory of hope, the sting of reality, the finality of death.

Every day, something.

*See December 30, 2018 blog post.

April 6, 2019—Koi Pond

Today, past and present converged. It was wonderful. I wish it could have been perfect.

One of my dearest lifelong friends flew in from Washington to see me. We are easy together. Where do you want to eat? I'm up for anything. How about True Food? Yes, let's do that. Want to shop? Always. How about we go home and open a bottle of wine? Sounds great.

After picking her up at the airport, we decided to go to Fashion Island to eat.

As we near the koi pond, I remember. Another forever friend, Lynette, took Chandler to Fashion Island when he was little, along with her little girl Brooke. Guess who ended up in the koi pond despite numerous reminders not to get too close? I know that memory is now bittersweet for Lynette. Hopefully it will become more sweet with time.

Although I wasn't there when it happened, my mind played the movie. Chandler could not bring himself to maintain a distance from water. He wasn't defiant. He just could not control the magnetic power that H2O held over him. I imagined his dimpled cheeks as he toppled into the water after teetering too close to the edge. That was my son. A metaphor for his life. Why stay on dry land when a world of fun awaits in the water?

We strolled past the koi pond and went on to have a delicious lunch at True Food. Then we strolled down Corona del Mar beach. I told Carole that it was much easier walking up and down the hill to the beach without a stroller, boogie boards, lunch, and all the stuff associated with bringing three little boys and a toddler to the beach. I would give ANYTHING to schlep all of my kids, ALL of them, up and down that hill one more time.

After the beach, we met Charli, Lynette and Brooke for coffee. Wonderful day. Wonderful. It would have been perfect, if…

If Chandler were alive and well on this planet.

That's just the way it is these days. Probably, or maybe, some-day my mind and heart will recalibrate "perfect" and it will be a fitting description.

I really don't ask for much. Simple things make me happy. It's the simple things in life that make for a perfect day.

It's pretty simple. I just want my son back. Then it will be…a perfect day.

April 8, 2019—Nothing to Write About

My friend Carole asked me tonight, "Do you ever get to the end of the day and have nothing to write about?" I replied, "If I do, it's a good thing."

Today, was one of those days. I'm grateful. So very grateful. No punches in the gut. A whole day of feeling relaxed, unhurried, at peace, and almost…normal.

Carole and I enjoyed breakfast and a perfect lavender latte at Ellie's Table on our way to a glorious spa day at a hotel in Dana Point overlooking the ocean. They agreed to match a crazy good Groupon deal I had found—bonus! We lounged by the pool for most of the day, then pampered ourselves—Carole with a massage and me with a facial.

After our spa day, we headed up the coast to meet our friends Dave and Lynette for dinner at Urth Cafe in Laguna Beach. The Reuben sandwich was delicious, but the hit of the evening was the blended matcha tea. Definitely something I will crave and order again, but I did discover in no uncertain terms it is imperative that I bring Lactaid along the next time I indulge in that tasty treat. Enough said about that.

Carole, Lynette, and I have known one another for 35 years. So many stories, so much history. No need to fill in the back story. We were together when the back story started! We only broke up tonight's 4 1/2-hour party because Dave had to be up at 4:00 a.m. It was a good time.

And now, as I end this day, feet up on my sofa, candles flickering, glass of wine by my side, I'm hearing my kids talk with a friend about their brother. I hurt with them and for them. They are processing as well as anyone could, but it still sucks.

I am reminded of this new reality. I've known it all day long. I've mentioned Chandler and told numerous Chandler stories. I've even said the phrase, "after Chandler died…." But somehow the harshness and finality was kept at bay until now. Maybe that was a gift to me. You have to have moments where it's not front and center. I had a lot of those today.

How would I describe today? The most fitting words I can think of came from my friend and fellow club member Christine a few weeks ago when she said…

It was as good as it gets.

April 9, 2019—Quiet

In quietness and confident trust shall be your strength.

~Isaiah 30:15

Today I was reminded that quiet time alone is not a luxury for me. It is a necessity. It pulls me back to center when my mind and body pull me toward frenetic activity and flurries of thought.

My mind never stops. I'm not exaggerating. Never. If my mind were a book, it would be *If You Give a Moose a Muffin*. I exhaust myself.

When I float*, my mind stops. I'm able to get some internal peace and quiet. I floated again today, my third time since last summer. I actually fell asleep—yes, asleep while floating on a bed of saltwater! I didn't wake up until the mysterious piped in music began playing in my sensory deprivation tank.

My sense of calm followed me to Newport Beach where I sat with my journal in the warm sand and let my feelings and thoughts flow onto the page. Other than in people, the place I encounter God most powerfully is in nature. Watching the waves roll out and crash back into the shore on the perimeter of an endless shimmering horizon reminds me that God is bigger. Bigger than my pain, bigger than loss, bigger than my abilities to cope in my own strength. He is bigger. Immense, vast, immeasurable, uncontainable. Like the ocean stretching out before me.

And yet, He becomes small enough to meet me in my little place. In my tiny corner of the planet. In my pain. In my tears.

I walked away from the silence of my saline sleep chamber and the reflectiveness of my warm spot on the beach with a hunch that if I lean into quiet spaces, God is going to do some important things in my heart in these next nine months—my year of firsts.

Quietness. Confident trust. Strength.

*Floating is done in a sensory deprivation tank of saline water. It can help with anxiety and promote a sense of calm and well-being.

April 10, 2019 – He Won

One of the infamous Chandler stories in our family is about the time Chandler burned his butt on the fireplace. I think it's worth recounting.

When the boys were little, they would engage in a little competition to see whose butt could get the reddest. This was most often accomplished by standing at the French doors in our family room, baring their buns, and pressing them against the sun-baked glass. Surely this has happened in other households.

One day Chip was watching the boys while I was out. As soon as I walked through the front door, Chip said, "Lis, come look at your son." Well, that's never good.

I walked into the living room to see Chandler sprawled out on the ottoman, his bare bottom glowing a radiant red.

"What the heck happened?!"

Chip responded, "Chandler thought his butt would get the reddest if he put it on the glass in front of the fireplace while the fire was going."

It did.

At one point, Chase came downstairs and assessed the situation. Thinking through how to best express honest sympathy for his little brother, he said, "Chandler, I'm sorry…that…you were dumb enough to put your butt on the fireplace."

The poor kid could hardly put on pants, and I was afraid he might get an infection. So I took him to the doctor the next day.

The doctor took a look at Chandler's blistered bottom, asked how it happened, and responded, "I've never really seen anything like this before." Of course not.

As with most of Chandler's wounds and injuries, eventually his bottom healed up.

And, what he would most want us to remember—he won.

April 11, 2019 – Family Picture

The danger of having pictures of your family in your office at work is that people ask about your kids.

When they ask about your kids, you want to talk about each one of them. When you talk about each one of them, what do you say when you get to the one who isn't here anymore?

It happened again yesterday. A nice young family came to tour our school, and the mom asked if all my kids live at home. I began with the immediate response I would have given before January 1—from oldest to youngest. When I got to Chandler, for a split second, I thought, *I shouldn't tell her this. It's just too sad. I don't want her to be sad.* But it's the truth. My son died. So I told her.

She was sad for me. I didn't stay in that space but quickly moved on to tell her that Charli is still at home and a junior in high school.

God knew I needed a boost today. A dear friend whose husband passed away four years ago texted me this morning to ask if I wanted to go to lunch. YES!!!

I told her it's so hard when people who don't know about Chandler ask about our family. It makes it too real to talk about Chandler in past tense. Not that I don't want them to ask. I do! I want to talk about Chandler. But I want to talk about him as if he were on a trip and will be coming back in a few weeks or months. Like when he did an internship in Washington, D.C., followed by a trip to India. I didn't see him for about five months. That was by far the longest time I'd gone without seeing any of my kids, but I knew he would be coming home. I would see him again.

My friend understood. She told me she had felt the same way for a long time after her husband died. She told me that someday I will be able to talk about Chandler without the deep sadness and pain. Without the feeling of heaviness. That I will be able to not feel punched in the gut when someone who doesn't know asks me about my kids.

I will keep my family pictures on display in my office. And people who don't know will keep asking. And I will keep sharing.

These are my kids. And this is my story.

April 13, 2019—Llamas, Dancing, Soda, and Pilates

You know it's going to be a great day when you encounter a camel and a couple of llamas in the parking lot before 10 a.m. And, no, I hadn't been drinking. They were for real.

Today Charli joined me for Animals Everywhere, a self-explanatory community event that Mission Hills, the school where I am admissions director, has participated in for a few years. Once again, our tub full of aqua balls were a big hit with the kids as well as our helium balloons.

Our booth was right beside the cutest llamas you've ever seen. Not that you've seen lots of llamas. If you had, you would know these ranked right up there with the cutest of them. As cute as they were, they weren't very cooperative when it came to posing with us for pictures. They were in the pen with a cow and a couple of tortoises. I was reminded how grateful I am not to be a tortoise or to be married to one as I watched one of the shelled creatures eat, yes eat, cow poop.

The DJ playing music for the event was so good! We sang along the whole day while blowing up balloons and tying them onto tiny wrists. At the end of the day, we joined in and danced to the Macarena, Cupid Shuffle, and ChaCha Slide. Charli killed it dancing to "Baby Baby" by Bieber. I had a flashback to the 4th grade Sacramento state capitol field trip. A dad had brought his guitar, and we were having a sing-along to "Baby Baby" on the tour bus, and sometime during or just after the sing-along, Charli's friend Jillian threw up on me. Luckily, no one threw up today. It was just dancing and singing. And eating cow poop…if you were a tortoise.

After the event, Charli and I used a Dickey's BBQ gift card generously given to us by a Mission Hills family when Chandler was in the hospital. Can I say how disproportionately happy I was when I discovered the soda machine? It's the kind where you can choose from a bajillion different kinds of soda, including Caffeine-Free and Diet—BOTH in one soda! AND…there was caffeine-free diet cherry vanilla Coke! What!??? Yes, I know diet soda isn't good for you, but I never have it, and when I got the chance to splurge with the cherry vanilla caffeine-free variety, I decided to throw caution to the wind.

When we got home, I jumped onto my Pilates reformer and did a workout. Reformer workouts are all love-love, no love-hate. I fell in love with the Pilates reformer machine last summer and decided it was much cheaper to have one of my own than to pay the monthly cost to go to a reformer class. I pull out my reformer, switch on my diffuser with some Thieves essential oil and a bit of lavender and turn on one of the many reformer workouts on John Garey TV. My time on the reformer helps me stay sane and is something I look forward to, a highlight in my day.

Once again, the simple pleasures of today brought exactly what I needed. A feeling of aliveness and an overwhelming sense of gratitude that—I'm NOT a tortoise.

April 14, 2019—One of Those People

I usually don't mind being one of those people.

I don't mind being one of those people who fits the definition of a Redneck. I was raised mostly in a trailer (mobile home if you want to get fancy about it) at the end of a dirt road.

Our trailer had three doors but only two sets of steps. We finally just nailed the third door shut.

Our trailer had no skirt on it. What that means is, dogs could go under there to be sick or die, especially after they'd been bitten by a snake. That happened to two of my dogs—Cuddles and Brandy. There was at least one snake that never got to my dogs—the one my mom killed outside the chicken house in the middle of the night in her robe and slippers with a hoe while I watched from the bathroom window at the end of the trailer.

We had a fire pit out front made of roofing tin, not for decoration, but to burn the leaves and other trash we'd rake up. And also to throw the dead snake in.

I played outside from the time I got home from school until it got dark. Climbing trees, crawling across pipelines suspended high off the ground below, crawfishing, playing with my dogs, and riding my bike through every square inch of the woods within a 5-mile radius of home.

The evening routine went something like this—stop on the top step, knock on the door, wait for Mama to come out and check me for seed ticks. If there were no seed ticks, I just hopped in the shower. If there were seed ticks, I had to take a bath in Pine-Sol. Unless one had stuck to me already. Then Mama had to put a match to the tick and hope it would let go. They usually did. Then the Pine-Sol bath.

I don't mind being one of those people who just happens to get lost everywhere I go. I've made peace with it. And I thank God every day for GPS. Although I'm also one of those people who gets lost even with GPS, prompting a meltdown of the GPS lady who insistently repeats, "Make a legal u-turn and proceed to the route."

I don't mind being one of those people who often let their kids stay up a little too late growing up because it was fun to hang out with them.

I don't mind being one of those people who is the shortest or the oldest or the last to finish the meal.

Here's what I do mind.

I do not like being one of those people who has lost their child.

Sometimes it hits me like a ton of bricks. From the middle of nowhere I hear a voice. "You are one of them." It's something no one ever thinks will happen to them. You don't prepare for it. Nor should you. It just happens, and you deal with it. But I don't want to be one of them. I never asked to be one of them.

And they didn't ask to be one of them. None of us did.

But here we are. We are those people. Those people who've lost a child.

April 15, 2019 – Thank You, Siri

On the way to meet friends for a morning hike, I decided to listen to music. Before thinking through what I wanted to listen to, I blurted out, "Hey, Siri, play…" I knew if I didn't fill in the blank quickly, I would lose her, so I said the first thing that came to my mind. "*Cry Out to Jesus* by Third Day." I don't know why I said it. I haven't listened to that song in years.

As I listened to the words, all kinds of pain from all kinds of memories and circumstances flooded in.

Allowing my heart to cry out to Jesus does not remove me from my circumstance. It doesn't wipe out painful memories, reverse bad choices, or bring my son back.

When I cry out to Jesus, I acknowledge a power greater than myself. I join with a love that is creative, redemptive, present, and without limits. I place myself in hands that were nailed to a cross for me—all because of love. I admit my great need and His greater abundance. This is not dogma for me. It is not theological mumbo jumbo. It is my reality. My source. My strength.

I'm grateful that this morning my mouth blurted out exactly what I needed Siri to play for me—a reminder as I begin this Holy Week. Cry out to Jesus. He is with me.

April 17, 2019 – Lightning Strikes

This morning I woke up to an envelope addressed to Chandler

sitting on the kitchen counter. Sometimes I open the Chandler mail. Sometimes Chip does. Whichever one of us feels up to it in the moment. It is never easy. I know it is completely unreasonable, but I want to call the person who sent the envelope and say, "Don't you know? How insensitive can you be?" Doesn't the whole universe know things are different?

I opened the envelope and saw a ticket to Lightning in a Bottle, a music festival in Central California. Chandler must have purchased his ticket well before December 15. I could imagine his ear-to-ear grin and dimples as he opened the envelope. My heart sunk. Another punch in the gut. I felt the wristband. He would have been so excited to slip that on his wrist.

He loved music festivals. He never met a stranger and always came home talking about all the new friends he'd met. And he loved to dance. Oh, how he loved to dance.

The festival will not be the same without him. He won't be dancing all day and lighting up the night with his smile. They will miss his contagious energy.

I hate this. Oh, I hate it. I hate seeing a sign of life—a party that Chandler will not be a part of.

I contacted the folks at Lightning in a Bottle and explained why my son would not be there. Their response was more than I could have hoped for. They refunded his ticket price, but more importantly, they asked for a picture of Chandler. They will honor him at the festival.

Chandler will be at Lightning in a Bottle in spirit. But I want his feet to be planted, physically, on the ground at Buena Vista Lake… dancing, jumping off things, walking to different campsites to meet new friends.

It will have to be enough that attendees will see his picture and remember Chandler from other festivals. And talk about the guy with the crazy dance moves, unquenchable energy, and a heart that welcomed everyone in.

April 19, 2019—Too Many Times

What a wonderful start to the day—an impromptu walk around the lake with a friend. Gorgeous morning. Great conversation. Exercise. Nature. All good stuff.

I got home and it hit me. I saw Chandler's picture and broke down. Not a quiet cry. A loud, gut level, uncontrollable cry. In those moments, the words just fall out of my mouth. "I miss you so much, son. I just want you to know I love you and miss you. I want to know that somehow you are here." The pain feels literally overwhelming. I don't know what to do with it. I can't redirect it. I can't see past or beyond it. I can't shape it into something different. I have to feel it. Just as it is.

Jesus, please help me. It's too much. It's just too much. I don't know how to do this. Please help me.

The sobbing slowly subsided. I did not feel hungry. I thought to myself, *I don't want to do anything. Nothing. And I don't want to eat.* But I remembered…

If you brush your teeth, you will probably get dressed. If you get dressed, you will probably go downstairs. If you go downstairs, you will probably get something to eat. Today I brushed my teeth and skipped straight to a walk with a friend, first thing. Now I had to tell myself, "Next, eat something." I didn't feel like opening the freezer and pulling out the ingredients. But I made my body go through the motions. In the end, I enjoyed one of my best spinach smoothies ever. I sat outside and soaked in the sun, savoring each sip of my green creamy concoction.

For lunch, I met my friend at the lake for a picnic. The RSM lake is taking centerstage as one of my new go-to happy places. Ducks, water, adorable dogs passing by, sunshine, delicious food, and easy company of a friend who gets it. Such simple pleasures and yet such rich food for my soul.

I needed that mid-day refueling of my emotional tank. When I got home, I had to deal with a bank issue related to Chandler's account. In that conversation, I had to say the word in some form too many times. "My son died…when my son passed…because Chandler died…yes, he passed away on January 1…blah blah blah death certificate."

Thankfully, I was able to end my day with more life-giving hours.

Book club tonight—we are actually speeding through this book at a pace of about five chapters a month! Go us! I brought the most amazing home-made from-scratch vegan gluten-free brownies for us. Got the recipe from our neighbor Lauren who made us a batch about two months ago and no one could believe they were gluten-free.

When I got home from book club, Chance was home with several of his friends from Bodhi Leaf where he has worked the past couple of years. They had come for a little going away get-together since Chance just started a new job. We listened to hip-hop, ate leftover brownies, and discussed all manner of topics including the merits, and possible lack thereof, of Casey Musgraves.

Thank you, God, for life-giving moments today that fueled me for the hard stuff. Including having to say it…too many times.

April 20, 2019—In Between

I've been thinking since January 1 how much I abhor the word *final*. I think anyone who has lost a loved one will say that the finality hits the hardest.

Final means there is no possibility for more. No more Chandler-ness in real time. No more of the dimpled smiles, the laughter, the hugs, the dreaming out loud together about what's next.

I walk into his room, and it hits me that there was a final time when he slept in that room. It won't happen again. There was a final time when he said, "Love you, Mom." Those words won't fall on my ears from his mouth again in this lifetime. There was a final hug, a final meal together, a final birthday present, a final Mother's Day card. I just didn't know it at the time.

When Chance was little and he wanted more of something he knew he'd already had more than enough of, he would say in his sweet little voice, his index finger indicating the single number, "One more, 'ass all." There are times when I feel like I would trade all my vital organs for "one more, 'ass all."

Final. I hate that word.

Here we are on Saturday. The day between what the Christian tradition calls Good Friday and Easter.

Friday is death. "…Jesus said, 'It is finished.' With that He bowed his head and gave up His spirit" (John 19:30). Death is final. No more.

So back to Saturday. What is Saturday if Friday is death, finality, and Sunday is…well, let's just cut to the chase. We know what Sunday is. Easter. The resurrection. Celebration. New life. We will talk about that tomorrow.

But today. What is Saturday, the day between *final* and *life*? Most of my days since January 1 have been Saturday, the day between.

Saturday, for me, is knowing there is a God who says there is life beyond this life, but today feels like death. Today is heavy. What I need is hope.

Saturday is straining to see hope.

April 22, 2019—Alive in Their Words

Today on Easter Monday, I have been reflecting on yesterday and how very grateful I am for our family and for our expanded tribe.

Yesterday afternoon, we had the Board & Brew gang over for an Easter BBQ. I love those kids. OK, young adults. Their hearts are so big.

I love hearing them talk about Chandler because he is alive in their words. Savannah and Emily told me he had bought them pizza the night before his accident. They worked his last shift with him. Troy told me he has built a small memorial for Chandler where they used to hang out a lot. He said Chandler is one of the best people he's ever known. Cody and Joey showed me their new tattoos—inspired by Chandler.

A common theme among conversations is—if you were on the fringe, Chandler would make sure you were included. He was a friend to the friendless. He had time for people whether they were the most popular or the least acknowledged.

Another true fact we all agree upon—Chandler was not vanilla. Not that there's anything wrong with vanilla. He just wasn't that. He was every exotic flavor, every interesting texture, every unconventional possibility, and every novel adventure. Chandler was not easy to forget. And…he remembered *you*.

There will be many more days like yesterday. Days to catch up, laugh, remember.

I'm grateful for a community that remembers with us.

April 24, 2019—Flashback to My Days of Whine and Noses

I was getting ready to leave work today when a young mom came in to register for our preschool summer camp. After making sure she was settled with the summer camp registration, our receptionist extraordinaire, Lynda, brought her into my office because she had some questions about our junior kindergarten program. I answered her questions and watched her adorable little toddler buzz about the office. As our conversation seemed to be drawing to a close, I sensed a sadness in this young mom. I asked, "Are you OK?"

I saw the tears. "I'm sorry. I saw your video at church on Sunday. I'm so sorry about your son."

She had seen the video I posted a couple of days ago that was shown at Easter in the Park—*Losing Chandler, Holding Onto Hope.*

My heart was so moved. Standing before me was a mom who had never met me and yet her heart was breaking with mine. She was hurting with me. It meant so much.

I hugged this young mom and told her thank you. "Savor every moment," I offered.

About that time, her little one buzzed by again.

I noticed her toddler's plumped up diaper, and from somewhere deep in my brain, I recalled words I'd written in a book called *Days of Whine and Noses—Pep Talks for Tuckered Out Moms.* "Yes, it will be easier after potty training, but *right now,* there's the golden opportunity to pinch those cute little buns when the diaper gets changed."

My prayer for every mom who read my book was that they would cuddle a little longer, squeeze a little tighter, and breathe a little deeper—that they would embrace the craziness of mothering young children and recognize the significance in everything from potty training, to teething, to snotty noses.

After earning a credential I wish I didn't have, my conviction about this truth is even deeper today.

I hope these words from *Days of Whine and Noses* will inspire you to lean into *this* moment with those you love:

By living with one foot poised anxiously in tomorrow, we rob ourselves of the beauty that is in today.

April 25, 2019—Another One of Those People

Today I had the privilege of spending time with a fellow club member. Her son died less than a month before Chandler.

We hadn't met face to face before but had been introduced online to one another through a mutual friend. We decided to meet at the lake in Rancho Santa Margarita for a walk—a gorgeous day for it!

I put on my name tag from church to give a visual cue that this was me since, despite what appears to be a widespread notion, there's really no tell-tale way to identify the mom in the crowd whose son died. We would joke later in our conversation about how people assume there's some kind of "look" you're supposed to take on after losing a child. "Oh, that must be her—she looks like she's lost a son."

What are we *supposed* to look like?

There have been plenty of moments with no makeup. Or makeup that's smeared with tears. Or eyes red from crying. Or public wardrobes that seem to have been assembled while blindfolded and drinking heavily.

But not always. Quite often, I fix my hair, put on makeup, and make an attempt at matching my clothes.

Another thing we talked about hearing a lot is, "You're so strong." Almost simultaneously, we said, "What choice do we have?"

Speaking for myself, it's not that I don't appreciate the sentiment.

It's encouraging and nice to hear, even though inside I'm thinking, "What else can I do? Crawl in a hole and not come out?"

For me, strong means I try to remember that other people in the world want me to be around. They want me to show up. So I will take care of myself the best I know how. Strong, to me, means I admit my ultimate dependence on God to carry me through this—in supernatural and natural ways. I will take little miracles and cold

kombuchas. Both bless my soul. And strong means I lean into the purpose God has for me on this planet, whatever that is.

One of the things that went unsaid, I think, is that each time one of us said a sentence containing any form of the phrase "when . . . died," it was piercing. We don't want to hear it. But it's the truth. Do you say the truth, or do you soften it with "when he passed" or "before everything happened" or some other linguistic gymnastics to refer to the fact that the child you have loved all their life will never hug you again on this earth?

A few blogs ago, I wrote about being one of *those* people now. My friend had not read my blog, and I hadn't mentioned writing about that. Toward the end of our time together today, she told me that soon after her son died, her husband said to her, "We are *those* people now."

I'm grateful to get to know another one of those people.

My people.

April 27, 2019 – The Gondola

Grief is like one of those gondola rides when you go skiing or sightseeing on a mountain. The gondola hits you from behind, and you have no choice but to fall into the chair and ride it out. Tonight the gondola hit me from behind.

It was an absolutely gorgeous day golfing in a couples tournament at Dove Canyon Country Club with lifelong friends. In our particular foursome, we (the wives) have only golfed a handful of times. Let's just say, when someone asks what my handicap is, I say, "Golf." So even though we ended in last place today, I'm pretty proud that several times, we hit the ball instead of the grass. And several times, the ball went up in the air and advanced more than 10 feet. We only lost about five balls, and we ended the day with approximately the same amount of clubs we started with.

When we pulled the golf cart up to the clubhouse at the end of the day, I could see there was a wedding taking place by the waterfall outside the restaurant. It hit me. All my mind could envision was Chandler lined up with Chance and Charli at his oldest brother Chase's wedding on that very spot in 2016. He looked so handsome in his grey suit. Our family. All together. Celebrating.

Tears welling, I told Chip what was going on in my heart and my mind. He hugged me. We went into the pro shop to report our score, and as I was telling our friend Gabe that I'd like to start recording my scores to get a handicap, I lost it. I had to just walk out of the pro shop and try to get myself together. I was not successful. So I went to the women's restroom and cried. So many tears. Loud sobbing. I'm grateful no one else was in the locker room.

When I thought I could join everyone for dinner without losing it, I emerged from the locker room, breathing deeply, the kind of breathing you learn when preparing to have a baby the natural way and haven't yet discovered the magic of an epidural. My Lamaze breathing got me to the dining room, but as soon as I saw my friend and started to tell her why I was late, the dam broke again. We left the dining room and sat for a few minutes while she listened and was just there with me. The very best thing you can ever do for someone who is heartbroken and grieving is to just be with them and help them hold their pain.

Later, and this is another way I know God is with me, I got a text from a friend saying she was thinking of me. I gave her a call and told her about my evening. She just listened and hurt with me. She lost her dad not so long ago, so she gets the pain of loss.

I said, "I don't get it. How could I hold it together to speak at my son's memorial service, but I can't keep it together to report my golf score?!" She reminded me that it wasn't long ago that we walked into that very place for Chandler's memorial and that maybe now the reality has sunk in more than on January 13.

THIS is GOD WITH ME. Friends who listen. Who care. Who hurt with me.

Looking through pictures tonight, I see images of my son in the hospital when there was still hope. Images when hope had begun to fade. And images of Chandler in all his glory—shirtless, grinning, hugging, biking, flipping, LIVING. I have to believe he is doing all those things right now. I don't know it for a fact. But that's where faith comes in.

So today I had planned to write about how I discovered the power of silence and reflection. It will have to wait for another day. Today, all I could do...was ride the gondola.

MAY 2019

It's been four months today.

I wonder how much time will need to pass before the 1st and the 15th of every single month don't punch me in the gut? I wonder how those dates will feel with each passing year?

Today started out rough. Then God showed up in the form of a friend popping into my office with the most lovely gifts—a hug and a green juice from Nekter.

I went to our Wednesday chapel service and stood in the back to catch a bit of the student awards and the worship time. The first song was "Blessed Be Your Name." With broken voice, tears streaming, I declared that even though my road is marked by pain and suffering, I will bless the name of the Lord.

As I wept, I felt arms wrap me. My Nekter friend had gotten up from her seat and come back to hug me. She whispered, "You're not alone." God showed up.

I went back to my office, put my head down on my desk, and cried. *I miss you so much Chandler. I just miss you so much. I hate this.*

Before noon, I'd gotten texts from four friends letting me know they are praying for me and thinking of me—including one friend who used WhatsApp because she's traveling in another country. God showed up.

At lunch, tears gave way to moments of joy. The Bridge Church treated us to Sol Agave Mexican food, and we sat outside around the table discussing must-try restaurants, telling stories about eating squirrel (more about that in another post about my Redneck roots), and even touching on one of my favorite topics—the Enneagram. Good food, good people, good conversation.

Tonight I went to Sweatstar again. I decided my intention for this evening's hot yoga session would be *peace*. I needed peace for my mind and soul and body. With every pose, I turned the words over in my head—...*peace that passes understanding* (Philippians 4:7)... *my peace I give you* (John 14:27)...*let the peace of Christ rule in your hearts*...(Colossians 3:15). Peace.

At the end of the session, I lay on my mat, eyes closed, tears streaming, trying not to let sobs overtake me. I felt warm hands smelling of rich essential oils gently touch my forehead—an anointing of compassion. In a packed, dimly lit room, the instructor somehow knew. She lingered as if to say, "I'm here. I'm with you in your pain." God showed up.

Four months. One day at a time. And only because God keeps showing up.

May 3, 2019—Managing the Pain

I went to Board & Brew last night to hear Alex Brown play. He was a friend of Chandler's, and Chandler was a fan. It is always good for my heart to hug my B&B tribe.

The place was packed, and the bar was hopping. For a minute, I let my mind play a movie of Chandler back there chatting it up with regulars, flashing his dimples, and winning fans. He loved engaging with people. No one was a stranger, and no one was beyond the realm of meaningful connection and conversation.

On the wall opposite the bar hangs Chandler's skateboard deck. He was never able to actually see it or do a kickflip on it. One of Chandler's best friends brought that skateboard deck to the hospital just a couple of days after the accident. Some of us signed it during the days of hope. We all prayed like we'd never prayed before that Chandler would leave that hospital and someday be able to get on that skateboard and scare us all with whatever crazy trick he decided to execute. I read the messages Charli, Chase, and Chance had written to Chandler. My heart broke for them. They love their brother so much.

So now I'm facing Mother's Day. I'm scared. I talked with a dear friend today about it. She is part of the same shitty club. I told her I'm not sure what I need for Mother's Day this year. I just know it's going to be hard. She is so wise. "I think maybe you are trying to manage the pain and the experience ahead of time, and you just can't."

So now I'm thinking through what might be the kindest thing to do for myself. I've thought of going on an adventure with my kids—maybe Knott's Berry Farm, San Diego Zoo, bowling…

I'm sort of thinking I don't want to do what we've always done. I can't bear to think of the kids all here at the house eating together and then playing games to indulge me, my usual request. Because it won't be like we've always done. Chandler will be missing.

It's not that I want to deny the pain or pretend like it's business as usual. I just want to be able to celebrate my other three amazing kids. I have done nothing in this life to deserve them. And yet…oh, how grateful I am that God blessed me with Chase, Chance, and Charli. They are my heart and soul. My best thing.

What does that look like? How do you celebrate the joy of mothering three kids when the fourth is not here? Will never be here again?

This journey toward Mother's Day can only be taken one day at a time. One step at a time.

Thank you, God, for bringing loving, caring people into my life to surround me as I live through some of the most difficult days of my life. I cannot manage the pain. I surrender it to You and ask You to help me recognize every single practical and supernatural way You are carrying me. I open myself to Your peace, Your presence, Your provision.

May 5, 2019—Turning Point in Trust

Friday, May 3, was a red-letter day for me, a turning point. I want to write about it as a touchstone of remembrance, of accountability. I want to return to Friday in my mind again and again.

I have been a person of faith since a young age. I have said that my trust is in God, that He is the ultimate source to meet my needs. I believe I've done my best to live that out, and I'm not beating myself up or bemoaning lost time. It's just that on Friday, a light came on, and I realized there's a depth of trust I've never ventured into because I've always been able to access other sources to meet most of my needs to some extent. I'm now in a season where I've come to know that there just aren't enough external resources to touch the deep chasm of need in my soul.

On Friday, I had conversations with a couple of friends who were helping me process some stuff that is just downright painful. One of my friends made an offhanded comment that I'm certain was not intended to result in some great "aha" moment on my part. But it did. As I shared my hurt and frustration about a particular situation in which I was feeling unheard and uncared for despite clearly communicating my needs, my friend responded, "It's like going to the hardware store for a loaf of bread."

She was right. That's exactly what it's like. You keep asking and expecting and hoping, and in the end, the thing you need most just isn't available where you're looking.

I'm especially grateful for how friends and family have supported me as I've commenced this involuntary grief journey. God continually uses people to demonstrate His love and care for me, to say, "I've got you." Just today, I got a text from one of my dearest friends that she was praying for me…at exactly the right moment.

But there are countless moments when I'm by myself, with my pain, with the gaping Chandler-sized hole in my heart. Where do I turn in those moments?

The revelation to me on Friday was that my deepest needs can only be met in God, the one who created me and knows me better, loves me more, than anyone ever could. When I expect to find a loaf of bread at a hardware store, I set an unrealistic expectation which will inevitably lead to disappointment—also known as a resentment waiting to happen. On Friday, I realized that I have been anxious, angry, obsessive, and irritable far too many times in my life because I have been focused on getting a loaf of bread from a hardware store instead of visiting the bakery.

Just because I had this revelation on Friday does not mean I'm going to walk this out perfectly right out the gate. You can't undo years of habits and thought patterns in a day or a week or a month. That's why I want to keep coming back to the moment of clarity on May 3 when something clicked and everything in me knew that I can trust God alone to meet the needs that inhabit the deepest recesses of my heart and soul. In that moment, I felt a sense of complete peace, hope, joy, and freedom. I want that every day, not just in an aha moment on a Friday when I realize the only place it makes sense to go is…

The bakery.

May 6, 2019–Both/And NOT Either/Or

Since January 1, I've been told a few times, "You just have to be thankful and celebrate the time you had." I completely get where they're coming from, and I'm not trying to be the grief police. My problem is with that little word *just*.

By some kind of magical emotional programming, wouldn't it be great if we could skip straight to the celebration part? The part where we relive the laughter, the family get-togethers, the milestones. All of the good stuff when we were together and couldn't imagine ever not being that way. And in the reliving, there would only be joy and gratitude.

But magic only happens in Vegas and on *America's Got Talent*. We are wired to grieve when we lose someone we love. If we try to skip it or skim over it, it will come out some way. We can't *just* celebrate.

We have to hold the pain, sit in it, feel it, move with it and through it. When it punches us in the gut, we have to admit that it hurts, maybe double over and hold on for a bit while we try to regain our breath. We have to let our minds and souls absorb the new reality—that we will not be making any new memories with our loved one.

I will never get to laugh at Chandler's always amusing responses in the board games we used to play, especially on Mother's Day when I held them hostage. I will never get to hear Chandler tell me about his next career plan. I will never get to be surprised by the hairstyle of the week.

Grief is not an either/or proposition. I can't *just* celebrate Chandler's 25 years. I have to honor my grief process. As much as I hate being in pain, it comes with the territory when you love.

It's both/and.

This week is especially hard. I'm not sure that today I can authentically use the word "celebrate"—my heart is not in celebration mode today. It might be a while before the celebration part overshadows the grieving part. But even now, they are both present to some degree, varying with the day or the week.

I celebrate and I grieve. I have to make room for both.

May 7, 2019 – The Evolution of Mother's Day

I was thinking today about how Mother's Day has evolved for me through the years, both as a daughter celebrating my own mom and as a mom being celebrated.

First, a tangent. I have to say how grateful I am for this morning. I woke up with the most uplifting, encouraging song running through my mind. It's old school—Kirk Franklin and God's Property (GP), "My Life is in Your Hands." I've been listening to it a lot these past weeks. The chorus is a declaration that no matter what comes my way, my life rests in the hands of God. I've held onto that truth through some very dark times, and now I'm clinging to it for life… quite literally.

So on to the evolution of Mother's Day.

When I was growing up, I remember my dad taking me to get gifts for my mom for Mother's Day. One year, I insisted we go to TG&Y, a Redneck superstore, where I picked out some pink flowered PJs, probably the cheapest material ever created. Bless her heart. My mom wore those cheap PJs even after the first wash when they shrunk to a size that would have fit her perfectly when she was eight years old.

After my mom died in 1983, it was a few years before Mother's Day brought anything except tears and an indescribable missing of my mama. With the passing of the years, the pain did ease, although I do remember wishing with all my heart that she were there when I had Chase and was the celebrated mom for the first time.

As much as I absolutely loved being a mom of young kids, all I wanted on Mother's Day when they were little was to NOT be responsible for them for a day. I would basically tell Chip, "You've got them." And I would go shopping, or go read somewhere, or just wander around aimlessly for as long as humanly possible until the witching hour when I had to return to the dishes, and laundry, and sibling skirmishes, and bedtime struggles, and mealtime pickiness.

As they grew older and were able to wipe their own butts, blow their own noses, make their own food, do their own laundry, referee their own bouts, and in general take care of their own necessities, the game changed. I wanted to go do something alone for part of the day and then have everyone come together for dinner and to just hang out. Usually the hanging out part includes games, which most of my family does not love, but I get to force them into because it's freaking Mother's Day, and I DESERVE a round of *Apples to Apples*!

This Mother's Day marks another point in its evolution for me. I am trying to suspend expectations. Like my wise friend told me, I cannot pre-manage the pain. I know it will be unlike any other Mother's Day before it. I'm grateful my kids will be surrounding me. They are amazing. Just being with them is healing for my heart. I don't know how I got this group of people that I love so much to be with, but I'm not going to argue about it.

The evolution continues. Five more days.

May 11, 2019 — Joy

I have found the cure for everything. GOAT YOGA!!! It is one of the most joyful experiences I've ever had. Charli agrees—we will definitely be doing it again.

I don't know who decided to put yoga and goats together. Was it a farmer who saw his baby goats frolicking with abandon in the field and said, "I bet yoga would help them get centered?" Or was it a yoga instructor who saw the fiercely determined scrunched up faces of their students trying to master the eagle pose who said, "These people need to lighten up a bit?" Either way, I'm certainly glad goat yoga happened.

I was a bit skeptical at first because while most goat yoga events are about $35/person, this one was FREE! My suspicion was that we would show up and find out we had the B-list goats—the ones that were too old or too heavy to jump up on our backs and play. Or maybe those narcoleptic goats that fall over asleep when startled. I was so wrong! From the git go, these goats were full of life, ricocheting off people's backs with their hooves, voicing their strong opinions, chewing our hair and clothes, peeing on our mats, and interacting with us yogis like any well-mannered young goats should.

One of the goats seemed to have a case of mistaken species identity—he really LOVED the lady in the front row. They may have exchanged numbers.

After goat yoga, Charli and I went to Stacks for breakfast. It's Mother's Day weekend, so I decided to honor taste buds over health considerations. We got guava French toast with toffee syrup—a thick, gooey sauce with real toffee bits in it. It was…oh, I don't even know a word for it. I just know my eyes rolled back, and I left my body for a minute after the first bite. As if that weren't enough, we also got the spicy chicken and bacon waffle with spicy mayo and cheddar cheese. It felt so good to be so bad. We will be back. Oh, yes, we will be back.

Tonight I did hot yoga. Word of the day…JOY. Bracelet I was wearing—Choose Joy. Scripture that kept running through my mind—"The joy of the Lord is my strength" (Nehemiah 8:10).

I began this day with such joy. I will end this day remembering that whatever comes my way, I have a God who is with me, who will carry me through the hardest of times, and who is able to plant seeds of joy in the soil of sadness.

May 12, 2019—Mother's Day

I have been dreading this day since January 1. There will be many firsts, some I'm well aware of and some that will sneak up on me. Mother's Day is the most personal. This is the day my kids write really nice words to me in a card just because I'm their mom. Their words mean more to me than anything. Being their mom means more to me than anything. So here's how my first Mother's Day without Chandler went down.

First, I began to receive texts that let me know so many prayers and big virtual hugs were coming my way. Throughout the day, these words of encouragement and scripture verses were the wind in my sail to keep me moving through the turbulent waters.

My first conversation today, the first live "Happy Mother's Day" I heard, was from Australia, one of Chandler's best friends, a young man I love dearly. With each Mother's Day text from Chandler's friends, my tribe, I knew Chandler was telling everyone around him, "See, I told you my friends are the best."

After I got off the phone, I sat down at the table and cried. I got up and wandered around the kitchen crying, lost, unsure what to do with myself. The phone rang. I saw that it was my sweet friend Christine who has been through several Mother's Days without her daughter. I managed some semblance of "hello" through the sobs. She cried with me. She didn't offer any solutions or spiritual platitudes. She just hurt with me. And she prayed for me. That conversation created emotional space for me. Since I was able to release some of my anguish to a trusted friend in the same damn club, I felt like I had more capacity to enjoy the gift of being with my kids later when we would get together.

When I got to Sweatstar for hot yoga this morning, I was greeted with a hug by one of the owners—such a compassionate soul. I cried as she hugged me. She said, "I know. I can't imagine. Just for this hour, put it all aside and just be on your mat."

I always choose a word or phrase, or more likely it chooses me, each time I come to my mat. I've chosen *joy, surrender, in Christ, let go and let God, strength*, and *peace*. The only word I could manage today was *breathe*. With each pose, the only way to get through the next few seconds was to breathe. I knew that was how I would get through the rest of the day. Breathe. Deeply. One breath at a time. Appreciating the gift of that moment and the next and the next.

On the way home, I decided to stop at the bike memorial. Of course, more tears. I just sat there, again feeling lost. Just lost. A lady walked by, stopped, and said a prayer. Through my tears, I said, "That's my son." She knelt down and put her arm around me. She told me that she walks by the bike frequently on her way to church and says a prayer for us every time. Apparently, she was walking to church the night of Chandler's accident and passed by that intersection just after he was taken away in the ambulance. I told her thank you so much for every prayer. When she walked away, I prayed, "Thank you, Jesus. You see me."

I went home and showered. I had told my friend Christine earlier that I had thought about reading old Mother's Day cards from Chandler, but I just wasn't sure if I could do it today. Maybe it would just be too much. Well, I got this wild idea that I would read through them and find Chandler's signature so I could take it and get his name tattooed on my wrist. I sat on my closet floor and cried as I read some of Chandler's words to me through the years. One of the signature lines was, "Love, your Chandler Man." That's the one. I want that tattooed on my wrist. Chance was the voice of reason and said, "Mom, maybe we should do some research and go to a reputable tattoo place instead of just what happens to be open on Mother's Day." So, that adventure will have to wait for another day. But it will come.*

The best part of my day came when all my kids—almost all my kids—climbed into the car and headed to the beach. These are my favorite people. Chase, Chance, Charli, and (because God smiled on us big time) Karen. They make me laugh. They challenge my thinking. They show up for me. They are good human beings. And I thoroughly enjoy hanging out with them. To say I am grateful and humbled to have them in my life is a gross understatement, but I don't know how to find words adequate to say what these people mean to me.

We drove to Laguna Beach. When Chandler was little, he used to

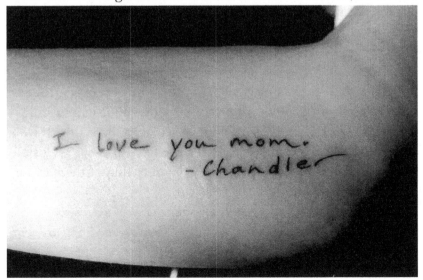

call it "li'l guna." There was traffic, but it didn't even matter. Having time with them in the car to talk and laugh was medicine for my soul…as always. We tried a new pizza place and then took a long walk on the beach. Then we stood in a LONG line for gelato that was worth every gram of sugar and fat. Chance got me some dark chocolate lavender truffles at a chocolate shop while we were waiting in line. Somehow every heavenly flavor found its way into those tiny truffles.

What did it feel like to be all together today but not really all together? There were moments when I almost forgot. I mean, there have been plenty of times in the past when all the kids couldn't be together at the same time on a holiday for whatever reason. One year, Chandler was in India on Mother's Day. There were other moments, like when we took our picture on the beach, that I thought, *This isn't right. There should be four of them.* Even though I didn't get my Chandler Mother's Day hug, I imagine he made sure my mom got a big, warm Chandler hug—"from your daughter."

If I had to name three words that capture the essence of this first Mother's Day with the gaping hole, they would be pain, joy, and gratitude.

Pain. I miss my boy so much. It feels like too much to carry sometimes. The pain is unfathomable and yet tangible. The ache. The finality. The missing. It is so deep and dark. It leaves me wandering around lost. It takes my breath away.

Joy. Being with my kids today brought me pure joy. Plain and simple.

Gratitude. Mother's Day is over, and I didn't disappear into an endless abyss of grief, never to return. I didn't do it in a vacuum. I couldn't have. This entire weekend, I have been blessed with texts and calls and flowers and a "C" necklace to help me feel close to Chandler. Every tear I've shed holds the reflection of these expressions of love and support.

Thank you, God, for being so good to me today. You brought exactly what I needed to get me through this day I have dreaded. You are with me. You see me.

I made it!!!

*That day came in January 2020 when a local tattoo artist replicated Chandler's written words to me from a birthday card—*I love you, Mom.* Followed by a perfect copy of Chandler's signature. Devyn, the artist, remarked to me, "If you look closely, his period looks like a heart." And it does.

May 15, 2019 – Go Me, Choose Joy!

Booyah!!! Tonight I finished my 15-day challenge at Sweatstar. I am celebrating with a Booch Craft orange/pomegranate/beet beverage. So refreshing!

Yesterday I learned of a family in our area that lost their 10-year-old son, hit by a car while riding his BMX bike. My heart aches for them. Those first days and weeks are almost intolerable. I am praying for them, and I know they will be surrounded by a loving community that will help carry them through this.

When I read about it, I relived some of the horrible feelings of December 15 and January 1, all rolled up into one. I was sick at my stomach. I saw the family's picture with their little guy and knew the pain they will feel every time they look at that picture and have to absorb the reality that he is no longer here. It really just feels like too much to bear. I want to tell them to be so gentle with themselves. I want to tell them—first, brush your teeth. Then get dressed. Then maybe you will be able to make your way to the kitchen and get a bite to eat or some coffee. Just put one foot in front of the other, even when it feels like you're trudging through wet cement. You will make it through this. And your son will live on because you kept putting one foot in front of the other and telling his story. Most of all, right now I just want to cry with them.

Today I grabbed my "Choose Joy" bracelet to wear. It was a gift from a friend after Chandler died, so it reminds me that I am absolutely not alone. It also reminds me that even in the middle of just plain crappiness, I still have choices. I can choose to isolate myself or to remain open to the love of people who want to hold me up. I can choose to obsess over every negative aspect of my circumstances or to turn my thoughts toward the positive, even just in this moment.

In this moment, I am breathing. I have access to food if I'm hungry. I'm sitting in a comfortable chair. I have a good book to pick up and read.

I can choose to sink into the painful images and memories that surround losing Chandler…and just stay there. Or I can allow myself to choose joy. Right now, that may mean recalling fun memories with Chandler or belly laughing during goat yoga or meditating on scripture that feeds my soul and reminds me that the joy of the Lord is my strength.

In this moment…I choose joy.

Also, GO ME for finishing my 15-day challenge at hot yoga!

May 20, 2019—Running to the Rock

Life doesn't stop when your kid dies. The clouds don't stop producing storms of pain and sadness and anxiety just because the river is already full to overflowing or the trees have been bent or broken in the wind. I wish just for a while, the only pain I would have to process is the pain of losing Chandler.

I was reminded yesterday on our hike that the only safe place my soul can hide when I feel like I'm drowning in the pain of life is in God. I picture myself under the rock that can withstand any storm that rages around it.

My God—the high crag where I run for dear life, hiding behind the boulders, safe in the granite hideout; My mountaintop refuge…(II Samuel 22:2).

It's not easy to get to the rock sometimes. I am distracted by my own attempts to control the storm or build my own flimsy shelter. When I give up and run to my strong rock, I know I can find real peace and security.

I think this is what Step 1, in 12-step recovery circles, is all about. Surrendering the illusion of control. Then Step 2, recognizing there is a safe place I can trust. And Step 3, choosing to run to that safe place.

God, I need a safe place. My heart and soul are aching. I know You are that safe place. I run to You, my rock, my security, my peace.

May 23, 2019 — Stronger

You never know how strong you are until your strength is put to the test.

As I was in my down dog yoga position tonight at Sweatstar, I realized that two of the rings on my outspread fingers represent two people I have lost. I have my mother's wedding ring on my right ring finger. And I have my *WWHC* (What Would Honor Chandler?) ring on my left ring finger. I did not check either of those boxes. I've lived through several difficult, even heartbreaking, circumstances for which I did not check the box.

As I moved through my first few yoga poses, the phrase came to me—*stronger than you think you are*. I held onto that throughout the next 55 sweat-drenched minutes.

I'm under no delusions. Whenever I'm hit head on with the hard stuff, I can no more scrape up enough strength within myself than I can scrape up sufficient change from my couch cushions to make for a decent college entry bribe.

What I have learned through time and life experience is that I don't have to look to myself as my own ultimate source of strength.

My grace is sufficient for you, for my strength is made perfect in weakness. (II Corinthians 12:9).

Even through the worst of circumstances, this scripture has been a shot of courage in my veins. It allows me to acknowledge my human limitations and fall into arms that are stronger.

We aren't stuck with just our own internal resources. In our weakness, God is strong. Even when we could never imagine facing down the giant in front of us…

We are stronger than we think we are.

May 30, 2019 — Chandler's Room

Chandler's room is now a guest room. It is still Chandler's room. I don't know if we will call it that forever. But for now, it just does not feel right to call it the guest room.* Chandler is supposed to be in there. Surrounded by his music festival clothes, his dirty dishes, his sleeping mats for when friends sleep over, his broken skateboards… all his stuff.

I'm not going to sugarcoat it. It was a hot mess, that room of his. But I would give anything—literally anything—to open his door and see a petrified plate of nachos on the floor and a new music festival t-shirt on top of his dirty clothes pile.

How can I even say how much I miss him? He is part of me. I carried him for over nine months because, like most of my kids, he didn't want to come out on time. His sweet face when he entered my world. The dimples that emerged. His little hand in mine. Countless trips to try out the newest skate or BMX parks…and the closest emergency rooms.

My other kids say that Chandler could get away with anything. It's pretty much true. There was a childish innocence about him even in his mischief.

My lifelong friend Carole was the first person to stay in Chandler's room since January, after it had been cleaned out. Yesterday, another lifelong friend, Pastor Bob Willis, who so beautifully officiated Chandler's memorial service, was the first to sleep in Chandler's room since we got a comfy sectional queen fold-out sofa a couple of weeks ago. This means we actually, for the first time in Espinoza history, have a designated space for our guests. I know Chandler is happy to welcome Pastor Bob, and tomorrow his wife MaryEllen, to his room.

To decorate Chandler's room, we used the Dallas Cowboys jersey his Board & Brew friends had made for him along with several pictures my friend Stephanie had blown up for Chandler's memorial. A few of Chandler's favorite things—golf, dancing, skateboarding, biking, the beach, and hiking.

A focal point of the room is one of Chandler's prized possessions—his orange lungi, a type of sarong that he got when he was in India. His friends joke about how Chandler just didn't give a rip what anyone thought. He would show up wearing his lungi because it was "comfortable." I love Chandler's free spirit, his joie de vivre.

Chandler, honey, I love that your room is now a welcoming, comfortable space for friends and family. I think you like that too. But I would give anything on earth to have you back in there with your hot mess. May your enthusiasm for adventure and your care for people infuse themselves into every single person who ever stays in your room. I miss you so much, my Chandler Man.

*Two years later, we are still calling it Chandler's room. That's just what it is.

June 2019

I wonder how long before the 1st of the month is just the 1st of the month? When will it slip my mind that it's the anniversary of the rest of my lifetime without Chandler?

Thinking back on these past five months, it's hard to comprehend the depth and breadth of emotion I've processed. In five months, I've gone from sitting on my couch, staring into space, wondering how I would get through the day, to getting back to work, having a normal schedule, and functioning at a level that seems to be not too far from my norm.

What feels different is that I don't have it in me to take on any new challenges. I feel like I need to operate in my zone, not above it. I don't have the bandwidth for that. And yet, every day, in some form or other, I find myself having to rise above my zone.

Oh, my heart—OK, this is real-time processing—Chance just ran out the door and said "Hey" to MaryEllen, my friend visiting from out of town, who is blow drying her hair in the bathroom, and it sounded just like Chandler. Just like Chandler as he would run out the door to meet his friends. I miss that voice.

Chandler could not have better friends. Brendan and Christian stopped by Chandler's bike memorial today and cleaned it up, added some flowers. My heart aches for them. Brendan spent more time with Chandler in the past few years than probably anyone. How many young adults lose their best friend? How do you even deal with that at such a young age?

Tonight, we are going dancing with our friends Bob and Mary-Ellen. The last time we all danced together was in Punta Cana last October, before our universe imploded.

Chandler, honey, I miss you so much. I hate that I haven't seen you in five months. I hate everything about not having you here. We all do. But we are going to be OK. We know you would want us to love well, to live in the moment, to do the next right thing. And to dance.

So tonight…we dance.

June 2, 2019—From Chase to Chandler

I have shared Chance's song and Charli's eulogy from Chandler's memorial. The following was shared by his oldest brother, Chase.

Reading through Chase's words tonight is difficult. There is an immeasurable depth of pain that accompanies the witnessing of your children's heartache. My heart literally hurts for Chase, Chance, and Charli. I want to take away their pain, but that's not possible. I suppose it wouldn't be advisable even if it were possible. Chase himself, shortly after Chandler died, told me that he did not want to shrink from what the pain had to teach him.

I believe that the character of my kids is being strengthened and their capacity for compassion being enlarged through the loss of their brother. It's not something I signed up for, and I hate that Chandler is gone. I hate that his brothers and sister have to figure out how to live their lives with this new reality, this gaping hole. But I believe in my kids. And I am so very proud of the human beings they are.

My brother is an enigma, scarcely understood in his entirety, but appreciated with fullness.

Time in Chandler's presence inspired me to be present and grateful for every moment.

Chandler was authentic and available, yet still there was, and remains to this day, a wondrous frontier within him yet to be explored.

He lived for, yet also feared, that frontier.

He pushed boundaries and thrived at the edge.

He encouraged others to discover new ground.

He tangled and tussled with the limits of his body, both enamored and skeptical of what the highest of heights, and fastest of speeds may bring.

Hold your breath and squint your eyes with fearful anticipation… you'll be astounded at what you see.

My brother flies, really.

A master of the physical world until his final day in the flesh.

The hardest moments of my life were spent in anticipation of losing my brother.

Driving his car home from his place of work on December 17 was like hell on earth.

His blood stain still fresh on Antonio parkway.

At the house, I sat in his car for what seemed an eternity.

A cascade of emotions and memories flooded through me like none I've ever had.

I clutched at everything in arm's reach, just to feel something of his.

I breathed deeply through my nose to capture his scent.

I needed him, any part, any trace.

I became frightened and crazed when my nose congested and I could no longer smell him.

I pounded the steering wheel with clenched fists and lifted my head to the sky in anguish, in pain, in sorrow.

Stumbling into the house, the door barely visible through the wells in my eyes.

I collapsed to the floor in a state of demoralized weakness, mumbling "I love you, Chandler. I love you buddy."

I miss my brother, I want him back, I'll do anything.

Chandler has encouraged me toward movement from that place of agony, though it still lingers in me just below the surface of my composure.

I'm not ready to be without him; none of us are.

I've pondered in my darkest moments, is he well without his body? Can he hear me without his ears?

Can Chandler feel me and speak to me without cells and breath?

Then I am reminded by the holder of purpose, the architect of meaning, that Chandler is bigger than his body.

Although I am not free of bodily limitations, and thus cannot receive Chandler in the way I have dreamed since a tragic December 15, the dream will one day be divine reality.

I want to hold my brother once again, to look at him, to speak to him, to absorb all that is him with fresh attentiveness.

Chandler is incomprehensibly free, and I long for unbounded unification of brotherhood.

Until then, Chandler, be with me, be with us as we struggle and as we rejoice.

My brother's spirit is magnetic and mysterious.

His upset did not last long, nor did ours.

Chandler had innocence in his voice, in his eyes, his soul, even when he was far from it.

I can't stay mad at Chandler, none of us could, and that's why he got away with everything.

Like a puppy who pees on the rug…one glance at him and all is redeemed.

Everyone felt heard and cared for by him.

He was the brother, the son, the companion we all want.

He welcomed and embraced all of our brokenness and celebrated us for the good.

He has many fans, but he was the biggest and most loyal of fans.

He was everyone's best friend, which sounds impossible, but it's not.

Chandler's curious, childlike grin was transparent.

You meet him for five minutes and feel you've apprehended all of him.

Yet somehow there remained more mystery behind his eyes than in anyone you'd ever met.

Conversations took unexpected turns and made me question my understanding of the universe, of myself, and of Chandler.

My brother disarmed those around him.

Even in heated conflict, he brought about peace and patience.

He didn't posture to be dominant or powerful, but he lent strength to those who are weak (apologies to those who caught one in the jaw; you probably earned it).

Chandler was a leader, but never self-proclaimed.

In these days since his body retired, I am both pained and proud to learn of who he was through his actions and words.

There is so much I would have loved to see and learn while he was here.

He did so much good, had so much influence.

But many of his best deeds were quietly appreciated.

I will take solace and pride in growing closer to his spirit through learning of him, and from him.

Once Chandler's life became a looming uncertainty, my understanding of the scope and breadth of his goodness to others was magnified one hundred-fold, at which time we listened and watched in awe of my marvelous brother.

The world is better for having you in it. My world is fuller.

Thank you, Chandler.

I see the world from a new vantage point; one of mercy, humility, acceptance.

Chandler loved without pretense, without prejudice.

He loved not in pieces, but in wholeness.

I want to grow up to be like my little brother.

June 3, 2019—Peace

"O God, you have let me pass the day in peace; let me pass the night in peace. O Lord, who has no lord. There is no strength but in you…Under your hand I pass the night. You are my Mother and my Father. Amen."

~Traditional African Prayer

I read this prayer the other day in a devotional called *Healing After Loss* by Martha Whitmore Hickman. As I went into hot yoga later that day, the sound loop in my mind was Jesus' words in John 14:27—*"Peace I leave with you, my peace I give you…let your heart not be troubled, neither let it be afraid."*

Grief is unsettling. It really is "an achievement," as Hickman says, to experience any length of time in peace when you're grieving.

If peace is like the smooth, unbroken surface of a tranquil sea, grief is like that same sea at the mercy of an unpredictable storm. There are moments of peace. And there are moments of unnerving turbulence, often arising so quickly and violently that the surface holds no memory of its prior smoothness.

Like when I drove by the bike memorial tonight. My mind was yanked back to an evening almost seven months ago when Chandler was riding his bike and never made it past that spot. It brought back a flood of horrific memories. I just kept driving. It's all internal. You would never know from outside appearances the tumultuous storm brewing inside.

Under the strong hand of God, I regain my peace. I know there will be more turbulence to come, but I am grateful for any amount of time that I spend in peace.

The fact that there is any peace at all…that is a miracle.

June 5, 2019—Chandler and the Monks

One of the pitfalls of being on social media is waking up to a pop-up memory that punches you in the gut. Facebook reminded me this morning that six years ago, Chandler was teaching English to exiled monks in the Himalayas. That would be so freaking cool if it weren't so freaking hard. From what I've heard and read, someday seeing that image of Chandler won't sting so much. My initial response will be joy, not profound pain and sorrow. But that's someday. Not today.

India was Chandler's happy place. Along with the beach, the skate park, the golf course, the mountains, the dance floor, and the seat of his BMX bike. He loved his lungi and his leatherbound journals from India, one of which we used as a guest sign-in book at his memorial. He treasured his friendship with Bob Ney, the mentor who took him on the trip of a lifetime.

He told me when he got home from India that one thing that really impacted him was traveling to areas where people had so little and yet were some of the most content, happy people he'd ever met.

He actually came home with the idea of starting a lungi business to benefit people in a certain village in India.

One of his many adventures in India was a silent retreat. He told me that he went into the retreat terrified of not being able to use words for a few days. Chandler LOVED words, as anyone who knows him will attest. But he said he learned to be OK with the silence and to calm the monkey mind that constantly diverts our attention away from stillness.

That reminds me of when I went alone on a spiritual retreat years ago and someone who knows my penchant for starting a conversation with any creature possessing a pulse reminded me not to try and chat up the priests who may be in the midst of some kind of vow of silence. I found an elderly priest, Brother Claude, who was not on a vow of silence of any sort and asked if I could talk with him. During that conversation, I asked, "Doesn't it get old…having the same exact routine every single day?" His response—"Oh, my dear, how could loving God ever get old?"

Chandler possessed a tremendous depth and breadth of spirituality. This was evident when, at four, with his cute little lisp, he said, "People don't mean it when they thay they have Jethuth in their heart, cuth Jethuth hath uth in *Hith* heart."

That's where it all has to start. Jesus has us in His heart. That's what matters most.

Jesus has me in His heart. He has Chandler in His heart. That's why I can start the day with a punch in the gut and end the day knowing it is well with my soul. And I will see Chandler again.

June 6, 2019—The Hardest Part

Today someone asked me, "What's the hardest part for you?" She said it like that because she too lost her son recently, and we each have our own "hardest parts," all of us in this club.

I think maybe the hardest part can vary depending on the day or the month. Today I would say the hardest part is when it settles in on me that Chandler really is gone, that I will never see him again while I'm breathing on this earth. Those moments hit me most when I see images of him, especially of that grin of his that always made it hard to stay mad at him.

One Sunday evening we were all around the dinner table. Chandler was probably about four. We had to be out the door for church on time because I was speaking at the service. I'd cleared the table and came back in to find Chandler covered head to toe in strawberry yogurt. "Chandler, what are you doing?" Grinning ear to ear, he said, "I'm pretending ith thunthcreen."

When those moments hit, it's like the veil that separates me a bit from this new reality is torn away, and I am left staring at a dark, deep, endless abyss where Chandler does not exist. Not in a way that I can touch or hear or smell. It is too much for me to hold. I can't stay there long. Maybe I should. Maybe I should set aside an hour or a day to sit and look through pictures of Chandler before scrambling to repair the veil. I think the veil, for me, is necessary. I really can't absorb all this at once.

The hardest part keeps coming…over and over and over again. And over and over and over again, I continue to breathe and live and smile and laugh and cry and love.

June 7, 2019 — Team Chan

Today was evidence that the greatest joy can commingle with the greatest pain.

It started with a trip to the dentist for phase two of a dental implant process. It's never my favorite thing to have someone stick a drill in my mouth, bear down with all their weight and drill a post into my bone. What made it worse—that tooth was pulled the day before Chandler died. All those memories and emotions of December 31 and January 1 poured over me when I walked into that dentist's office. I texted my friend and said, "Please pray for me…I can't cry in this chair." She did, and I didn't. Pretty much everything about the first two hours of today was painful.

But then…there was joy.

My friend Tracey Desmond and her husband Mark run a nonprofit called High Hopes dedicated to rehabilitating traumatic brain injury victims. Chandler would have gone there had he left the hospital. When Tracey asked if we would be interested in playing on Team High Hopes for a golf tournament benefiting victims of traumatic brain injury, I knew this was going to be a special day. So after getting a post drilled into my bone, Chip and I met two of Chandler's best friends, Grant and Brendan, at the golf course to spend the day doing something Chandler loved and supporting a cause with which we now have a heart connection.

It was one of the best days ever. Lots of wonderful and lots of difficult right up next to each other. We used Chandler's ball marker, and Chip played with a ball that had a picture of Chandler and him on it. Chip's driver cover was a roadrunner that he had bought for Chandler for Christmas just before the accident. Our hearts went out to those families we met whose lives are impacted every single day by traumatic brain injury.

Lots of fist bumps and high fives and laughter and Chandler stories. It was good to see Brendan and Grant having fun, ripping the ball down the fairway. They miss Chandler so much.

So now I sit here, mouth throbbing, images of today playing in my mind. Especially the image of me sinking a 20-foot putt! And I'm reminded once again that all the best stuff and all the worst stuff can bump up against each other in the same day, even in the same hour. They can even converge to bring laughter through tears. And it can be a good day.

June 8, 2019—Just for Today

Today I couldn't do anything hot—no hot yoga, no hot pilates or cycle, NOTHING hot—because of getting that post screwed into my gums yesterday. So I decided I would carve out a couple of quiet hours for myself before tackling a looming household project. You could also call those couple of hours "avoidant behavior" since the project is not something I was looking forward to. I choose to call it intentional time for reflection and personal growth. That sounds better.

I went to a local tea house and ordered the special—turmeric coconut latte. It did not disappoint.

Then I perched myself at an outdoor table, pulled out my Faith, Hope, Love journal, my blue gel pen, and my 12-step book. I opened it up to Step 2: *Acknowledged that there is a God who is able to restore me to sanity.* Each question in the book helped me flesh out what that looks like in my life.

One question in particular really spoke to me: *What can I gain from believing I could be supported and loved by a power greater than myself?*

I responded:

I can gain an unshakable sense of security and courage to do the hard things—like look at my own faults and make decisions that may not please everyone I would like to please. And courage to try new things, to take chances, because I am in the hands of one who loves me always, simply, unconditionally.

Sometimes we can choose to do for a day, or for a few hours, what we could not fathom doing for longer periods of time. It helps to use the phrase "just for today" or "just for the next three hours."

Just for two hours today, I chose to focus on God—His power and love and ability to address my deepest needs.

Thank you, God, that I do not have to rely only on my own inner resources. I'm grateful that you are bigger, that you care for me, and that you are able to meet me right where I am with every resource I could ever need. Amen.

June 18, 2019—Gone

Today at work, I did a tour for a delightful young family who has three little boys. Three little boys. That's what I had. Two are all grown up. The third...is gone.

I loved hearing about their little guys, and I told them stories about my boys as if everything was normal. It felt good for a few minutes to just retell the stories with lightness and joy. They mentioned that one of their boys has some bruises from a recent moto-cross injury. Of course, I told them about Chandler who never went a day without some evidence of his love for defying gravity. In all our story swapping, they never would have suspected that one of my three boys wasn't here anymore.

The last couple of days, I've been really feeling it. I went into Chandler's room tonight and looked at pictures of him doing his favorite things. This is exactly what I've been thinking today...

He can't be gone. How can he be gone? He was my baby boy. I held him, I rocked him, I watched him skate and bike and dance and laugh, and he never hesitated to give me a hug, and he loved people, and he was so alive! How can he be gone??? HOW????? Oh, God, how can he be gone???!!!!

It doesn't feel possible or real. But it *is* real. I know it's real because he hasn't come home in six months. I know it's real because he didn't write me beautiful words on Mother's Day. I know it's real because his room is quiet and far too orderly. I wonder if there will ever come a day when I absorb the entire reality and stop questioning—*How can he be gone? Is he really gone? Is this real?*

God, how I need you. I have no words for the depth of pain I am feeling. It's just too much. I throw myself into your strong arms. I know that you are enough for me. I trust you with my heart, my pain, my grief, my life. Amen.

June 26, 2019—Grief and Chewing Casualties

I had an aha moment the other day.

Don't you hate it when you're enjoying your food, blissfully savoring every single bite, when all of a sudden you bite your tongue?! That happened to me about a week ago, only it wasn't the side of my tongue like normal people—it was the flap of skin underneath. Ouch! The pain sent a shockwave through my whole body. I was with people, so I tried not to make an audible response, but my eyes started tearing up immediately. I kept chewing, trying to forget how much it hurt. No one ever knew.

In that moment, it occurred to me, my aha moment. That sudden, piercing pain that catches you completely off guard, sending shockwaves through your body, is like the unexpected stab of grief. You're going about your business, having a somewhat "new" normal type of day, when a searing pain pierces your heart, and the reaction is immediate.

Sometimes you disguise the pain. Maybe because you don't want others to feel uncomfortable. Maybe because you're afraid you won't be able to pull yourself back up out of the well if you fall into it. Maybe because you have decided for the moment to postpone the pain, to give yourself a bit of space to focus only on feeling happy instead of sad.

Sometimes you can't disguise it. You can't act like it's not happening because there is a physical response. Tears well up and spill over onto your cheeks. You can't speak because you have to work to catch your breath. And anyway, you know that anything you try to say will just end in wordless sobs.

I know that as long as I plan on eating, I will bite my tongue again, and it will hurt. It's just part of the deal.

And I imagine that as long as I don't have Chandler here with me, I will experience plenty more out-of-the-blue stabs. It's just part of the deal when you lose someone you love.

June 27, 2019—Happy Birthday, Chance

Twenty-eight years ago today, we woke up to sad news. Grandpa Reggie (Chip's grandpa) had died unexpectedly during the night. He was one of Chip's biggest fans and would call daily or weekly just to check in.

On that same day, God allowed a precious little 8-pound baby boy to enter our lives. We named him Chance Dakota. I am reminded today that life and death are intertwined. There's no life without death, no death without life. Today, we remember Grandpa Reggie and celebrate Chance's birthday.

Chance was adorable, let's just be honest, and he was the mellowest of the four Espinoza babies. I remember one night hearing a slight noise in the hallway, only to discover Chance had figured out how to get out of his crib for the first time and was crawling down the hallway. Not screaming or yelling. Just quietly crawling.

Chance has always had a strong moral compass. When he was in about second grade, he witnessed a skirmish just outside his elementary school. Somehow, he got in trouble for being on the scene. His teacher made him write a letter about it. In second-grade-style (original spelling retained here), he wrote, "I should of ran away to be safe…I had never been this roton…I need someone even wiser than my parents. I don't know how to stop it!"

When he was eight years old, he got in trouble for throwing dirt on a neighbor's house. He'd actually done three pretty mischievous deeds that day, so we were having a little chat about it. At one point, he crinkled up his forehead, obviously in turmoil, and said, "Mom, I'm trying so hard to be honest right now and tell you the whole truth. Timmy didn't make me throw the dirt like I said…It's so hard to be honest!"

I can always trust Chance's ability to cut through the crap and find the wisdom in a situation. About 12 years ago when a book I'd written had just come out, I got a call from the TV show *Wife Swap* asking if we'd be interested in being on the show. I was slated to go live for a week with a family back east that raised llamas. My first thought was, "That will be a great platform for promoting my book!" I'm not proud of it, just being honest. When I talked with the family about it, Chance said, "Mom, why would we be on that show when we've said before, 'Only an idiot would be on that show?'" I never got to live with the llamas. (I apologize for offending anyone who has been on *Wife Swap*. It just wasn't our gig.)

Chance has brought us so much joy. I love hearing him write music up in his room. I love having long conversations with him about philosophy, faith, politics, the Enneagram—he is wicked smart. I love his sense of humor. I love that he has never once hesitated to give me a hug, even when he was a teenager with friends watching.

I pray that this next year will bring deep comfort to my middle son who misses his little brother tremendously. I pray that he will have more and more opportunities to live out his passion for writing, performing and producing music. I pray that he will continue to find great fulfillment in the job he loves. I pray for many more memories with the best friends a person can have. And I pray that he will always know without a doubt that he is loved beyond measure by God, even if he throws dirt on the neighbor's house.

June 30, 2019—Surrender to the Moment

I've heard from those who know firsthand as well as those who are professionals in the area of grief—don't anticipate or try to pre-manage the pain of an upcoming "first." I've actually lived through it a few times so far, especially on Mother's Day. There is an unspeakable terror that resides in the gut—what is it going to be like? How will I be able to withstand the pain? But then you get through it. Not without tears or a hurting heart. But you don't shrink into nothingness and disappear from your life. At least that's been my experience thus far.

So today I'm trying to be in this moment. Because tomorrow and Tuesday—Chandler's birthday—will not be easy.

This morning, I slept in…YES! Then I went to Sweatstar to meet two of our tribe, Chrissie and Trisha. We sweated like pigs together, down dog-ed, and vinyassa-ed. My word today?

Surrender.

Afterward when we were saying goodbye, I lost it. I miss him so much. They miss him too. It is comforting to miss him together. We're not alone. We shared sweaty hugs.

The rest of the day was spent hanging out with family. Aunt Cho came down. That's always a treat. The best conversations are with these people. So grateful for them.

This afternoon I replanted two succulents I bought at Lowe's yesterday. That's a pretty big deal for me. I hate gardening! I love plants, flowers, and all things green. I just hate being the one in charge of making them live because I suck at it. We'll see how long my newest acquisitions thrive. I'm hopeful. They're succulents after all.

Here's my strategy for tomorrow and Tuesday.

Surrender to the moment. Take it as it comes. Don't anticipate the pain. Don't create a story about what it will be like. Just be in each moment. Whether that moment brings tears, joy, laughter, quiet sadness, even temporary paralysis. It's OK. I will get through it. I will come out on the other side.

And I'm not doing this alone. I have family. I have our tribe. I have a strong, compassionate, loving, present God who is nearer than my very breath. He is with Chandler, and He knows all is well.

This is my strategy. Let's see how well I follow it.

July 2019

On May 23, 1996, at my MOPS (Mothers of Preschoolers) group in Costa Mesa, one of our moms spoke about keeping a notebook of the amusing and funny things our kids say and do. Then for our craft time, we each made our own three-ring binder with dividers for all of our kids' names. I look at that journal from time to time and am reminded how very grateful I am for every single memory… even the ones that involved me being publicly humiliated by some form of bodily excretion inappropriately deposited.

This week is a tough one. Today…six months. Six months since I've touched my baby boy's face. Six months since I looked into his brown eyes. Six months since I held his hand and felt its warmth. My heart literally hurts. It hurts so damn bad. It doesn't feel possible that I won't see him again on this earth. Every day further from January 1 is one day further from his physical presence. It is a mixture of sorrow and terror. How do you deal with never seeing your son again? Thank God the intensity of these feelings doesn't linger indefinitely. It hits and then subsides. It hits hard on days like this.

Tomorrow is his birthday.

Tonight I'm looking through the pages behind the "Chandler" divider. Here's some of the Chandler-ness.

3-5-97—Chandler, you had to go with me the other day to a doctor's appointment. You were quite aware of most of what went on. Last night you wet your pants outside and later said to me, "I pee outside and it make Jesus very, very sad." I said, "Honey, Jesus doesn't care if you pee outside, I do." You replied, "But you pee in the cup at the doctor."

12-22-97—Today you said, "Mom, I'm gonna marry you when I grow up 'cuz I love you so so so so much. Even much-er than dad (meaning I love you even more than Dad loves you)." I'll never forget that, though someday I'll watch you wed the real girl of your dreams. Well, we've had our day. I guess I'll let her have you.

2-8-98—Today the phone rang, and you answered it for me because I was on the couch feeling sick. You talked for about a minute, then hung up. I asked, "Who was it?" You replied, "I don't know. I have no idea." I asked, "Who did they want to talk to?" You said, "Me."

God, we need you—every one of us who is missing Chandler so desperately. There is no cure for this pain. It is a symptom of love…for which we are truly grateful. I just pray for awareness of your presence and openness of heart to receive your comfort, in whatever form it may come. Amen.

July 2, 2019—Happy Birthday, Chandler!

Today was just a tough one. Probably the toughest so far.

Charli and I went and got smoothies at Nekter (Chandler worked

there before Board & Brew), and then we got balloons to put on Chandler's bike memorial. Charli reminded me that he loved green and pink, so that's what we went with. Later, I saw that someone had brought fresh flowers. That always makes me happy.

Then I went to hot yoga. Voice shaking, I told the instructor, "My son would have turned 26 today." She said, "Just get on your mat. He will be with you." My word for the day—"here." I chose to be "here" in the moment during the hot yoga session and also for the rest of the day, knowing it would hold some challenges. I knew that being "here" would mean emotional connection with both celebration and loss.

So many tears today. On my yoga mat. In the shower. In my reading chair. In the kitchen. In the car.

I think it hit me especially hard today because I realize the enormity of loss, not just for our family, but for everyone Chandler's life impacted. He loved people well. He listened. He defended. He was present. He lived in the moment. He made people feel like they mattered.

I can't even find words to express how I feel right now. The emotion, the breadth and depth of it all, is wet on my face. It is indescribable—the missing, the ache, the longing, the desperation for more of Chandler. Every story, every video, every picture...I want it.

Tonight, a lot of Chandler's friends came over to hang out. It was so good for my heart. I hurt for them. One minute, you have the world by the tail. The next, you're trying to figure out how to do life without one of your best friends.

My heart aches for Charli, Chase, and Chance. They lived life with Chandler. The everyday stuff. His stinky room, his birdie-ing milk from the carton, his late-night philosophical conversations. I hate that they have to go through this, that they have to figure out how to be three siblings without the fourth.

In the days to come, I will share some cute, funny stuff from Chandler's section of my mom journal. But today...today, I am hurting.

I celebrate Chandler's life. But I hate that he's not here.

Most of my energy today is in the missing.

I celebrate Chandler's life. I'm grateful for our 25 years with him.

But today...today the pain of not having him here is so great that I'm not able to fully celebrate and just be grateful for the time we had.

I understand from reading others' accounts that this will eventually morph into a different kind of missing. That memories will, at some point, be met with a smile rather than with tears.

Today that is not so. Today…so many tears.

Chandler, today you are celebrating an existence with no gravity, no limits. You are visiting with Grandma Ruth, with Grandpa Bill, Grandpa Reggie, Grandma Trinnie. You are more alive than ever. But I am here without you, and it's just so damn hard. You know that I, we, will be OK. This is just part of the journey. Until I see you again, son, thank you for 25 years of adventure. Never, ever, a dull day. I love you so much. So much.

"Don't know what it is about Chandler Man's lovin', but I like it, I love it, I want some more of it."

July 3, 2019 – Obsession

Obsession. Sometimes it's too strong a word. Sometimes not strong enough. To one degree or another, it describes my state of being since January 1. Last night, it was good, and hard, to celebrate Chandler's life, with others who are obsessed as well.

Why are thoughts of Chandler infused with every other non-Chandler thought? Why do seemingly unrelated events or images trigger a memory of him? Why do I feel drawn to read his old report cards? To look at every picture I can possibly find of him? To hear and re-hear every Chandler story?

Because that's all I have.

I have no more future days with Chandler. What I see and feel and hear and remember—that is what I have. I don't have Chandler.

I was not obsessed with him when he was here. I didn't cling to every moment as if it were his last.

I know people say you should live each day as if it was your last or your loved one's last. But I'm not sure how realistic that is. If this were my last day, or my loved one's last day, I probably wouldn't clean the bathroom or wash clothes or get groceries. I probably wouldn't take time to exercise or shower or go to work. I would probably suspend most everything in my life except for spending time with the people I love.

It's just not feasible to set aside the everyday-ness of life and live as if this is the last day. Unless you know it is the last day.

The challenge is to figure out what it looks like to cherish the people in our lives fully in the middle of laundry and work and school and car repairs.

I don't apologize for being obsessed. It's what I have now.

That said, here's more Chandler-ness from my journal:

11/28/96—Chandler, we had a visitor with us for Thanksgiving today. In the middle of dinner, you mooned him!

9/29/97—Tonight while we were reviewing the family contract, you said, "If you blow up the house, you get a sad face."

3/21/98—Tonight at Claim Jumper, I gave you some yucky green beans to try. You tried them and then retorted, "I think they were poop until it was this."

July 4, 2019—Blue Sugar

Lots of people have told me they've experienced times when they knew their loved ones who have passed on were somehow present. I hadn't had any experiences like that...until July 2.

The morning of Chandler's birthday, I woke up smelling his cologne—Blue Sugar. The scent is distinct and unmistakable.

I opened my eyes and looked around to figure out where the smell was coming from. It's like he was there, letting me know he was OK on his birthday, a day that was going to be one of the toughest for all of us.

He wore that cologne often when he was going out dancing. He would squirt it onto his white shirt or onto his shirtless chest, semi-covered with his leather fur-lined jacket.

I like to think Chandler was dancing on his birthday.

After hanging out at our house on Tuesday, some of his friends went to Focus, a local dance club that they used to frequent together on Tuesday nights. They graciously invited me to go, but I said I thought I would probably need to be on some sort of psychedelics in order to fully appreciate the particular type of music they play at Focus—it sounds like EDM (electronic dance music) to me, but what do I know? What I did know for sure was they weren't going to be playing "Brick House" or "Super Freak," so I hugged everyone and sent them off to have a great time.

Chandler absolutely loved to dance. I think maybe he was right there in the middle of his friends, the unseen guest of honor, digging his jam, smelling like Blue Sugar.

God, I don't pretend to know or understand what happens beyond the realm of the visible. I just know I woke up to the smell of Chandler's cologne on his birthday. Whatever that was, thank you. It meant the world to me. Amen.

July 6, 2019—Enjoy Saterday

Back when the boys were young, everyone had chores to do on cleaning day. Sometimes I would write the "to-do" list on a whiteboard in the kitchen. On this particular day, Chandler decided to erase what I'd written and replace it with what he felt to be a more appropriate goal:

Enjoy Saterday.

This is how Chandler lived. He settled in and enjoyed the moment. Whether he was at the beach, on the dance floor, in his room watching a televised golf tournament, working at Board & Brew, on his

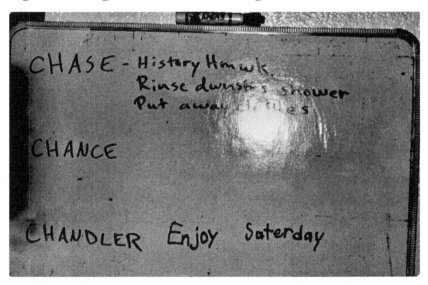

bike or any other set of wheels, hanging out with friends. He lived in the moment.

I live with a tension between enjoying the moment and getting stuff done. Historically, I have tended to put off enjoying the moment until I got a predetermined amount of work accomplished. The "enjoying" was my reward. I've gotten better, but sometimes it takes discipline.

I will NEVER get all the work done. There will ALWAYS be more to accomplish in any given day, week, month. That means that most of the time, I will need to create a stopping point for myself and move on to the "enjoy" part even though there is still much to accomplish. Some days, some seasons of life, it's easier than others.

Today, it was easy. I was able to focus 100% on Chandler's cleaning day admonition—Enjoy Saterday. I did.

And now, more Chandler-ness:

9-8-98—Jesus and God don't get diarrhea.

10-2-98—(bedtime prayer) Thank you, God, for this beautiful world and the great things in it.

11-9-98—Today you learned to turn your bike by putting your foot down. You keep saying, "I love my life! I just love it so much." At one point, you said, "I love my bike as much as God loves me... except I even love God more."

July 7, 2019 — This Backpack

This backpack hung from the shoulders of a strong, rugged, adventurous young man as he ascended hills and mountains. Today it hung from my shoulders as I climbed up to a secluded lake in the mountains near Lake Tahoe, and I felt that young man with me. Not physically. Not like I smelled his Blue Sugar cologne on the morning of his birthday. But I did feel like he was near.

Chandler was never one to sit on the couch and play video games or watch movies. He would always opt for anything outdoors—hiking, biking, skating, running, golfing—mostly without a shirt. Well, except to golf. It's a rule.

I loved Chandler's adventurous spirit. I carry that spirit with me every time I am out in nature. Like this weekend when I'm with my Adventure Sisters hiking in Lake Tahoe.

Today, we saw cascading waterfalls, babbling brooks, vibrant green meadows, magnificent rock formations, and even a bear! To say we took our time and enjoyed the journey would be an understatement. It took us four hours to get up to Grass Lake and only one and a half to get down. There were just too many gorgeous vistas begging for our attention on the way up—logs to sit on while dangling our feet over the water and rocks shaped perfectly as little benches on which to chew our snacks ever so slowly.

Today, I sank into the moment, drank in the fresh mountain air, laughed, contemplated, and gave thanks. All while carrying this very special backpack.

And now, more Chandler-ness:

4-24-99—"Mom, you know that dark that was back behind this day?" (You were trying to say 'last night.')

9-26-2000—"Every second, God has a new finger, 'cuz we're his fingers."

5-27-03—The other night, Dad took you to a game (Angels) and you caught a ball. You gave it to your friend Tanner and said, "I get to come to these games a lot. You can have this." What a heart!

July 10, 2019—Inspirare

Tonight I had the privilege of visiting with Kyle, one of Chandler's best friends. Most of their time together was spent golfing. I asked him to tell me one of his favorite Chandler stories, expecting to hear about some crazy thing Chandler had done on the golf course.

Instead, Kyle said that he will never forget when he and Chandler were taking an English class together at Saddleback College. Professor Beckham was a really tough but gifted teacher. Kyle dropped the class because he didn't get a very good grade on one of the first essay assignments. Chandler hung in there and got a B in the class. Kyle told me that the professor was absolutely blown away by Chandler's essays. But what stuck with Kyle most was that Chandler encouraged him and said that the professor was really disappointed that Kyle had dropped—that he really liked Kyle.

Kyle recently graduated from UCI. He said that the experience with Chandler and the English class impacted him, that somehow his academic performance seemed to take on an upward trajectory after that.

The word he used was—"inspired." Chandler inspired him.

The word inspire comes from the Latin *inspirare*, meaning *to blow into*. Chandler blew into Kyle's sails and moved him further toward his goal of earning a degree.

Kyle and I agreed that the ability to inspire is a special gift. Some people seem to naturally inspire others…effortlessly. That is what my son did.

Chandler proved that you don't need a degree, a lot of money, special credentials, or a prestigious title to inspire others, to make a positive impact on the people who cross your path.

In yesterday's post, I asked the question, "What would you do if you weren't afraid?"

I believe that somehow this question is connected to today's conversation with Kyle. To the idea of inspiration. To the conviction that I don't, that we don't, need anything more than we have right now to be able to blow the wind into someone else's sails and help move them toward something positive.

Today's Chandler-ness: five special three-year-old Chandler words:

hangin' berg—hamburger

pantses—pants

ikesream—ice cream

burkane—Burger King

li'l guna—Laguna

July 12, 2019—Celebration

I couldn't have asked for a more perfect birthday today. It was a day that filled up my soul with all the good things. And my belly! I had to unzip my pants.

Woke up to a beautiful birthday card from Chip on my nightstand and a necklace I will always treasure—a pendant displaying one of my favorite pictures of Chandler and me. He also got me a snuggly blanket with that same photo on it.

At Sweatstar this morning, the words I focused on were "celebrate me." As I lay on my mat, I got a sense that God was saying to me, "I'm glad you were born."

Why does it sometimes take decades of life and a horrible tragedy to open our eyes to the reality that we are truly, deeply, unconditionally loved by God and that He is crazy about us? We are worth celebrating. I am worth celebrating. I'm not sure where we got the notion that it's godly to love and celebrate other people but prideful to love and celebrate ourselves. I am as much a precious child of God as anyone else. I am learning that it is OK to like myself and to SAY so.

As I left my hot yoga session, I prayed, "God, please give me some moments today where I rise above the dark cloud and feel pure joy, where I don't feel the rope tugging me back down. I know

I'm asking you to suspend the natural process of grief, but please, just a few moments."

Then I took my sweaty self to Newport Float Therapy in Costa Mesa. I don't know what it is about floating in a dark, silent chamber of saline water that turns off the constant barrage of thoughts that bounce around in my head—I just know it does. It's like when I make a pot of beans in my pressure cooker. After the beans are done, I flip the pressure valve and the steam explodes from the lid, slowing until it completely dissipates. That's what my brain feels like when I lie down in the float chamber. The pressure dissipates, and all I experience is peace and relaxation.

Next on my agenda was to hit the beach with my journal and some books for two or three hours. Probably because my mind was in a clear space due to hot yoga and floating, I wasn't too terribly tweaked when it took me over an hour to find a place to park at Newport Beach. When I finally found a spot, my phone wouldn't let me connect to the ParkMobile app that you had to use to pay for parking. I almost gave up. As I was driving out of Newport Beach, I saw a spot with a meter that didn't require ParkMobile for payment. I pulled in, only to find that the meter wouldn't take my credit card. And I had no change. I went into a nail salon and, probably sounding just a bit desperate, told the owner, "It's my birthday and I just want to sit on the beach for an hour. Could you please give me change for this dollar bill?" I was never so happy to get four quarters. Here's the thing. If I had followed Plan A, to take my journal and some books to the beach, maybe I would have gotten lost in my overthinking. Since I only had an hour (the limit on these parking spots), I only took my phone and keys.

I walked a couple of blocks to the beach and sat down a few hundred feet from the water's edge. Not having pen, paper, or books, I was free to just gaze out at the waves, to swirl my hands in the warm sand around me, to simply sit with thoughts of gratitude for the gifts in my life. And to discover the perfect moment to receive the perfect birthday message.

I have known for months that when this day came, I would want to listen to a special voicemail left for me on July 12, 2018.

After Chandler died, I had scrolled frantically through my voice messages to see if I had any that I'd kept from him. Thank God, there it was.

I wasn't sure exactly when to listen to it today because I didn't know how badly it would wreck me. I really didn't know how I would feel. As I sat there on the beach, I knew it was time. I scrolled through and found the message. I clicked the arrow. My sweet son's voice began singing Happy Birthday to me. He was calling to see if he could take me to lunch for my birthday. And, "…if you can't, I will probably just go to the beach until work."

This was the perfect moment, the perfect place, to hear Chandler's birthday message. The beach. He loved the beach. It felt like he was meeting me there. I'm grateful I didn't give up on claiming my spot in the sand today.

Before I left the beach, I prayed, "God, thank you for my life. Whatever this next year holds, please be my strength, my peace, my security, my provision, my guidance, my confidence, my joy, my comfort, my source."

This evening, I met Chip and the kids at Boomers for miniature golf followed by dinner at the Cheesecake Factory. Time with them is the best time. Simply the best. Period.

By the way, that dinner was a reminder that we are not alone—we paid for it with gift cards given to us in January to bless us in our time of loss. Thank you!

Thank you for all the texts, messages, and phone calls today. Each and every one is truly appreciated and does my heart good.

Thank you, God, for some moments of pure joy today, with my head emerging above the dark cloud. Thank you for my family and friends who made me feel so loved and celebrated today. Thank you for Chandler's birthday message. Thank you for my life. Amen.

July 16, 2019—Facebook and a Whole New Wave

The shower is a good place to cry. The hot tears mingle with the hot drops of water pouring down over your head, and you feel immersed in a mix of water and anguish, not just anguish. You hope that maybe when you turn the water off, the anguish will end too. It doesn't. But you're cleaner, and you smell nice. So there's that.

I had no idea Chandler had a Facebook account. Tonight I did a search for "Chandler Espinoza" for the sole purpose of finding a link to a video that Aunt Val wanted. I saw "Chandler Espinoza is on Facebook." I figured it was my blog, so I clicked on it. A wave of emotion washed over me as I saw new images and new sentiments about Chandler that I had not seen before on his Facebook page, from most recent back to when Chandler was posting. I only read back through December 15. That's all I can take for now. I will revisit it because I am obsessed with Chandler. I want to read everything, see everything, hear everything. It's all I have.

There is not a single cell of my body that doesn't throb with the pain of missing my son. I see pictures friends have posted of Chandler's beaming smile and words that describe a vibrant, loving young man who was present for the people in his life. I feel robbed. His dad has been robbed. His siblings have been robbed. His friends have been robbed. Our world has been robbed. We had a priceless treasure for 25 years, and now he is gone.

As a mom, the aching is primal. I long to stroke his hair, to kiss his cheek, to smell his scent. To hold his face in my hands, look into his brown eyes, and say, "I love you, son." And to hear him say, "I love you, Mom." Just one more time.

It's too much. Just too much.

July 24, 2019 – Life-Giving

Just finished *The Next Right Thing* by Emily P. Freeman. One of the exercises she suggests is making a list of Life-Draining things that have recently been present in your life and a list of Life-Giving things presently in your life.

My Life-Giving list included: time with family and friends, being out in nature, exercising, eating good food, prayer and quiet time, meditation, writing, and my work. There was another item on my list—"Feeling what I feel."

As I sat back and reviewed both my lists, I was surprised. "Feeling what I feel" would not have been on my Life-Giving list if not for a corresponding item on my Life-Draining list—GRIEF.

I would have chosen any other way imaginable than losing Chandler to learn how to feel what I feel. But since this is how the lesson came wrapped, I accept the gift with gratitude. Don't misunderstand. I don't welcome Chandler's death with gratitude. But since I can't change the fact that he's not here any more, I can honor him by accepting with gratitude every gift that comes to me through the grief process.

With grief comes a myriad of emotions, often overwhelming, and sometimes not easily distinguishable from one another. They are deep and demand your attention. You can stuff them, ignore them, express them in logical terms, or try to keep moving so they don't catch you.

Or you can acknowledge them, name them, sit with them, feel them. My tendency is to think about and talk about my feelings. That's easier than feeling them. Analyzing and expressing in concise language how I feel allows me to sidestep the experience of just sitting with my feelings.

I'm learning that when I feel afraid, or sad, or disappointed, or angry, or whatever emotion resides in me at any given moment, I can feel it and be OK. It won't overtake me and control my life unless I allow it to. I can acknowledge and honor my feelings because they are valid, and they give me good information. When I allow myself to feel my feelings, I am more alive, more fully human. It seems I have access to a wider range of every emotion, including greater depths of the ones I really like—joy, contentment, serenity.

Oh, if you're wondering what else is on my Life-Draining list...I refuse to testify for fear that I might incriminate myself. I will say that my Life-Giving list was way longer than my Life-Draining list.

Another gift for which I'm deeply grateful.

Tonight's Chandler-ness:

(Preface: I am known in our family for having no spatial sense, therefore running over curbs on a regular basis)

Guy in front of me ran over curb.

Mom: I just want to go tell him, "Don't feel bad—happens to all of us—well, some of us."

Chandler: "Or maybe just us."

July 30, 2019—Reflection

Water is healing for me. It occurs to me that several of this year's summer travel opportunities afforded to me have been connected to water—lakes, waterfalls, ponds, the ocean. Even swimming pools! I believe that God knows exactly what I need and is offering me the space to be there.

This afternoon I was in Laguna Beach for an appointment. I was planning to come straight home, but because of rush hour traffic, I thought maybe I should hang out at the beach for a bit before the drive home. I was right. Not because of the traffic but because of my soul.

I found a coveted parking spot. Pageant of the Masters is happening right now, so parking spots are few and far between. Grabbed my journal and pen and walked a few blocks to the beach. The sand was warm, and the temperature demanded neither a bikini nor a sweatshirt, which was providential since I was wearing a short-sleeved shirt and jeans. I looked out over the endless expanse of water and remembered how vast, how limitless my God is. With that in mind, I read through the reflections I'd written during my glorious quiet time alone in Palm Desert last week.

Here are a few:

- God's love is healing. It will carry me. It will console me and fill up the deep places of emptiness. It is enough.
- Be grateful for all the gifts in my life when I'm tempted to lament and long for a different set of past circumstances.
- I am enough. Christ lives in me. Everything I need is already here.
- Forgiveness frees me and detaches me from the hurts that rob me of being who Christ intends for me to be—a fully alive person, not defined by or bound by anyone else's actions, reactions, or lack thereof.

As if sitting in the sand next to the waves with my journal weren't enough, the remainder of my evening included time with a cherished friend and a conversation with one of Chandler's best friends who is doing something Chandler would be…IS…so proud of.

Amidst painful thoughts that drifted into my mind unbidden, this day unfolded with many welcome gifts, affirmations, and joys.

Tonight's Chandler-ness:

3-5-97—Chandler, the other day in the van, I said, "Chandler when we get home, you can have a little snack." You immediately piped up and said, "No, I already did take a nap." I said, "Snack, not nap." You thought that was so funny, you continued a few days later to say, "Hey, Mom, say that you ready for snack'"— and we go through the whole thing. It's like our own little knock-knock type joke.

AUGUST 2019

August 6, 2019 – 99.9%

A little over 19 years ago, I was loving being Mom to three active boys. They were my pride and joy. They were all in school at that time, and I began to think about what it might be like to have another child. I talked to Chip about it.

After Chandler was born in 1993, I had given Chip what I thought was a very reasonable choice—celibacy or vasectomy. I will give you one guess.

So his response when I asked years later if we could think about having another child was, "I'm not getting a reversal."

Lisa: "But can we pray about adopting?"

Chip: "Sure, we can pray about it (wink, wink)."

I did pray about it. One day I wrote in my journal, "God, do you have it in your plan for us to adopt? And even if your plan was for me to be pregnant, it could happen, even though Chip had a vasectomy." I didn't actually think of that as a legitimate prayer request, just an acknowledgment that God can do anything.

A few months later while getting ready for a Christmas banquet at church, I couldn't zip my pants. Any of them! I was lamenting to a friend that I had just eaten too much on our recent vacation to New York City or that maybe I was in perimenopause and was just bloated. She suggested I take a pregnancy test. "Why would I do that?" I asked.

That night, I went to the drugstore and bought a pregnancy test (to appease my friend) AND a box of Pamprin, convinced this was some weird kind of bloating. I've never been more shocked than when I saw the plus sign appear on the stick. Shocked and elated. But elated doesn't really capture the explosion of joy and gratitude in my heart in that moment!

The next morning, I returned to the pharmacy with the unopened Pamprin and said to the clerk, "In a strange turn of events, I'd like to exchange this Pamprin for another pregnancy test."

Another plus sign on the stick, despite the 99.9% effectiveness rate of vasectomy.

After Chip recovered from the news and asked me to run my prayers by him from now on, we sat the boys down and told them they were going to have a sister or brother. I will never forget their quizzical response—"But Dad had that ice pack." We had explained to Chase and Chance in simple terms after the birth of their baby brother that Dad had the ice pack so we wouldn't have any more kids. This news was baffling to them.

I didn't care if it was a boy or a girl. I was just grateful for an answered prayer that didn't even seem like a real prayer at the time.

We went for an ultrasound. They told us we were going to have a baby girl.

God spoke to my heart and said, "Every time you look at her, remember how much I love you."

Now 18 years later, I am as much in awe of this girl as I was when I saw the plus sign on the stick. She is beyond anything I could have dreamed. She is intelligent, strong, wise beyond her years, articulate, witty, courageous, honest, ambitious, hard-working, inclusive, and compassionate. I just absolutely love hanging out with my daughter. She challenges my thinking. She makes me laugh. We can be quiet together and do our own thing. Or we can dive into one of our missions together—to try all the boba, all the pho, all the sushi…all the good stuff we can find to try. Also, we can thrift shop. We both love a good deal.

Today I took Charli to Nekter for an acai bowl because she wanted something light before tonight's soccer practice. Chandler worked at Nekter for a while. I remembered seeing him behind the counter. I thought of how Chandler would have texted Charli today to say "Happy Birthday." He probably would have told her he wanted to take her to lunch, maybe for Thai or Indian food.

I think Charli had a really good birthday today. I know she wishes she could have heard some form of "Happy Birthday" from Chandler. I hope she knows, deeply knows, how proud he was of her and how much he loved her.

Dear God, "thank you" doesn't begin to express the gratitude in my heart for the privilege of being Charli's mom. A million "thank yous" to you for placing Charli in our family—against all odds. Amen.

August 16, 2019—Losing Stuff

There's a lot of hard stuff in life. Most of it boils down to loss of some sort.

I'm thinking tonight of friends and acquaintances who have recently lost loved ones, who have lost their health, who have lost financial stability, who have lost meaningful relationships. Who have lost a sense of hope.

I hate losing things. I do it on a not infrequent basis. Usually I find what I thought was lost. Where are my glasses? On my head. I can't find my phone! Oh, I'm talking on it. Where are my keys? I left them in the pantry when I grabbed the oatmeal.

Just today, I was thrilled to find a pair of comfy pajama shorts that I'd been missing for a couple of weeks. I thought they were lost for good. I love it when what I thought was lost gets found. Such a sense of relief. That all is well with the world again. I can stop searching.

A few years ago, at the end of the workday, I went to grab my keys from my desk and head out to the car. They weren't there. I searched all over the office. I called home and asked Chance to grab my extra key and bring it to me. There was no extra key in the drawer where it would usually be. Chance picked me up, and I called the dealer to find out how much it would be to get a new key made. It was the kind with a chip inside, apparently a a tiny chip so special it is worth $375. It just has to unlock a car, not fly it to the moon! I was sick. Just sick all night. How could I have lost my keys?

Bright and early the next morning, I got a call from a friend at work. "Lisa, are you missing a set of keys?" Instant relief! All was well with the world. Well, almost. I bought two magical chip keys on ebay for $12 and programmed them using a YouTube video. With a spare key once again on hand, indeed all was well with the world.

I wish all loss could be like that, could end with instant relief. No more searching.

Every day I grapple with the reality that Chandler will not be back. I have lost him. For good. Yes, I believe I will see him again when I take my last breath. But all my finite mind can really wrestle with right now is—my son is not here today. He won't be here tomorrow. Or next month or year. Or the next.

But still I search. I scan my surroundings for some visible sign that Chandler is present somehow. Some people believe their lost loved ones send butterflies or rainbows or a certain number. They have amazing stories, and even pictures, to prove it. I know it sounds terribly greedy, but I want my sign.

From what I've heard and read, there will come a time when it will feel, once again, like all is well with the world. Like I don't need to be searching constantly.

Lord, for every friend and acquaintance who has recently experienced loss or who is facing impending loss, surround them with practical help, the kind of boots-on-the-ground support that is getting us through losing

Chandler. And grant them supernatural help—a deep sense of peace that transcends their circumstances. Amen.

August 18, 2019—Slow Time

This morning I dropped Chip off at the airport about half an hour from our house and decided I would visit a church nearby. I had been there several years ago with Chandler for a school assignment. He was supposed to visit a church different from the church he would usually attend and write about the experience. He really enjoyed the liturgical aspect of this church—different from any church he had previously attended given our faith background.

First off, there were two dogs in the back of the chapel when I walked in. That's my kind of church! One was a service dog, a goldendoodle, that I fell in love with. The other was held in its owner's arms. Not sure what the deal was with that.

It was standing room only, so I stood.

Despite standing the whole time, I enjoyed the simplicity of the worship music, the liturgical readings, and the sermon that challenged me to look at Philippians 2:5-7 in a way I hadn't before.

I was blessed by the whole experience. But the final prayer, the benediction, touched a deep place in my soul. Rather than comment on it, I will simply share it with you. Before you read it, ask the Lord to let it speak to you right where you are. Whatever your circumstance or emotional state or season of life. Let Him meet you in this prayer.

Above all, trust in the slow work of God. We are, quite naturally, impatient in everything to reach the end without delay. We should like to skip the intermediate stages. We are impatient of being on the way to something unknown, something new.

And yet, it is the law of all progress that it is made by passing through some stage of instability—and that it may take a very long time. In the places of uncertainty, may you know God's peace. In the places of grief, may you know God's comfort and care.

In the places of weariness, may you know God's rest. Gradually, may you return to yourself having learned a new respect for your heart and the joy that dwells far within slow time. Amen.

August 19, 2019—Let Down

Last night while baking a pan of scrumptious paleo banana bread to redeem four criminally overripe bananas, I turned on some worship music to sing along with. One song that I especially love came on called "King of My Heart." Over and over the chorus declares that God is good...good...good.

I believe that to be true. I believe God is good.

There's a bridge in the song that says God is never going to let me down. When I sing that part, I try hard to mean it. But I don't.

God has let me down. I prayed and fasted for my mom to survive lung cancer. More than that, I prayed from the earliest age I can remember that she would not get lung cancer. She smoked. I knew people who smoked were more likely to get lung cancer. Somehow in my childhood spirit, I knew it wouldn't end well if she didn't stop. So I prayed. As much and as earnestly as any child possibly could. My mom died of lung cancer when I was 18.

Chandler was in the hospital 18 days. I prayed, "God, please let him leave this hospital. Whether he walks or not, let him live and find your purpose for his life." He died on January 1, 2019.

I can name lesser instances where I have felt let down by God. The prayer I prayed was not answered in any way that looked like an answer. It looked like God wasn't even paying attention when I prayed.

Whether or not God lets me down is not the point. My faith in God is not based upon whether He performs to my liking.

How arrogant of me to think that all my plans and hopes and intentions and desires are the highest, best, and wisest. That if I'm disappointed, God must have dropped the ball.

When God allows the opposite of what I want, what I pray and beg for, I can admit that I feel let down. I don't need to defend God and make excuses for Him. This is part of the tension of faith—I feel let down by God...and I also believe He is good.

God, you are my God. Your thoughts and your ways are not mine. For starters, I cannot create and sustain a universe. Even when I feel let down, help me always choose to trust you. In the midst of my broken heart, my disappointment, my pain, my confusion. Where else can I go but to you? Amen.

August 26, 2019 — XXooo

Today I was talking with a friend about how sometimes with our families we get into a routine of hugs, kisses and "I love yous" that can sometimes feel like going through the motions. It's not at all that we don't love them. Just that it can become a conditioned response in the same way "Bless you" is an automatic response to someone's sneeze.

I have always hugged and kissed my kids and my husband. We rarely get out the door or off the phone without exchanging "I love yous."

Since Chandler died, when I kiss Chase, Chance, or Charli on the cheek, I feel their skin. I smell their scent. I take it in and store it somewhere in my soul. When I hug them, I absorb every inch of the hug. When I say, "I love you," I mean that they have my whole heart and are the greatest joys of my life.

I remember the last kisses on his cheek, the last smell of his skin, the last caresses of his hand. I relive them, but only for a few moments. It's too hard to sink into those lasts.

Chandler, my sweet boy, my heart aches for you. It's just too much. Too much.

August 27, 2019 — Paralyzed

So this just came in the mail—*Wings*, the Santa Margarita Catholic High School magazine. There it was on the last page. My sweet, handsome boy, a proud graduate of SMCHS.

As I cry, whispering over and over again, "I love you so much, Chandler…I miss you so much," I realize I am just doing what you do when you lose your son. When you lose anyone you love.

You cry. You talk about them. You feel sad. You long for one more hug, one more conversation. You wonder if this is the day when it hits full force and you are completely undone.

And you just keep getting up, brushing your teeth, and going about your life. Your different life. The one you didn't choose.

I'm not saying there won't come a day when I feel like I literally cannot…do any of it.

Paralyzed.

If that day comes, I will look down at the ring on my left hand, the one that says WWHC—What Would Honor Chandler. By the grace of God, carried by the love and support of friends and family, I will find the strength to move.

WWHC.

*My deepest sympathies to the family and friends of Cindy Bobruk pictured beside Chandler. It is wonderful to know that your loved one is remembered. But it is also a punch in the gut to see it in print. It's real.

August 29, 2019—Mixed Bag

I'm assuming the phrase "mixed bag" originated with something like a bag of candy that didn't just contain one type but a variety. Maybe there were Hershey's Kisses mixed in with SweeTARTS and licorice sticks. Personally, I would eat the Kisses and give away the SweeTARTS and licorice sticks. Others may have a violent reaction to chocolate (how could I live??!!!) and scarf down every last SweeTART. Taken to the next level, even within a piece of candy can reside a mix of yum and yuck. Have you ever bitten into a piece of See's candy and loved the outside only to discover the inside was some weird nougat concoction with no apparent relation to its decadent chocolate covering?

Today was a mixed bag. Even a mix of yum and yuck.

For the past few years, I have taken a picture on the first day of school at Mission Hills with a couple of my dearest friends, Stephanie and Alice. Today was different. This is the last year Stephanie will be taking that picture with us as the mom of a Mission Hills student because her daughter will graduate in 2020. This is the first year I've taken a back-to-school picture when Chandler isn't here.

I see us together, and I'm so grateful for these friendships. And I remember that things are different…that next year will bring more changes. And it's a mixed bag.

Tonight I attended back-to-school night at Charli's school, Santa Margarita Catholic High School. I love meeting her teachers, saying hi to folks I know, and walking around the campus that my daughter has called home for the past three years. I am so proud of my girl—who she is in this world. Her willingness to speak her truth and unwillingness to allow someone on the fringe to be exploited. I could go on and on.

I tried to focus on this night.

My mind wanted to drift back to 2008, 2009, 2010, and 2011... back-to-school night at SMCHS for Chandler. I look for connections. Did he have this teacher or that teacher? Did he do a back flip off that tree? There's the diving board where he qualified for CIF semi-finals with no diving experience but a spirit of no fear.

It's a mixed bag.

This is what it's like, this grief thing. You can't separate it out. You can't tell it, "This is my daughter's night...take a back seat." So you enjoy every freaking moment you can enjoy, and you keep your brain steeped in the context at hand. But sometimes it refuses to cooperate. You either expend your mental and emotional energies refusing to acknowledge that everything is different or you allow yourself a brief time to live into what was...what you thought would always be and would eventually weave itself into what is.

In the first class I visited, the mom in front of me asked about my kids, and in the course of the conversation, it came up that Charli is my second child to go through SMCHS. I showed the mom Chandler's picture and said, "Charli looks a lot like her brother."

Then I came back to now and the evening that is Charli's back-to-school night.

There is no right or wrong here. Only a figuring out a day at a time. A moment at a time.

It is a mixed bag.

August 30, 2019—Silhouettes

One of the first images to enter my slowly awakening consciousness this morning was a picture featured in a Facebook memory—the ones they throw at you randomly out of nowhere.

When I saw it, so many memories surfaced. I guess that's what Facebook is aiming for.

The summer before her 8th-grade year, Charli dyed her hair with Splat hair coloring. We were sure it would fade completely by the time school started. It didn't. This was a problem because her school would not allow "unnatural" hair colors. I think her particular red color was in fact a natural color for a Polly Pocket doll or My Little Pony. It just wouldn't work for Mission Hills Christian School.

A week before school, we were desperate. We washed it with various detergents and even tried coloring over it. It was still a very "unnatural" pinkish red. We had to cut it. SHORT. So not only did she have an UBER-short haircut not completely unlike that of PeeWee Herman back in the day, it was almost black due to the dye we'd used to color over the pink. Charli had the best attitude ever, "It's just hair. It will grow back."

The picture in the Facebook post that popped up this morning was taken with her new haircut while sitting at a sleek glass desk we'd purchased for $15 at Goodwill to transform part of her closet into a study space, complete with New York City skyline lampshade and Ed Sheeran pillowcase wall decor. So much fun executing the closet makeover. She loved it!

All those memories...but here's what took my breath away. Charli's silhouette in this picture bears a striking resemblance to one of my favorite pictures of Chandler, contemplative, the sun illuminating his face.* Charli is inextricably linked to Chandler—in his life and now in his death.

Last night, I completed a survey for Charli's school counselor. Honestly, it's hard for me not to just brag obnoxiously about my daughter. I tried to stay on point. One of the questions was, "What event has been most impactful during your student's high school career?" Charli had to answer the same question on her survey. We didn't compare notes but, as you can guess, had similar answers.

I won't tell Charli's story, but I can tell mine. I have seen my daughter witness her brother suffering what no one should ever have to suffer. I have seen her grapple with the reality of her brother not coming through that front door, strolling into the kitchen for a snack, and talking to Charli while she does her homework till the wee morning hours. I have seen her examine her experience, and Chandler's experience, in the light of years of Christian education, church attendance, and bedtime prayers to begin formulating her own worldview. The faith she will have on the other side of this will be her own. I have seen her loosen her grip on things that before Chandler's death would have been a source of considerable anxiety. I have seen her internalize the lesson we all learned after December 15—the best gift you can give is to be present for people, to love them, wherever they are on their journey.

Chandler was so proud of Charli. He loved that she spoke her mind, that she played hard on the field or on the court, that she questioned and did not accept everything at face value. That she thought deeply about things that matter.

These two silhouettes. Separated for now. But not forever.

*Charli and Chase now have this image of Chandler permanently tattooed on their bodies—Chase on his left side, a nod to Chandler's coveted side tattoo, and Charli on her left wrist.

September 2, 2019—Thai Food

This morning's Facebook memory— a year ago today Chandler met Charli and me for Thai food. Four and a half months later, I wore those same jeans to his memorial service.

I want to look at this picture and just remember the fun we had at lunch and how he and Charli jumped up together in front of the fountain outside for a photo op. I'm grateful we had that time

together. There is a shadow cast on the gratitude—the searing reality that a lunch like that will never happen again.

I was comforted a bit when I read a passage from *Healing After Loss* this afternoon:

What would our loved one want more than to see us lifted from our sadness? And indeed, the truth of who the person was can come to us much better once some of the grief has passed. In the early stages, we are preoccupied not with the memory of our loved one, but with our own pain.

Is it really possible that one day I will look at pictures of Chandler, pass by his bike memorial, watch a video of him on wheels, or read the words he wrote in my Mother's Day cards and feel pure joy even though I know there will never be a new picture or skateboard trick or Mother's Day card from my sweet boy? This is not a rhetorical question. I want to know. Is it possible? Will there come a day when I will be able to see those Facebook memories that pop up and not feel punched in the gut when Chandler's face is there?

Chandler, thank you for hanging out with Charli and me over Thai food. I think I remember you going skateboarding afterward before you went into work at Board & Brew. You always were adventurous with food and with life. We are trying to live into that ourselves and make you proud. Today your dad threw some apple into his salad! We love you. It hurts so much to not have you here. I hear it gets easier. Well, maybe not easier, just different. Whether it does or doesn't, we have each other, and we will be OK.

September 4, 2019—Marathon

A few days ago, a text thread with my Adventure Sisters went something like this....

Dawnell: Want to go see *Brittany Runs a Marathon* on Wednesday at 7 in Irvine?

Lisa: Brittany who?

Dawnell: Haha

Lisa: I'm so confused.

Dawnell: It's a movie...*Brittany Runs a Marathon*, based on a true story.

I had no idea there was such a movie out right now. I thought Dawnell was suggesting we go see a mutual friend named Brittany run a marathon—I didn't know which Brittany or why she was running a marathon so late in the evening.

Once the message became clear, she had me at "based on a true story." My kids make fun of me because they know that's all they have to say to get me to watch anything—from a Netflix series on basketweaving to a movie about penguins that make shoes for a living. It doesn't matter as long as it's based on a true story.

So tonight we grabbed a bite to eat and went to see Brittany run a marathon on the big screen.

In the beginning of the movie, Brittany is told by a doctor that she needs to lose weight and get healthy. After being shocked by the membership price tag at the local gym, she decides that since running is free, that will be her ticket to following the doctor's orders. She stands on the sidewalk in front of her apartment, contemplating the energy it will take to propel herself forward, and whispers to herself, "One block." She runs the block. It's not easy, but she remembers the advice of a friend—"Small goals." Then she runs two blocks. Then a mile. Then she signs up for a 5k. She eventually decides with two other friends to train for the New York City Marathon.

Along the way, Brittany tends to push people away rather than allowing them to help her on her journey. Her brother-in-law tells her, "Brittany, when people want to support you, let them."

I'm not dropping a spoiler here because...look at the name of the movie. Eventually Brittany does run the marathon. She is, of course, exhausted as the miles wear on, but she hears the voices of her friends yelling her name, cheering her on. It gives her the inspiration, the strength, the determination to keep going.

Random experiences that before January 1 would have held no connection to Chandler now steer my thoughts and emotions toward my son. I wasn't obsessed with Chandler until he wasn't here anymore. Now I see him and hear him in places I never would have before. It seems all roads lead to Chandler. And tonight, Brittany's marathon led me there.

When Brittany stood staring at the sidewalk ahead, unsure how she would be able to run the entire block, I remembered how it felt lying in my bed on January 2 wondering how I would be able to get up. But I did. I brushed my teeth. And I went downstairs. I remember another small goal was to make a spinach smoothie for breakfast. Eventually, I did it. Another goal…go to the grocery store. I did it. And another goal…go back to work. I did it.

Tonight as I watched Brittany's courage well up in the last grueling miles of her race, fueled by the presence of loving friends, I felt a kindred spirit with her. I am in a grueling race with no finish line in sight. I hear the voices of friends cheering me on. I accept with deep gratitude every bit of support. I know I can't run this alone.

Grief is not a sprint. It's a marathon.

September 5, 2019 – It's Just Different

Yesterday on the way home from work, I pulled up beside a very sexy man. We were obviously taking the same route to our destination. I flashed a grin as I passed him on the left.

Just ahead, we both saw it. The ambulance, the damaged car on the side of the road, people gathered around, someone sitting on the curb. We slowed down and both prayed, I'm sure, for everyone involved.

I passed the accident and pulled into the parking lot of RSM lake where I was planning to go for a run. I immediately grabbed my phone and texted that sexy man.

"I hate seeing that."

The sexy man who approached the accident the same time that I did has a decal on the back of his car just like mine—a silhouette of Chandler getting air on his bike. He hates seeing the flashing lights and the somber scene as much as I do. We have different details coloring our thoughts, but in the end, we both remember that our son was at the center of that scene on December 15.

I know it is supposed to get easier. In some ways it does. And in other ways, it's more difficult. The best word I can use to describe it is "different." It's like comparing the pain you experience when you first burn yourself on the stove to the pain that comes later when the blister pops exposing raw tissue underneath. They both hurt. It's just different.

I've always prayed when I approached the scene of an accident. I still pray.

It's just different.

September 6, 2019 – Indian Food and Chandler's Pants

My friend Cathy took me to lunch today for my birthday. Our schedules just didn't coordinate for July and August, so I'm all for extending the celebration into September. In discussing where we wanted to eat (both of us are adventurous foodies), she threw out Thai or Indian food. Then she said, "Let's go Indian. Chandler loved both foods, but I know he loved his India experience. We can honor him."

When Chandler came back from India raving about how much he loved the food, I attempted somewhat successfully to make Indian dishes like dal and curry chicken. One holiday, I don't remember if it was Thanksgiving or my birthday, Chandler said how much he appreciated my making Indian food for him. On second thought, maybe he said "trying" to make Indian food. He was being gracious.

Everything on today's lunch menu at The Clay Oven looked delicious. We ordered three meals cuz, why not. Three meals. The third in honor of the young man who inspired us to go with Indian cuisine.

When the food was served, it covered most of the table. Every bite of each new dish was followed by a mouth-full version of, "Mmmmmm...that is so good."

Amidst the tasting and savoring and mmmmm-ing, I said, "If Chandler were here, he would be in heaven.... Actually, he is in heaven."

When I got home, I was hit between the eyes with the reality of that statement. A pair of black slacks and a pair of Lucky jeans were on the pool table. Chip said, "I think those are Chandler's. I found them in the garage."

I picked them up and folded them, buried my head in the jeans hoping to smell Chandler. They just smelled like jeans. The slacks offered no scent of my son either.

There is something surreal about holding Chandler's belongings and knowing he will never touch them again. Never need them. It was surreal today when I mentioned something that had happened,

"After Chandler died." It catches me off guard every time I say it. Like somehow every time I utter those words, it makes it more final.

This is what it looks like. There's no way to anticipate exactly what a day will be. You just ride the waves the best you can and catch your breath when they subside.

Other than a kitchen sink pipe breaking leaving us sinkless until Monday, the day ended well. More about that next week.

God, thank you for time with my friend today over the food that Chandler loved. Thank you for Chandler's India adventures—a highlight of his short life. Thank you that I don't have to ride these waves alone. Amen.

September 10, 2019 – Thirty-two Years

Thirty-two years ago today, I became a mom. I can't even believe they let me take a baby home. On the videotape of Chase's homecoming, you can hear me asking Chip, "What do we do with him now?"

Through the years, I've probably made every mistake you can make. There have been high highs and low lows. There hasn't been a day that I wasn't supremely grateful to be Chase's mom.

I am proud of my son for who he is. He is fiercely loyal to family. He possesses an unrivaled work ethic. He is generous, offering to give us his savings to pay for Chandler's spinal and brain rehab when there was hope that we might be going in that direction. With three siblings coming along after him, Chase never once expressed the slightest degree of jealousy or resentment. Only pride in his little brothers and his sister.

Chase is a champion for those who need a champion. In elementary school, he came home excited to tell me he had volunteered to be a big buddy for a child who was developmentally disabled. At church, he volunteered to be a big buddy for a young man with Down syndrome. Chase did not serve them out of pity but out of a shared sense of friendship and shared dignity.

Chase is a master of learning. It doesn't matter if it's mastering the art of making smoked cheese in his new smoker or reading the latest academic journals related to his career, Chase is exquisitely curious and willing to put in the work to sate his curiosity.

When Chase was in fourth grade, Mrs. Price gave him an award for being a "Divergent Thinker." This was music to these parents' ears. We knew our son was pretty flippin' smart, but his curiosity, eagerness, energy, and innate tendency to think outside the box (and SAY it out loud) often got him into trouble. Mrs. Price affirmed in Chase a quality that would serve him and the world well. As a forensic psychologist, divergent thinking is one of Chase's greatest assets. Thank you, Mrs. Price.

Last Friday we celebrated Chase and Karen, both September birthdays.

For their special birthday dinner, they chose homemade pinto beans, enchiladas, cilantro lime rice, guacamole, posole, and green chile. I made gluten-free fudge brownies with mocha sorbet for dessert. I'm not gonna say the brownies were a huge hit with the fam. However, I managed to finish the entire pan of leftovers in about a day.

If God had lined up all eligible young ladies and let us pick the one we wanted for Chase, we could not have done any better than Karen. She is a treasure. Beautiful inside and out (yeah, it's cliché but if the shoe fits…). Karen has a deep wisdom about her. When she says something, you would do well to listen. She is a hard worker, a quick learner, and a genuinely kind soul. And she puts up with us with such grace.

Family birthday celebrations are tough these days. Our favorite place to be is all together, and we're just not.

September 11, 2019—September 11

On September 11, 2001, I dropped the boys off at school and returned home with newborn Charli. I sat down in my comfy glider in the living room, nursing pillow resting in my lap with Charli nestled on top, and flipped on the TV to catch up on the news while my baby girl enjoyed her morning nourishment. It took a while to understand what was happening. Every channel blasted news of a plane crashing into the World Trade Center in New York City. We had stood on top of the WTC just ten months earlier.

As the horror played out on the screen in front of me, I continued to glide back and forth, back and forth, while Charli lounged in the most comfortable seat in the house. She had no idea that the landscape of her world was changed forever. She looks for seats closest to the end at a concert and for the closest exit on a plane. She weighs the possibilities for terrorism inherent in any travel opportunity.

To a large degree, all of us are out of control of our grief process. We can't control the triggers, the waves, the pain, the timeline. But in a sense, at least it is ours to own.

For families of those whose lives were lost on 9/11, there are constant reminders in the form of political banter, media commentary, and a yearly commemoration. Standing at my vantage point today, my heart goes out to these families whose grief process is not their own. It intersects with the world's process of remembering, honoring, debating, politicizing.

While the world was processing at a macro level the complexities of the 9/11 atrocity, families of those who died that day were also processing at a micro level. *They can't be gone…. I just kissed them goodbye this morning. My son will never know his father…or his mother.*

The grief is different for them now than it was 18 years ago. Just different. Not gone. And still, it is simultaneously global and intimate.

I am by no means minimizing or comparing the pain that accompanies any loss. The degree of pain and the manner in which the grief process occurs is different for all of us. I'm just saying that today, my heart and mind remembered 9/11 in a different way than ever before.

God, bring comfort even now to those who are missing their loved ones, lost in the horror of 9/11. Bring redemption through good works, loving acts of kindness, carrying out of justice, and lives continuing to honor those who were lost. Amen.

September 12, 2019 — Three Things

My friend Gail, who has been through some tough times of her own, texted me this today.

In hard times
she had learned
three things…
She was stronger

than she ever imagined,
Jesus was closer
than she ever realized,
and she was
loved more than
she ever knew.

I don't know who wrote this, but I'm sure they've gone through some stuff. That's how they know.

This touched me so deeply. These three things I have found to be absolutely true.

God you are so good. I didn't choose to lose my son. I never would. But through this crappy reality and all the other crappiness I've been through, I am grateful that you have taught me these three things. Amen.

September 15, 2019—New Car

Yesterday morning, another Facebook memory popped up and punched me in the gut. They come from out of nowhere. How do they pick what memory to throw at us on any given day? Do they not know I don't have Chandler here anymore?

I'm sure on September 14, 2011, when Chandler was riding with me, breathing in that coveted new car smell, he had no idea that seven years later, he would be driving the white Toyota Highlander and making payments to me for it. I have $40 cash left from the last payment he made stashed in my dresser drawer. He held that money in his hands. I will keep it forever.

One of the worst days of Chase's life was when he had to pick up that car from Board & Brew after the accident and drive it home. Drive it through the intersection where it happened. Over the asphalt still stained with his brother's blood.

Now it's Chance's car. It serves him well, hauling his music gear here and there. Even though it made sense for Chance to take over the Highlander, you can imagine how difficult it was.

The Highlander served me well the seven or so years I drove it. It was the first car I ever shopped for, picked out, and paid for myself.

Some of my favorite memories of that car have to do with the game Charli loves. It carried us to and from countless soccer practices and games. When I bought it, I told the salesperson, "I want a car with good gas mileage, low maintenance, and enough room for Charli and her soccer pals to pile in with their gear—that's non-negotiable." The Highlander did not disappoint. Through the years, it has seen a whole lot of sweaty, grass-covered, pony-tailed soccer players. It has been host to a lot of laughter, loud singalongs, and on-the-road banquets.

A car is just a car. The memories it creates, the family time in close quarters, the space for community to happen…that's what makes it special.

September 17, 2019—Jackie

Like I said yesterday, you never know what a day will bring.

You know how it is. You're just fine, and then all of a sudden, it dawns on you that you can't live another day without a haircut. I called the salon to see if Jackie was working. I hadn't been in to see her for months. It was just too hard. But today felt like the right time.

For the past several years, every hairstyle Chandler rocked, like only Chandler could, was thanks to Jackie. Well, except when he got hot, not unlike Pedro from Napoleon Dynamite, and shaved his head at home. Charli or I often cleaned up the back to make it even. I would give anything on earth to walk into the garage and find a pile of Chandler's freshly shorn hair followed by, "Mom, can you fix the back?"

DETOUR: This reminds me of one of Chandler's frequent psychosomatic episodes. Once when he shaved his head, he saw a red bump, probably a pimple or an ingrown hair. He was convinced there was something in there that needed to come out. He squeezed it mercilessly. He made us squeeze it. We finally convinced him that he was fine. He did not have a rare form of scalp cancer. That was such a Chandler situation.

I sat down in Jackie's chair and, after some small talk, told her the reason Chandler hadn't been in. It is a surreal experience breaking the news to someone that your son is dead when they only remember him alive and vibrant. You instantly relive the day that is permanently imprinted in your brain…into your very being.

It took a few minutes for the news to sink in.

The mood lightened when Jackie began recalling memories of Chandler in her chair.

She said, "Chandler was so happy. And crazy! You could tell he wanted everybody around him to be happy. His happiness was contagious."

For a split second, I felt pure joy—my son was on this planet for 25 years and made people smile, made them feel seen…significant… relevant. And we got to be his family. Then I was dropped back into today, and I just wanted Chandler back. I wondered if that pure joy would ever replace the nagging pain, the constant sense that something is missing.

Jackie said that when she would walk into Board & Brew, just a few doors down from her salon, Chandler would yell, "Hey, Jackie!" Not one to draw attention to herself, she would say, "Shshshsh." He would respond, "Everybody needs to know you cut my hair, and you're awesome!" Or he would yell, "I'm coming in soon, Jackie. I know it's too long."

The last style Jackie did for Chandler was a fohawk. When he requested that rather edgy cut, she asked, "Is your Mom going to kill me?"

The fohawk, what remained of it after they shaved his head for emergency surgery, was with Chandler when he breathed his last breath.

It's just hair right? Not for Chandler. It was part of the adventure of life…of self-expression.

Jackie, you "got" my son. Your expertise and artistic genius accompanied Chandler to every music festival and every all-night dance party. Your keen skill and sense of style joined with Chandler's sense of adventure and made its way into so many of the images we now treasure so deeply on this side of January 1. A part of you was with him on his last day here. Mama Chan is deeply grateful to you, Jackie. Thank you.

September 25, 2019—Last Stop

"Last stop."

That was the text beneath the photo Charli sent me on Saturday. While I was galavanting about NYC with my friend Carole, Charli was preparing to go to Homecoming at Santa Margarita. I had told her and Chip to send me pictures. They kept me in the loop and sent some fun pics.

We had just finished a late dinner when I received this last picture. Tears welled up and over.

My beautiful girl paying a visit to her brother's bike memorial before heading to Homecoming.

My heart was smiling because Charli had the gift of Chandler in her life for 17 years. He was always so proud of her. He was her fan. And it was smiling because Chandler had the gift of Charli. She loved him—loves him—so much. They had each other. I am forever grateful for that.

My heart was weeping because Charli won't have her brother present for any more of the milestones or special occasions in her life. She will have to visit some place in her heart and mind to bring Chandler into those moments. Or she can go to the bike.*

For as long as it will be allowed to stand, the bike memorial is a physical location where we can go to feel a special connection to Chandler…a representation of his presence.

I showed the picture to Carole, her daughter Jenny, and Jenny's best friend Jessica. They were so gracious. They asked if I needed to go back to the hotel.

"No, I will be OK. This is just how this goes."

We paid our bill and began navigating the NYC sidewalks toward our final adventure of the day—Slate, the dance club with the slide. Chandler would have thought it was so cool that I went dancing in NYC, literally sliding down into the club, and that Carole bought hideously ugly closed-toe shoes (who knew a dance club had a footwear regulation) at CVS Pharmacy (the only place to find shoes at 11 p.m.) just so she could get in. He would have wholeheartedly endorsed our last stop.

God, my heart aches for my girl who misses her brother so much. Please let her know you are with her in her pain…that she is not alone. Be more real to her than ever. Amen.

*The bike memorial at the site of the accident has been replaced by a bench in Chandler's honor.

September 28, 2019 – More Than Music

Last night Chance did a show with his band, Dad Legs, about half an hour from where we live. I wanted to go, but I'm sort of still on NYC time and fading earlier than my usual midnight bedtime. Plus, Charli had an early soccer game today, so no sleeping in.

Chance said the show started at 8 p.m., which in "band speak" means 9 or 10 p.m. Sure enough, he texted me from the club that it might be 8:30…then "no later than 9:30." I left the house at 7:50, confident that they would go on by around 10.

I felt kind of like a big deal when I told the person at the door I was Chance's mother and got in free because I was on his guest list. Once inside The Wayfarer, I surveyed the young crowd. It occurred to me that I must look like quite the cougar, and I wished I had worn a t-shirt that said, "My son's in the band."

After a few minutes, Chance and two other band members saw me and came to give me a hug. Now I was a cougar with definite targets. Again, the t-shirt would have been handy.

I love that Chance has never shied away from giving his mother a hug in public, even during the cool teen years.

Somehow the stars aligned, and they actually went on at 8:30. I don't know if I could have grinned any wider watching these young men do what they love to do. They are fantastic musicians and songwriters, but more importantly, they are very cool, very fine human beings.

I've watched Chance grow from a young kid teaching himself to play a bass guitar that was bigger than him into an accomplished musician, songwriter, and producer. Music has been his therapy, his catharsis, his prayer through a lot of hard places.

From downstairs or down the hall, through the years we've heard melodies and phrases coming to life as Chance's heart weaved its way into song after song after song. As he sat in his room the week before Chandler's memorial on January 13, I could hear unfolding a song of love, of anguish, of heartache, of all the emotions converging. The song no brother ever wants to write and no mother ever wants to hear being written.

Chance, my son, I love you so much. Thank you for using your gift to bring beautiful music into the world. I hate that you have to live without your brother. I'm grateful that you have your music. It is good for your soul. And for ours. Thank you for pouring your pain and your passion into "Head First." If things go like I imagine, I'm sure Chandler is bragging to all who will listen about the song his brother wrote for him.

September 29, 2019—Run for Chandler

If things had gone differently, Chandler would have been where Charli and I were this morning.

Six years ago, she and I did our first 5k together. Today we did our third. Today's race held a whole new meaning.

Each year, our community hosts the Dove Dash benefiting Ryan's Reach, an organization dedicated to helping individuals who have suffered brain injuries and providing support for their families. One of the specific beneficiaries of the funds raised by the Dove Dash is High Hopes, the first non-profit charitable brain-injury rehabilitation program in the country. My friend Tracey Desmond and her husband Mark are the owners and champions of High Hopes where the most determined, persistent, courageous people come every day to work toward their recovery from brain injury. My friend Tracey had told me that when Chandler got out of the hospital, he could come to High Hopes every day.

Along the race route were people in wheelchairs providing encouragement and inspiration. Chandler would have been one of them, cheering everyone on. Or maybe he would have tried to sneak into the crowd and wheel himself along.

Less than halfway through, I was regretting my decision to wear a thermal undershirt and running pants. My abhorrence for being cold got the best of me at 7 a.m. when I got dressed. What was I thinking? It's Southern California in September!

I run some, but I'm not a hardcore runner. I don't do long distances due to knee issues (and also because I hate to run long distances), so my goal was to run the race, keep pace with my Run playlist, and cross the finish line. Every time I hit a hill and started to lose steam, I reminded myself how grateful I am to be able to run, and I told myself—you can do this for Chandler...if he is watching, he is proud of you.

As I turned toward the last leg of the race and saw the balloon arch over the finish line, I kicked it in gear and sprinted to the end.

Walking through the booths of local businesses set up after the finish line, I felt a wave of gratitude. I love our community so much. I have felt their love and support since December 15.

So many of these places have been part of my journey, before and after. Club Pilates introduced me to the Reformer, and it was love at first try. HotWorx has been so good to me and allows me to work out 100% on my schedule and get double the workout in half the time. AMP Sports Med has gotten Charli back on the soccer field after injuries in record time and worked the kinks out for both Chip and me. LocoCycle—yep, I've done that too, and side note, the owner's mother took care of Charli in the church nursery when she was a baby. Athlete's Choice, where my daughter has trained and worked as a trainer for a few years, was also there for the event

Then there was the High Hopes booth. I hugged Tracey and Mark and met Brett Hickman and his mom Patty. He is a long-time friend of High Hopes with his own story of brain injury. Dressed to the nines, he told me how he is finishing up a book and plans to speak to young people about staying away from drugs. I asked if that is part of his story. It is.

To be honest, I wish I didn't have this deeply personal connection to High Hopes. I wish I could admire them from afar. I wish I still had the vantage point of seeing brain injury as something out there that happens to other people. But my life and my family have been rocked to our core, changed forever, by brain injury.

Thank you, God, for legs that can run swiftly, lungs that can breathe deeply, and arms that can hug tightly. Thank you for my community. Thank you for the opportunity to support such worthy causes as Ryan's Reach and High Hopes....

To run for Chandler.

Amen.

September 30, 2019—Then We Will Swim

This I will do, for best it seems: so long as the beams hold in the fastenings, here I will stay and bide what I must bear; but when the surge batters my raft to pieces, then I will swim.

~Odysseus

Like the Greek hero Odysseus tossed by treacherous waves on his epic journey back to his island home of Ithaca, those of us who have experienced loss find ourselves on turbulent waters, desperately searching for the safety of home. For the peace and comfort of our old normal.

But home is different now than before the storm pulled us like a magnet into the darkest tempests of the ocean.

Home is still where we belong. It is our safe place, though the landscape has changed. Empty spaces that once vibrated with life now silently question their purpose.

We strain with everything in us to catch any glimpse at all of the shore. For evidence that home is still there. That we won't be on this raft, tossed about forever.

And we stay the course. We lash ourselves to the raft if we must and ride the waves.

And when the surge batters our raft to pieces....

Then we will swim.

OCTOBER 2019

Nine months. That's how long Chandler resided in complete comfort and safety before making his entrance into the world. I felt him kick and roll. Undoubtedly practicing some upside down maneuvers he would repeat later on a bike or off a bridge. I would often push down on my protruding belly to try and coax his tiny heels out from between my ribs. I loved him more than can ever be imagined before I ever laid eyes on him on July 2, 1993.

Nine months. That's how long it's been since I last saw my son's chest rise and fall.

I saw him take his first breath. And I saw him take his last.

It is too much to grasp. Just too much.

I have prayed for signs, for anything that hints at, "Mom, I'm here. I'm OK." This morning I opened my *Jesus Calling* devotional. There on the first page of October's readings was an image of a burning candle. I got in the car to drive to work and turned on my *Pray As You Go* app. The image accompanying today's reading was a burning candle.

As Charli so poignantly expressed at Chandler's memorial service, Chandler means "candle maker."

I sat down in my office and looked at the beautiful candle my sweet friend Daisha gave me—Chandler's words about me from his instagram account illuminated by the flickering flame.

Is it candles? Is that my special sign? I don't know. I just know that this morning, I felt like Chandler was trying to tell me everything is going to be OK. That he is OK. That his light still burns brightly.

Tonight I went to his bike memorial. I cleaned up the dried-out flowers and replaced them with fresh flowers. I had stopped by Trader Joe's to pick up daisies, and when I checked out, the young man asked, "Are you Mrs. Espinoza?" Turns out, I know him from his days as a Mission Hills student, and he knows Chance from worship band back in the day. He knows our story. He went and grabbed a bunch of bright, colorful flowers to take to the bike. To honor Chandler. Thank you, Austin.

None of us know what the next nine months will hold. What I do know is that, for me, these past nine months have been marked by the worst and the best. Let's just be clear—I would trade all the "best" to change the "worst." Since that's not on the table, I want to say how grateful I am for family, for friends, for community who have come alongside and been our advocates, our encouragers, our providers on so many levels. I am grateful to wake up to this morning's reminders of my son—my Candle Maker.

Thank you, God, for carrying us through these nine months. My trust is in You. You will carry us through nine more. Amen.

October 2, 2019—Heart Path

Yesterday was tough. Today I needed to recalibrate.

I was able to spend time with three close friends, one wise counselor, and a partridge in a…never mind. Overdone.

I'm not happy that other people have problems, big ones, real ones. But I'll be honest…it makes me feel good to be able to listen to other people's struggles for a change. I feel like I'm not just sucking the life out of the universe by always being the needy one. I'm thankful to have friends who are real and open and will give me the gift of sharing their crap with me.

This afternoon I had a counseling appointment. We talked about following your "heart path," his words, not mine.

My path has been circuitous. Can I just tell you how many things I've done in my life?

Department store clothes model, cashier, bank teller, church secretary, administrative assistant, various product sales (massage chairs, Jafra, Avon, Cookie Lee, Apriori), medical transcriptionist, ASL interpreter, professional speaker, recording artist/songwriter, author, editor/ghost writer, small groups director, admissions director, and speech pathology assistant.

What I now know for sure is that I must write. It's in my soul. It's my passion. I knew I loved to write. But I didn't know how deeply it ran in me, that it is my DNA, before Kimberly goaded me into posting on CaringBridge and I found writing to be my refuge, my place of processing and healing. My place to have a conversation with others grappling with their own pain.

After today's session with my counselor, I'm trying not to complicate everything by analyzing all the possibilities in the world (that is SUCH an Enneagram 7 thing!), but rather to gently ask myself, and to pray—"What is my heart path?"

In the past, I have tended to scapegoat God. Instead of trusting myself to make a good decision, I have asked for big signs to point me in the right direction. And then if the outcome seemed less than optimum, I could say, "Gosh, I just followed all the signs I thought God was putting in my path." In other words, somebody screwed up, and I'm pretty sure it wasn't me.

I am learning a new operating system. The Creator of the Universe—wise, powerful, loving, merciful, gracious—is my very heart and soul. Do I really need a message written across the sky? A series of vivid dreams? A billboard that says, "Lisa, this way!" Can I not trust the still, small voice within?

I can follow my heart. It knows the way.

October 3, 2019—Consider the Waterpik

I have gum disease. Let's just get that out of the way.

As a result, I have a Sonicare, an Oral B Pro 1000, and a Waterpik water flosser on my bathroom counter along with a giant jug of Crest Gum Care mouthwash. And in the drawer below the counter, my Oral-B Gentle Glide floss, Sensodyne, Arm & Hammer baking soda toothpaste (it's gentle on the gums), and Parodontax toothpaste. My dental hygiene paraphernalia requires its own zip code. That's what you do when you like your teeth and prefer not to lose them. I don't mean to brag, but my hygienist says I'm doing a really good job keeping my gums from receding.

So my first Waterpik broke a while back. It still worked to floss my teeth, but the flossing attachment holder cracked and fell off, so I had to lay the flossing attachment on the counter after use instead of sliding it neatly back into its stand. After a while, the rest of the contraption decided to follow suit, and I had to buy a whole new Waterpik.

I had been using my new Waterpik for quite some time when one day I noticed something. The flosser attachment was lying on the counter. I picked it up and slid it into its unbroken, perfectly functional stand. It dawned on me that ever since getting my new Waterpik, I had been putting the flosser on the counter…right beside its stand.

I had become so accustomed to adjusting my behavior to accommodate my old broken stand that I forgot I had any other choice. I was acting out of habit.

I wonder how often I engage in certain behaviors because I forget I have a choice in the matter? How often am I operating on autopilot? Out of force of habit?

I'm so used to the way it's always been, the way I've always been, that I forget I am a growing, changing person who is not limited by past habits. Just because I reacted poorly to some particular situation in the past, it doesn't mean I don't have new tools, resources, or resolve to react differently now. Just because something worked well for me in the past, it doesn't necessarily mean that's the best option for me today.

God, help me keep my eyes open for habits that don't make sense anymore. That don't serve me or others well. And give me the grace and courage to do something about it. Amen.

October 4, 2019—Soul Care

I had been looking forward to having a soul care day today. Tonight, my soul is thanking me.

This morning I got to spend some time with an incredible mom…a mom who's missing her son. Just like I'm missing Chandler. There is so much you don't have to say when you're with someone who already gets it. But sometimes you say it anyway because there is a deep connection, an understanding between the two of you, that is reassuring, comforting. The knowing nod, the tear in the eye—these are not obligatory or courteous responses. They are rooted in a shared experience, a common grief. Her pain is my pain. And mine is hers.

This woman is so wise and runs so deep. I took her words with me to the beach after our time together at the coffee shop.

I paid for four hours of parking, strapped on my beach chair, umbrella, and backpack, and headed down the steep hill to Salt Creek Beach.

The phrase that echoed in my mind throughout my entire four hours was, "This is perfect."

The sky was the most calming yet vibrant shade of blue. The waves, aaahhh, the gently rolling waves. Just the sound always speaks peace to my soul. The sand was warm and welcomed me to set up my space for the day.

I reclined my beach chair, closed my eyes, and allowed myself to just be.

After a while, I propped up my chair, pulled out my journal and my purple gel pen, and began to write down some of the things my friend and I had talked about this morning. I want to remember her words. She doesn't just say stuff. It's like she has this wisdom filter that her words go through before they exit her mouth, so when you hear them, you want to write them down.

Next, I opened up my latest read, *The Choice*. It's the true story of a Holocaust survivor and her path to freedom, physically and emotionally. One of the passages I underlined in purple was:

To be passive is to let others decide for you. To be aggressive is to decide for others. To be assertive is to decide for yourself. And to trust that there is enough, that you are enough.

~Dr. Edith Eva Eger

That's a lot to digest. It speaks to my current learning curve—to be confident in my decisions, to trust my heart.

I took a break from reading to go for a long walk on the beach. When I reached the end of the stretch of accessible beach, I turned around and decided to run back to my spot. It's crazy how much harder it is to run in sand than on hard ground! Let's just say if Rocky Balboa had trained on the beaches of SoCal instead of on the streets of Philadelphia, his first fight may have taken a different turn.

Post-run, while sitting on my chair munching on my Trader Joe's broccoli kale chicken salad, I listened to my heart and made a decision about something that needed to be decided today. I refrained from overthinking and analyzing my decision or backpedaling. It took less energy to simply listen and follow my heart than to take a couple of steps toward following my heart and then begin dissecting every part of the decision to check for logic, practicality, worst-case scenarios, how it will affect every person's life on planet Earth, etc., etc., etc. My plan is to continue utilizing this new "follow your heart path" operating system.

I trudged up the hill ten minutes before my parking pass would expire, grateful that my legs would carry me up that incline packing all my stuff.

Tonight I went to dinner and a movie with friends. I highly recommend the Kilauea (pepper-crusted burger with spicy jack cheese and crispy onions) at Islands.

Today—from morning until pre-bedtime—only things that fed my soul. And my belly.

Thank you, God, for every intricate detail you designed in nature. The magnetic forces that pull the foaming waves toward the shore, the vast array of colors landscaping the cliffs by the ocean, even the shades of blue painted across the sky. Thank you for good people to share life with. Thank you for health. For books to read that inspire and challenge. Thank you for a nice, long soul care day. Amen.

October 5, 2019 – Thrive

We are overwhelmed by loss and think we will never recover a sense of self and purpose, that we will never mend. But despite— and, really, because of—the struggles and the tragedies in our lives, each of us has the capacity to gain the perspective that transforms us, from victim to thriver.

~Dr. Edith Eva Eger

I want to be a thriver. I know it is possible because Dr. Eger thrives despite the atrocities inflicted upon her and those around her, including her mother and father, as prisoners during the Holocaust. I know it is possible because of her mentor, Viktor Frankl, who thrived despite the same unspeakable circumstances.

I am in no way comparing my experiences to those of Holocaust victims. That was a horror rooted in evil and injustice.

But we do share this in common—a profound sense of loss that renders us different people than we were before. The question is, what does different look like? Are we now angry, bitter, resigned, hateful? These are all valid responses to injustice, to pain, to loss. They all make sense.

What I know from experience and from reading works like *The Choice* and *Man's Search for Meaning* (by Frankl) is that we become our own jailers if we allow those feelings to persist longer than is healthy or appropriate and to suck us under like quicksand.

Through the years, I've waded through some quicksand. Losing Chandler is a different kind of quicksand. Watching him in the hospital, then saying goodbye to him, it was, it IS, the worst kind of excruciating pain I can imagine. I'm ever aware of the quicksand. Sometimes I'm pulled along by friends and family, and sometimes it feels like I've managed to extricate myself from the mire and move on to more solid ground. Then…a picture, a Facebook memory, a smell, someone's laugh that sounds like Chandler's. It could be anything or nothing at all that reminds me how deep I am. That every day, I have to make a choice to keep moving or become stuck and begin to sink.

By the grace of God, I will not sink. I will be a thriver.

October 7, 2019—Pre-Op Day

This time next week, I will be laid up on the couch watching TV… hopefully on my way to a pain-free left foot! I've done physical therapy, cortisone shots, sensible shoes (uugghh), plantar fasciitis inserts, rolling, stretching, resting, icing, essential oils. Now it's time for the big guns—platelet-rich plasma injections. And while they are down there, I've asked them to throw in a bunionectomy. I'm hoping that the most painful part of the whole deal is the fact that I have to arrive at the surgery center at 6 a.m. YUCK!!!

Oh, and if your foot fell off after bunion surgery, please don't tell me.

As I sat in the doctor's office this morning for my pre-op appointment, I started having flashbacks to the hospital. I don't know why my mind does this. I had to use deep breathing and tell myself, "That was then, this is now. Chandler would want you to get your foot fixed so you can do all the things you love without the pain." It's the medical stuff that gets me. I was in that office voluntarily. I will enter that surgery center next Monday voluntarily. What echoes in my brain is—Chandler didn't volunteer for what he went through. He had no idea this time last year that in about two months, he would be hit by a car and end up with tubes and needles and stitches, and....

The nurse asked if in the past two weeks I've had feelings of sadness or hopelessness. It's part of their routine. I just said, "No." She doesn't need to know.

So then I had to go to the lab for bloodwork. I threw a big, huge hissy fit in high school when I got my blood drawn for a tonsillectomy. It had to have been embarrassing for my mom. I seriously screamed and kicked and flailed about. That's how much I hated needles, and the idea that someone could force me to have one poked in my arm to suck out my blood was simply unacceptable. I wasn't going to let them get by with it easily.

Then a few years later, I had kids. Needle, schmeedle.

Still, having my blood drawn is not my favorite thing. I won't sign up to do it for fun and leisure.

Today's blood draw was difficult in a different way. My mind insisted on flashing images of Chandler and all the needles, and I wondered if he was scared. Did it hurt? Of course, it hurt. I had to mentally walk myself through getting this simple blood test done.

I am trying to be gentle and kind with myself. Trying not to force anything that I'm not ready for. But sometimes I feel like I just need to say, "NO! I will not let these images settle in my mind right now!" "NO, I will not turn away from doing something I need to do because past trauma is threatening to overtake me!"

This is on a day-by-day, case-by-case basis. I may be faced with a similar situation tomorrow, and my heart, soul, mind, and body may adamantly proclaim—"You are not ready for this. Take it easy." I will be prudent to consider their wisdom.

This evening, I went and put new solar lights on Chandler's bike memorial. The old string of lights is getting a bit dim. Fingers crossed—after tomorrow's day of sunshine, the new lights will shine brightly as night falls. As I was sitting there trying to figure out what "S" and "F" meant on the "on" switch of the light string, someone knocked on my window. I was ready to cuss out anyone that was going to reprimand me for pulling over to the curb beside the memorial. It was a friend saying he had seen my car stopped by the bike. He helped me figure out what "S" (steady) and "F" (flashing) meant and then helped me string the new lights on the bike.

Tonight…lots of tears. Chip and I talked about Chandler. The missing is a physical ache in our hearts. I told him about my flashbacks at the doctor's office. Our minds are processing this very differently. At the same time, we have a completely synchronous experience and understanding of this—losing Chandler is the worst thing, and we will never be the same.

October 9, 2019 — Stepping In

I used to think that if I let grief in, I would drown. But it's like Moses and the Red Sea. Somehow the waters part. You walk through them…you get to discover that living a full life is the best way to honor him.

~Dr. Edith Eva Eger

These words were spoken by Dr. Eger during a counseling session with a bereaved mother who struggled to move through the grieving process after losing her son. Having lost family members and friends in the Holocaust, including both her parents, Dr. Eger is well qualified to speak to those of us who grieve.

She knows it all firsthand.

The hollow places of loss. The spaces that were once occupied by someone you love that you could actually touch and see and talk with. And now you can't. How inconceivable it seems to just go on with life, and certainly to enjoy your life, when those deep recesses threaten to swallow up everything. And how dare we laugh and eat and play and pursue goals when our loved ones cannot.

What I have learned and am continuing to learn is that the only way to get through this acute stage of grief is to step right into it. You take a deep breath and say to yourself, "This sucks. It's going to suck for a long time. But my feelings will not kill me. I will feel what I feel…and I will keep moving."

Dr. Eger likens it to the parting of the Red Sea. You take a step forward, and the water begins to separate to make way for you. You just keep moving forward a step at a time, and the water keeps parting. It's a frightening trek—after all, I'm still in the middle of the sea. I've come this far, but tomorrow will the walls of water come crashing down and drown me right where I stand?

Then comes the next part of Dr. Eger's sage wisdom to a hurting mother:

Living a full life is the best way to honor him.

I honor Chandler when I don't allow my fear to keep me from appreciating and enjoying the simple gifts offered to me each day. When I don't let it stop me in my steps and keep me stuck there.

I honor Chandler when I love well, enjoy the moment, and do the next right thing.

Right here in the middle of the parting sea.

October 15, 2019 — Two Kinds of Pain

For most of the day yesterday, I was somewhat annoyed at not being able to feel my foot. About midnight, I decided that not feeling my foot was actually a preferable option. The nerve block started to wear off, and the throbbing was pretty bad. I took my first post-op pain pill and finally got to sleep about 2:30 this morning. Then a dose of ibuprofen at 8 and another at 4.

This morning, Teri brought me a decaf iced vanilla almond milk latte, 2 pumps, and we visited for a while. I also worked today. I miss my peeps at school, but I'm grateful to have work I can do from home when necessary.

I am obeying doctor's orders to take it easy and keep my foot elevated, but I did manage to boil some eggs, make a pot of decaf jasmine green tea, and wash a few dishes.

My territory is bathroom, kitchen, couch. I strongly dislike the idea of being sedentary for days on end. But I've decided to allow myself the freedom to be less productive than usual and to enjoy all the benefits of being ordered to lounge on the couch. Reading, working in my pajamas, binge watching Netflix (specifically at this point *Breaking Bad*), asking my kids to wait on me, and accepting the rest as a good thing.

What I haven't allowed myself to do is feel how much I miss Chandler. I know this surgery was so minor compared to jillions of other medical procedures people have to deal with. Still, I don't have the bandwidth to manage the two kinds of pain right now. Not today.

Yesterday I had to summon gargantuan amounts of mental discipline to keep from having a panic attack and calling off the surgery right there in the prep room. All the medical stuff—the IV, the waivers, the hospital bed, the sound of a monitor on the patient next to me, the antiseptic smells. It was all too familiar.

I kept steering my mind back to the present, a hard turn, not an easy veer to the left or right. I had to wrestle with my thoughts and let them know they were not going to overtake me. I am here now. I'm getting my foot fixed. That's all this is. Here and now.

Tonight on the couch with my ever-awakening, throbbing foot propped up on the pillow, Chandler's beautiful face staring at me from the frame on the bookshelf, I am doing my very best.

Here and now. With two kinds of pain.

October 20, 2019—Alexithymia

Alexithymia.

This is the Greek term for not having words for feelings.

Often alexithymia refers to individuals who have been abused or traumatized in some way and are unable to identify and describe what they are feeling.

I can find lots of words to describe my feelings since December 15.

Terrified.
Shocked.
Hopeful.
Frustrated.
Angry.
Scattered.
Focused.
Desperate.
Heavy.
Lost.
Devastated.
Anxious.
Numb.
Sad.
Happy.
Paralyzed.
Confused.
Panicked.
Grateful.
Determined.
Joyful.
Weak.
Strong.
That's just off the top of my head.

None of these words fully capture or adequately convey all that churns within this 5'1" container.

I love words. I use lots of them. I could write words every day for the rest of my life—use up every synonym for pain, loss, grief—and I could never come close to describing this reality.

Lots of words, and yet none at all. That's what this is.

Alexithymia.

October 23, 2019—Ibuprofen and Eger

This morning I woke up with a headache and my foot throbbing. I was a bit bummed about not feeling well. I gave myself a little talking to.

It's OK not to feel good. You just had foot surgery a week ago. Take some ibuprofen, get back on the couch, and give yourself a break.

I made some headway on my latest read—*The Body Keeps the Score—Brain, Mind, and Body in the Healing of Trauma.* Then I watched an interview with Dr. Edith Eva Eger (author of *The Choice*), my new mentor. I would love to meet that lady. I want to be her when I grow up. She lives in San Diego where, at 92 years old, she still practices as a psychologist. A survivor of Auschwitz, she is passionate about helping people find healing and freedom after trauma and loss. If you want to be inspired, google her and listen. Or read her book… the one she wrote at the young age of 89.

The ibuprofen and a dose of Eger-ism brought me back to myself, and I began my workday. I can't even express how thankful I am for the ability to work from home.

You would think with all this time alone during the day, stuck on the couch, I would have pondered all the mysteries in my life and come to some profound conclusions. Instead, I have to reign in my thoughts, give them some boundaries, because they tend to visit every category, every topic, every universal possibility, leaving me overwhelmed. That's how my brain works. Always has.

Still, there are some questions that I find myself rehearsing often. I don't know if today, this week, this month, or even the rest of this year is the time to pursue answers in earnest. But the questions are there.

One such question is…what's next?

My friend Monica, who lost her precious son Jojo last year, spoke the gospel truth when she said to me recently, "We are changed forever. We will never be the same as we were." I replay those words and can't help but believe that this truth will shape what's next.

So today on the couch, as the question formed once more, I prayed….

God, you know what's next. I don't have the energy to grapple with it right now, but I trust you. You know the desires of my heart. Help me know when to move forward and how. And when to stay still.

Amen.

October 25, 2019—End the Call

A couple of weeks ago, Charli and I were headed home from the airport after our college tours in New York. It was about 10:30 at night, and I knew our trash cans had to be out early for Monday's trash pick-up. I called Chance to ask him to pull out the cans. For some reason, Siri misunderstood my voice command. Instead, she announced:

Calling Chandler Espinoza, mobile.

Instantly, a feeling washed over me that I cannot describe. Shock, fear, frustration. Why didn't I say it clearer? My audible response was instinctual, panicked, primal—"Shit."

I don't even remember how I stopped Siri from dialing the number from which would come no answer. Maybe Charli intervened. I just know it was a moment of unreality colliding with reality. Siri is calling Chandler, but I can't let it ring, not even once! I can't bear him not hearing the ringtone, not answering, "Hey, Mom."

Before losing Chandler, I rarely had a potty mouth. I remember two occasions where I pulled out the mother of all bad words. Well, maybe three, but who's counting. The first was when 8-year-old Chance was beating his head on the headboard with an excruciating migraine, and the nurse on the end of the line kept putting me on hold. The second was a few years back when a girl on the opposing soccer team intentionally pushed Charli really hard from behind, knocking her to the ground where she hit her head. Charli lay there for what seemed an eternity before she could get up. The ref appeared to be doing nothing about the girl who pushed Charli, so I may have charged the field with a choice word or two about the need for decisive action.

So it seems my potty mouth switch turns on primarily when one of my kids is in pain or in danger. Chandler's accident and death crashed through the thresholds of both.

The point here is not my potty mouth or lack thereof. The point is, it freaking sucks to lose your son. It shatters your heart, rips you to your very core. It squeezes your soul like a ravenous python with no predictable point of release. No language, the potty variety or otherwise, can do it justice.

Sometimes, there are words. Sometimes, there are none.

Either way…sometimes you just have to end the call.

October 2019—This is Me

When our whole sense of ourselves seems wounded and vulnerable, one of the ways we can claim our rightful presence in the world is to claim the legitimacy of our grief. That is who we are right now, and it is a valid way to be. In time we will see ourselves again in broader terms. But if, for a while, grieving is the main aspect of our being, then so be it.

~Martha W. Hickman

December is not far away, and I am keenly aware of my identity.

Throughout my life, I have played many roles—compliant child, eager learner, conscientious employee, supportive friend, mourning daughter, doting mother, curious adventurer, adoring bride. That's just scratching the surface. Until January 1, on any given day, I could have answered, "Who are you?" in a number of ways, with no one aspect of me dominating the rest.

As I turn the pages of my desk calendar at work and see that just two turns remain before December, I am very clear about who I am. A heartbroken, heavy, grieving mother. This is the way it is right now. It won't be forever.

If I do not embrace this reality, I will not learn what grief has to teach me. And I know from experience, it will come back later to bite me in the butt. Unprocessed grief will someday, somehow find its way out.

Lord, I know You are with me. I know I am surrounded by the love and support of family and friends. I know that Chandler would not want me to become paralyzed by fear and sadness. Because these things are true, I can turn the pages of the calendar and trust that I will get through this. Please help me to feel what I need to feel, knowing that these feelings, these unwelcome images, these fears will not kill me. I am a grieving mother. And I will be OK. Amen.

November 2019

November 3, 2019 – View From Above

This is one of the first pictures in Chandler's baby book. Chip's mom probably took it from upstairs while I stole a few minutes of sleep, newborn Chandler snoozing peacefully on my chest.

The caption I wrote underneath 26 years ago…

I wonder if this is what God sees when he looks down from heaven.

I wonder what Chandler sees when he looks down from heaven?

I believe Chandler is more alive than ever. What I don't know are the ground rules where he lives now.

Does he see me—on the couch, tears flowing, whispering, "Chandler, I miss you so much, honey…I miss you so much?" Does he see all those times when the grief waves roll in, and I struggle to come up for air?

Does he see when I take his shirt sleeve and hold it to my cheek? Does he see when I hold his picture and tell him how much I love him?

Any of these would bring Chandler to tears. If there are no tears in heaven, are his eyes graciously blinded to his mother's broken heart? Does he only see the happy stuff? Running through bubbles in a 5k, trying a new kombucha flavor, laughing at the dinner table with our family, enjoying a good book, watching *Breaking Bad*?

I hope he sees a mom who loves him beyond anything he could have even comprehended with his earthly Chandler mind. I hope he sees the boundless love that exists for him on this planet...and I hope he sees that it's because of who he was. I hope he sees me and his dad and his brothers and sister loving and missing him fiercely and moving forward—honoring him by choosing to live in the moment, love people well, and do the next right thing.

That's what I hope Chandler sees when he looks down from heaven.

Today's Chandler-ism:

6-28-2000—"I would rather worship than stick up my middle finger."

November 4, 2019—The First One

The picture says it all. His first concussion.

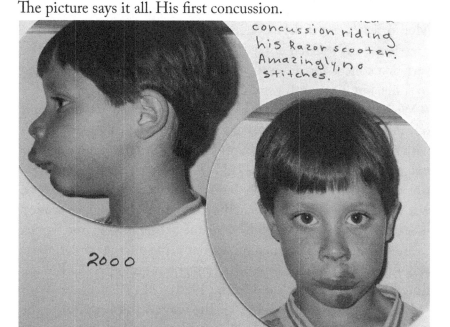

concussion riding his Razor scooter. Amazingly, no stitches!

2000

Here's what I wrote in my mom journal the day after:

Last night we were in the ER for almost four hours with you. You fell on the ramps and got a concussion. It was SO bloody! The scariest part was that you immediately began dozing off on the way to the ER. You were such a stud! You stopped crying once we got to the hospital, and that was it for the tears. Your dad got my message and dismissed his class in LaPuente and headed to the ER. Chase was with us; Chance was with a friend. He cried and was afraid for you. The CT scan was normal—thank God! Today you look horrible. Earlier you put on a rubber glove from the ER, got it wet and said, "I'm Dr. Wetglove. I clean things and do all kinds of things with wet gloves." You're funny even with a radically fat lip.

I've been looking through Chandler's photo album the past couple of days.

For a while I was a good mom. Each kid's acid-free, sticker-filled, chronologically accurate photo albums were current.

Public service announcement: Don't down a margarita while writing important dates you need to get right in your album.

I closed the album and opened up my journal full of Sayings, Memories & Stuff. My eye immediately fell on today's Chandler-ism—my journal entry the day that picture was taken. His very first concussion at seven years old. Believe it or not, he wanted to smile, but his mouth wouldn't let him.

We had the most awesome skate ramps that the boys would drag out into our cul-de-sac every day after school. Grandpa Bill was with us one Christmas when Santa brought the quarter pipe, and he helped Chip put it together. Daddy loved watching the boys have fun on those things, probably because given the chance when he was young, he would have done the same thing. Instead, he made a living balancing on sky-high 6"-wide metal beams as an iron worker.

The day Chandler crashed on the ramp, the only car at the house was Aunt Cho's Isuzu stickshift. Talk about quick recall! The last time I had driven a stick was in the 1980s.

I kept talking to Chandler all the way to the hospital, so he wouldn't fall asleep, praying for him and for me—that my feet would hit the clutch, the brake and the gas in the right order and my hand would shift the stick to the appropriate gear.

Glen Rouse, a family friend and pastor, met us at the hospital. He wasn't shocked. This was Chandler.

My little guy was so brave. No stitches that time, but there was a different visit to that same ER from a "wheels" accident that entailed some stitches to the chin.

As Chance wrote, "He always went head first."

November 6, 2019 – That's It

Social support is the most powerful protection against becoming overwhelmed by stress and trauma…being truly heard and seen by the people around us, feeling that we are held in someone else's mind and heart.

~Bessel Van Der Kolk, M.D., *The Body Keeps the Score*

That's it.

I won't say there haven't been plenty of moments since December 15 when I've felt absolutely overwhelmed, like the simple task of brushing my teeth was too much. Like the pain was saturating so much of my body and soul that there was no space left for joy or freedom. Like the prospect of living into some semblance of a new normal was beyond the realm of possibility.

But I have not been overwhelmed to the point of prolonged paralysis. To the point of losing hope in Christ. To the point of withdrawing from my life.

Here's what's truly overwhelming. The constant love and support of family, friends, and people I don't even know ever since the day of Chandler's accident. Without reservation or exaggeration, I can say that every text, phone call, Facebook post, prayer, meal, vase of flowers, bottle of kombucha, hug, word of understanding—every single act that reminds me that I am being "held in someone's mind and heart"—that is it. That is why I have made it this far and will continue one…day…at…a…time to honor Chandler's life by living mine the best I can. I am speaking in first person, but you can insert "we" because this has been our family's experience as well, not just mine.

"Social support." That's one way to say who Chandler was for so many who crossed his path. I have had friends of his tell me that Chandler was there for them when no one else would listen. The love that was poured out in his hospital room and at his memorial service were simply a "giving back" of the love that Chandler brought to his corner of this planet.

He started early. In kindergarten, Chandler received the Meadow Park Pride Award—for being a "kind, caring friend."

November 8, 2019—Friendship, Fresh Plants, and Faltering Lights
This time last year, I drove through the corner of Via Honesto and Antonio every day with no idea that this spot would become a landmark. The worst kind.

The past few weeks, I've not been too happy seeing the leaves pile up, forming mounds behind and around the bike. And the solar lights I'd strung through the spokes and handle bars not adequately fulfilling their one job. I know it's just a bike. But if it's there, it should shine like Chandler. It should be a point of light after the sun sets.

So today I picked up my friend Kelly, and we embarked on our mission. Usually I would just go by myself. Not this time. The purpose of today's partnership was two-fold: pain and pain.

Doctors orders are to lay low and not begin easing back into normal activities for another two and a half weeks. He doesn't have to twist my arm. My foot starts cussing me out after just a few minutes of weight bearing, and I'm grateful to hit the couch with a pillow and an ice pack. In order to avoid that level of pain, I knew I needed help to minimize clean-up time.

Then there's the other pain. The one that won't go away in two or three months or a year. Or with a pillow and an ice pack. I didn't want it to wreck me today. It's never easy to stand at that spot—Antonio and Via Honesto. With my dear friend there, I knew my mind would be occupied with conversation and perhaps not so prone to its usual unsolicited screenings—scenes that insist on filling in blanks, providing details that leave me mentally nauseous, grasping, distraught. And I knew if I lost it, that would be OK with her too.

What could have been a pretty crappy morning became an

occasion for smiles and laughter and Chandler stories as we swept up leaves and strung new lights and watered plants. Kelly brought a mini Christmas tree, Chandler's first of the season, to add to the collection. Whoever brought the mini pumpkins and the fresh potted plants (kalanchoes I believe?)—thank you!!!! Every new plant or trinket or candle or golf ball or note…these are reminders to us that Chandler is not forgotten.

Our mission was followed by a lovely lunch of delicious BLTs on toasted gluten-free bread and the world's best passion iced tea at Latte Da Bagelry in RSM. If you go there any time soon, come prepared…it's BYOTP. Luckily I had a tissue in my purse. The distinct smell led me to believe the bathroom had just been painted and all extraneous items, including a toilet paper holder, paper towels and hand soap, had been removed in the process. It's a minor inconvenience worth enduring for the mouth-watering lunch selections. Again, just come prepared.

Tonight a friend who has been in this club much longer than I came over to hang out. On her way, she passed by the bike and noticed…no lights. Well, this is simply unacceptable. I will give them one more day to charge in the sun. If they don't work by tomorrow night, Sunday's to-do list will read: Return piece-of-crap solar lights and buy a string that is worthy of its calling.

Today's Chandler-ism:

11-17-98—"I'm thankful to God for all my body pieces because they can do so many neat things."

November 13, 2019 – Sundown…Brighter

Tonight the bike is shining even more brightly. One of Chandler's friends bought another string of lights that I strung on it this afternoon before sundown. I had to drive back after dark to see. Beautiful.

The time change has been tough. The first step toward a re-creation. The days keep moving me closer. I know better than to anticipate the pain. Despite my earnest effort to remain in this day, in this moment, too often my thoughts take the form of sentences that begin, "This time last year…"

I don't have a lot of words.

November 14, 2019 — Ebb and Flow

This is my boy at Sheep Hills dirt jumps in Costa Mesa when he was 14. We used to travel all over, wherever there was a dirt jump, a ramp, a bowl to ride. We had to park and hike quite a ways back to these jumps. It was worth it.

Today felt a bit lighter. I loved being at work. I loved being able to spend 15 minutes getting my heart rate up in the HotBlaster sauna. I loved coming home to whip up some chimichurri chicken with brown rice for dinner. And I loved just being on the couch with my foot iced and propped up while Charli did homework on the couch to my left and Chip made himself some dinner in the kitchen to my right. Don't judge me—he has way different taste than Charli and me, and he loves to cook.

If you're looking for a decadent tasty treat after dinner, try SO Salted Caramel Cluster cashew ice cream. Perfect choice if you stay away from dairy, but it's so creamy, anyone would love it unless their taste buds are wacked. Literally one of the most delicious food items I've ever put in my mouth. I'm gambling cuz my IBS doesn't usually play well with cashews. It might be worth it. We'll see.

It's completely normal and yet feels so not normal—the ebb and

flow of grief. One day your head is above water, the next submerged. The next you come up for air for a few hours and then a wave hits and knocks you under. You wake up seeing sunshine and feeling ready for the day. The next morning, you wake up seeing clouds despite the clear skies and the sun's rays beaming through the window. I think I've become somewhat accustomed to this ebb and flow, push and pull, over and under, light and dark.

I appreciate what Martha W. Hickman says, "We need to remember that recovery from grief is not a smooth uphill path…these 'tempests' and setbacks are all part of the process. So let us expect them, accept them when they come, then take a deep breath and move on."

I ask myself if I'm doing all the things I should do. Am I feeling everything I need to feel? Am I feeling too much? Am I stuck in certain memories and images? Do I need to sit with those images and let the new reality seep further into my pores and cells and neural pathways?

For tonight, exactly what I'm doing is exactly the right thing.

November 15, 2019 – Worth It

> *There is no safe investment. To love at all is to be vulnerable. Love anything, and your heart will certainly be wrung and possibly be broken. If you want to make sure of keeping it intact, you must give your heart to no one, not even to an animal.*
>
> ~C.S. Lewis, *The Four Loves*

We know this to be true. We also know the converse to be true. As Lewis continues, if you encase your heart with protective layers, keeping it to yourself, it will become "unbreakable, impenetrable, irredeemable."

That is not the most human option. We mostly choose to love. We love deeply and without reserve.

Thus, we grieve. We mourn. We lament. We sob. We are faced with the work of figuring out life without. Without the one we loved since before his or her birth. Without the parent who held us when we were afraid or lonely. Without the sibling who conspired with us to make the most entertaining kinds of mischief.

Without the friend who was the first to hear about our victories and our defeats.

The love is worth the grief. But, oh, how it aches.

November 16, 2019 – Natural

Chandler was a natural athlete. Whatever he decided to do, he did it well whether it was basketball, baseball, track, diving, skateboarding, or biking.

When he was little, he was bummed because he couldn't ride a bike. One day he came in and said, "Mom, I figured out how to ride a bike." We pulled out his bike, gave him a push, and sure enough…he had figured it out by watching the big guys. That was the beginning of his lifelong love of biking. But not just plain biking. BMX trick biking. The kind that makes those who love you pray really hard.

In one of Chandler's first bike competitions, he took off for a practice run, and I whispered to Chip, "Oh, my gosh, I think he's thinking about doing something crazy." He rode back around, picked up speed, flew off the ramp and threw a back flip. We lost our breath, and he won a medal.

Baseball got off to a bit of a rough start. In t-ball, the most entertaining part of the game was watching Chandler in the outfield, back to the batter, scooping up dirt with his glove and dumping it into his baseball pants. He was the youngest and smallest, but he infused the game with Chandler-ness. By the time he was in little league, he had learned to use the glove for catching rather than dirt dumping.

As a freshman in high school, Chandler decided to dive for Santa Margarita. Other than jumping off the high dive since he was knee-high and hurling himself off bridges or rooftops into pools, he had no experience with formal diving. He began training with a local dive team, and from the first day, the coach could not believe this was new to Chandler. His lack of fear meant he would try anything. He ended up lettering in diving. That jacket is a treasure, a symbol of Chandler's sense of adventure, natural athleticism, and willingness to persevere through the learning curve.

I am grateful that throughout his life, Chandler was able to do the things that made him feel most alive. Even until the end.

Today's Chandler-ness:

3/12/98—Today was your first t-ball practice. You were so excited and cute with your cleats, glove, and Blue Jays cap. Afterward, I asked, "Did you catch the ball?" You said, "No, I didn't because I couldn't run as fast as the other guys. (pause) That's a bummer." You're the smallest, youngest kid, probably in the league. You said, "It was great."

November 18, 2019 — Invitation

This is the day that the Lord has made; let us rejoice and be glad in it.

~Psalms 118:24

For some reason, that scripture came to me this morning as I limped slowly across the floor to the bathroom. There's no such thing as hurrying to the bathroom, or anywhere else for that matter, on a healing foot. Gives you time to ponder things I guess.

I had to be honest. I didn't feel much like rejoicing, and I didn't feel terribly glad. I sort of felt blah. And I said to myself, "It's OK to feel blah. You have permission."

In the past, I've thought of this scripture as a mandate. You are hereby commanded to rejoice and be glad because how dare you NOT do so when God has so generously gifted you with breath today!

This morning I saw it from a different perspective. Rather than a command meant to jerk us out of our sadness or grief or anger or fear and into a seemingly opposite state of mind, it is an invitation. Not a slap on the wrist for feeling like a human being but rather a gentle reminder that no matter what is happening, God has created a new sunrise with new possibilities. We have the freedom, the opportunity, to live into this new sunrise and believe God will meet us. That certainly is good reason to rejoice and be glad.

God has boundless compassion and grace for us in our times of sorrow and pain. He hurts with us. Even when "rejoice" is like the word you can't seem to find on the word search puzzle. You know it's there. You search and search, but it eludes you. Then out of the blue, the sequence of letters begins to appear. And there it is. Rejoice.

God, I know that "rejoice" is a good word, a fitting word. But some days it feels hidden. Thank you for the invitation and also the grace to be where I am, trusting that you are right here with me. Amen.

Today's Chandler-ness:

11/9/98—Today you turned by putting your foot down! You have ridden intermittently throughout the day. You are beaming with pride and excitement and joy at your accomplishment. You keep saying, "I love my bike. I just love it so much." At one point, you said, "I love my bike as much as God loves me. Except I even love God more." You are precious.

November 20, 2019 – Chandler School

I had the privilege of homeschooling Chandler for 3rd and 4th grades. During those two years, I witnessed firsthand my little boy's ripe imagination, curiosity, and intrinsic drive to physically engage with the world around him. If you look up the definition of "kinesthetic learner," Chandler's picture will be there.

I remember when he was working on math, I pulled out a cookie sheet, covered it in shaving cream, and had Chandler form the math problems with his fingers in the white foam. He loved the multi-colored math manipulatives we used for learning multiplication. Everything came to life when we visited the Santa Ana Zoo's ring-tailed lemur, the subject of one of Chandler's assigned wildlife reports. For one of his science experiments, we used cornstarch and a couple of other household substances to create a sort of magical goo that reverted to its original shape no matter how much it was squeezed and contorted.

Most days his school "uniform" consisted of his boxers. He always had a stuffy nose from allergies, thus the roll of toilet paper residing on the kitchen table (aka Chandler's desk). After getting his big brothers to school and baby sister Charli involved in her own "schoolwork," we would open up our lesson plans for the day. It was a relaxed, rich time of learning. I gained deep insight into this amazing little guy we named Chandler.

One particular snapshot sticks in my mind. I had left Chandler with his reading assignment and gone into my office to work on a column I wrote for a parenting magazine at the time. I came back some time later to find him…staring intently, transfixed by his pencil eraser. He hadn't written much. But the pencil eraser was fascinating.

I learned that Chandler thought deeply about things. That his mind never went blank. It was simply preoccupied with its own unique trains of thought, spurred by anything from a pencil eraser to a jug of milk.

God, thank you for giving me those two very special years with Chandler at home. I was grateful for them before, but now...

Today's Chandler-ness:

3/21/98—Today you said, "Mom, I want to marry a clown." Yesterday you said, "Mom, when I'm this age, can I be in a pie-eating contest?" You are living in quite a world of your own.

November 23, 2019 – Time Is a Gift

Chandler-ness is up top today because it contains the seeds of two ideas about which I am passionate. I'll talk about Idea #1 today and Idea #2 tomorrow.

Today's Chandler-ness:

1-21-98—Chandler, on Monday we had you tested for kindergarten readiness because of your early birthday. I had a feeling I knew the outcome as I eavesdropped through the door. The evaluating lady said, "Chandler, can you put these in a sequence like this." With no interest in her directions whatsoever, you replied, "I can do thighn language." Sure enough, they recommended that we seriously consider giving you the "gift of time." So I have you home with me one more year. I'm excited!

Chandler's assertion that he could do "thighn language" (he hadn't quite mastered his "s") was off-topic but accurate. I had been teaching him sign language for several everyday words like "home," "mom," and "dog." That apparently seemed to Chandler far more germane to the conversation than putting something in the correct sequence.

SO...

Idea #1—Cherish...treasure...embrace...live into every moment with your little ones.

When a child has a secure attachment with a parent—when they know that there is a person who lights up because of their presence—a foundation is laid that will help that child as they grow into adolescence and adulthood and experience the inevitable disappointments and smack-downs of life. That kind of secure attachment happens when a parent settles into the mundane moments of parenting, knowing full well there's nothing more important. It happens when Mom or Dad hugs tightly and listens closely. And when clock time takes a back seat to the richness of pure presence.

The season of raising young children, with all their innocence and wonder, has much to teach us—be curious, say what's true, be naïve enough to think that your hugs make a difference.

If our children were the only beneficiaries of our learning to be present in our parenting, it would be worth it. But selfishly, I've found that the most fulfilling, joyous moments of my life were when I gave myself permission to BE with my children. To lay aside my to-do list and my driven-ness and just play.

Before starting to work full time a few years ago, I devoted my time through music, speaking, and writing to encouraging young moms to lean into the significance of that very special, and VERY exhausting, season of life. That passion has never waned as my own kids have grown and, in fact, has now taken on a whole new dimension. I wouldn't trade my special times with Chandler for anything on the planet.

When the evaluator recommended the "gift of time," she had no idea the breadth and depth of gratitude that would fill this mother's heart 20 years later.

Time is indeed a gift.

November 24, 2019—Don't Rush It

Yesterday's Chandler-ness spurred me to share two parenting ideas about which I'm passionate. I talked about the first yesterday.

So today, here's Idea #2: Don't rush it.

As an admissions director, I tell parents who are looking at kindergarten that we assess the kiddos for developmental readiness. In response, quite often I hear some version of, "Oh, I know my child is really smart, so he/she is definitely ready for kindergarten."

I get it. That would have absolutely been me with my firstborn, Chase. When he started kindergarten over 25 years ago, I had no clue about anything except that he turned five on September 10 (back then the deadline was December 1) and was supposed to start kindergarten. Had I known there was such a thing as "the gift of time" or a "bonus year," there's a good chance I would have scoffed and said, "I'm confident he's a genius, and I will do irreparable damage to his psyche and intellectual capacities if I hold him back from kindergarten for a year."

By the time Chandler and Charli came along, I knew better. I knew that there was no rush to get them into kindergarten. I knew that it had nothing to do with "smart" and everything to do with time, especially for kids like mine with summer birthdays. When Chancy & Bruce (the educational assessment company) recommended the "gift of time" for Chandler and Charli, I did a little Snoopy dance inside.

For parents, especially of little ones, it's so tempting to wish for the day when they will sleep through the night. When they will begin to hold their own bottle. When they will start to walk. When they will be potty trained. When they will start preschool or kindergarten. We look forward to those various milestones partly because we assume things will be a bit easier.

Fast forward to the teen years. Yes, it is easier when they learn to drive and your schedule becomes freer than you ever remember. Easier doesn't mean better or worse. It's just different.

Every season of parenting has its points of exhaustion and frustration and also its incomparable joys and moments of sheer bliss. I have learned along the way that if we keep one foot anxiously poised in tomorrow, we rob ourselves of the gifts that are right here in front of us…today.

Maya Angelou once said something to the effect of, "You can't do better until you know better." I'm glad I learned better somewhere along the way.

Don't rush it.

Today's Chandler-ness:

10/3/98—Chandler: God was never a baby.

Mom: Jesus was a baby.

Chandler: Yeah, but he grew up and became God's partner in teaching people to do the right thing.

November 25, 2019—Four

Today's Chandler-ness up top:

You told me you didn't want to wear boxers (or anything) to bed because without them it's "fresher."

Chance had a migraine, and you brought him an ice pack and said, "Here, Chance. This will make it feel better." It's awesome how you love your brother so much.

I hate that my kids have to miss their brother. I would rather they do what siblings do—complain about this or that pet peeve, argue, try to outwit or outdo one another.

It's one thing as a parent to carry a perpetual gut/heart/soul-ache because you miss your kid so damn much. It's quite another to watch your other kids try and go about their lives with one of them gone. Their lives are intertwined with one another. They have common stories and traditions and connections. And a common scapegoat—their crazy mom and dad!

I love that they are friends who can laugh and talk amongst themselves about the quirks and foibles and—I have to be real here—the mistakes of their parents. I love their camaraderie. And thankfully, amidst our abject imperfection as parents, they know we love them beyond what can be said or sung or written or painted or expressed in any measurable way. They share the common bond of having Chip Espinoza and Lisa Vickery Espinoza as their parents. Only they share that—Chase, Chance, Chandler, and Charli.

One of the four isn't in that loop anymore.

They've talked about how they just knew that someday their kids would have loved their "cool" Uncle Chandler. Their imaginations of the future never included a scenario in which one of them was missing.

Oh, God, how my heart hurts for my kids. Please show up for them in the days and weeks to come in ways that speak to each one of them uniquely…in the specific language of Chase, of Chance, and of Charli. Amen.

November 26, 2019 – One More Kiss

I want to write something uplifting and inspiring. Some life lesson that came to me today that I think might be helpful to someone else. Maybe something clever or funny.

All I can manage tonight is to put my fingers on the keyboard and tap out each painful letter—I WANT MY SON BACK!

It is a deep well, this well of grief. Dark, echoing with memories, bottomless. I know I won't stay down here indefinitely. I am not free-falling. I am holding, white-knuckled at times, to the rope. I will find it in me to, hand-over-hand, pull myself out, or I will find myself ascending through no efforts of my own. Likely, I will discover upon the first glimpses of light that it was my family and my friends who never let go of the rope and are hoisting me up into daylight again.

God, I know you are with me in the dark. You are my advocate, my strength, my security, my comforter, my provider. The dark is OK. It is part of life. You created us to love, therefore, we grieve. It is worth the grief. Amen.

Today's Chandler-ness:

3/12/99—Yesterday you and I went on a date to see *October Sky* and have lunch at Chili's. It was an "it doesn't get any better than this" time. From the movie, you said you learned not to give up and not to launch your rockets in a bad place.

November 28, 2019 – Grateful....and Yet

It's Thanksgiving morning. I opened my eyes at about 8:15, and my very first thought was, *I'm still here. And I'm not feeling terrified or hopeless.*

I've been lying in bed reading for the past hour or so and making mental (and physical) note of what time each component of the feast gets put on the stove or in the oven in order for us to eat by 5:00, after the Cowboys game. I've done the same traditional Thanksgiving meal for almost our entire marriage, and yet I still have to pencil it all out to make sure everything gets on the table at approximately the same time and not burned or undercooked.

I decided to write a bit this morning and then add some more at the end of our family day of Thanksgiving.

The emotions and thoughts that accompany the grief process are vast and vacillating. My pre-Thanksgiving day prayer:

God, please give us the grace and freedom to feel what we feel today as we celebrate our first Thanksgiving without Chandler. Give us sensitivity to one another and space to allow for what the other needs. Our natural inclination is to fear the pain. Help us to allow fear to dissipate and to be replaced by the reality that even in the depths of our pain and missing, You are with us, and the pain will not ultimately overcome us. Bathe us in Your sustaining presence. Amen.

Tonight...

My heart is grateful. It was a relaxed, simple day with family. Aunt Cho worked at the hospital all night and came straight here to spend Thanksgiving with us.

A few minutes after we started eating, Chance made the apt observation that this was about when Chandler would have entered the room, shirtless, explaining that he'd been surfing and offering, "Oh, this looks great!" as he grabbed a plate.

There was a palpable absence. A missing chair. Had Chandler been here, we would have eaten around the pool table (we have a fancy top that converts it to a dining table). Today, we all fit around the kitchen island.

I am grateful that we have each other. I'm grateful that I genuinely like these people...my family. These people for whom my love has no limits.

I am grateful for friends. For nourishing, delicious food. For health. For a home. For the crackling fire and Charli's bare feet propped against the mantle.

For the hope I have in Christ...that I will see Chandler again.

Usually, my predominant attitude on Thanksgiving is exactly that—thankfulness. It is my favorite holiday because there are no expectations except...be grateful. Today, I am deeply grateful. But the weightier proposition today was "Just be present and enjoy your family." I indeed felt joyful, and there was lots of laughter. But the deep missing was, is, like a heavy blanket draped around my shoulders whether laughing, chatting, eating, cooking, watching TV.

Chandler's absence was the underlying presence today. Even in the midst of gratitude.

Tonight, God, I thank you for a day filled with the simplest and best. As Chip prayed at dinner, "Please give Chandler a hug for us. We miss him desperately. Amen."

Today's Chandler-ness:

8/3/98—We were talking about your loose tooth and how when it comes out, your new one will grow in. You said, "Do you have to water the space?"

December 2019

December 1, 2019 — A Plan

It's the morning of December 1.

It helps to have a plan. And to hold loosely to the plan in case things go sideways.

Pre-December 15, it was a fairly safe bet that most or all of the items on my daily to-do list would be marked out by day's end (actually deleted one-by-one from Notes on my phone). Didn't really matter if I felt like doing something or not…if it was on the list, it got done. That's just how I'm wired.

These past months, I've developed a different relationship with my to-do list…my plan.

I've been learning more than ever that it's important to listen to my soul. What does it need most today…or for the next hour?

Of course, that only goes so far. If my soul doesn't feel like getting gas, my car may not take me where I need to go. If my soul doesn't feel like getting my work done, lots of important things fall through the cracks. If my soul doesn't feel like washing clothes, hopefully the people around me lack a keen sense of smell.

I've also been learning that sometimes when my energy is low or I'm feeling down, when the last thing I want to do is anything, if I can just push through and check off some of my to-do boxes, I gain a sense of accomplishment and satisfaction and, usually, more energy than when I started.

In general, I find it wisest to limit the number of items I assign myself on any given day if I can help it. But if I over-assign and I don't have it in me to do the next thing (or five) on the list, I will probably let it go and give myself grace. I will read or watch TV or make something good to eat or drink…or take a walk, once I get the all-clear from my foot doc.

Today's plan: Pilates reformer workout, laundry, lavender hot chocolate, unpack Christmas decorations, soccer, fire in the fireplace to end the day.

We'll see how it goes by day's end.

It's 9:00 p.m., and today's plan went smoothly.

It had its moments. Like unpacking the cheesy Christmas clothes I wore last year. Poinsettia leggings, Snoopy Christmas tree sweatshirt, sequined green sweater, angel earrings, and so on…I wore them every single day at Mission Hospital last December. The memories came flooding in. I don't know how to disassociate the sweater from standing beside Chandler in that sweater stroking his forehead, singing to him. For a few seconds, the thought crossed my mind to get rid of every single piece of cheesy Christmas clothing and start fresh. Instead, I decided that tomorrow, I will wear the Snoopy Christmas tree sweatshirt to work.

The only item left on today's agenda…hot chocolate by the fire. That's the plan.

Today's Chandler-ness:

11/30/99—At Universal Studios when they flipped on the Christmas lights, you exclaimed, "This is just like Las Vegas!"

December 3, 2019—Missing…Hurting…Celebrating

Despite its reputation for possessing a perpetually sunny disposition, this morning Southern California showed its chilly, grey side. As I lay snuggled under my cozy microfiber sheets and my down comforter, I didn't want to get up. The sun seems to draw my feet to the floor more readily. Since it wasn't there to greet me this morning, sheer force of will got me to my toothbrush.

Standing in my closet, I saw the red-and-white striped fur-lined Christmas knee socks with the rubber sticky bottoms that I wore at the hospital. Up and down the hall. To the patient refrigerator for a kombucha, then back to Chandler's room. In and out of the double doors to ICU, bringing friends in to see Chandler or taking a break to visit in the waiting room. Those socks that lent comfort and warmth threaten to suck the joy out of Christmas for me. The socks are not the only culprit. Everywhere I look, there are visible reminders of last December's nightmare.

Looking at those socks, I made a decision in my closet this morning. Well, maybe not so much a decision, but a wordless, resolute prayer of hope. I will not allow grief to steal every bit of joy from a season I love. A season whose meaning—God with us—is the central truth of my existence. Especially now.

It would not honor Chandler, a young man who was wearing a Santa hat on December 15, if I shrank from celebration.

So before heading to work, I sat down at my computer and ordered Christmas pillow covers for my couch. Never even thought of it before, but it will bring some extra cheer to our hang-out spot, so I'm going for it.

Instead of feverishly working to get all the Christmas decorations done in a day or two, I'm going to take my time, whenever the mood strikes, and enjoy the process. I'm going to be good to myself. To

cry and remember the really shitty parts when I need to. To miss my son like crazy. To look at pictures of Chandler and smile as best I can. To relax by the fire with a Christmas mug full of hot tea and watch *Die Hard* (yes, it's a Christmas movie).

I would be naïve to think that all the minutes and hours and days coming up, days rife with triggers, will only be full of smiles, laugher, and levity. But experience tells me that even though I will feel the weight and the darkness and the sense of bottomless pain, it will always give way to something lighter. Not normal. But also not smothering.

God, by your grace, help me…help Chip, Chase, Chance, and Charli… find times of deep joy in this Christmas season. Help us to honor Chandler in our missing and in our hurting but also in our celebrating. Amen.

Today's Chandler-ness:

1/7/97—Chandler, my Chandler. You exhaust me. Within a one-hour period of time (during which my mild headache became severe), you put ALL the towels in the bathroom into your bathtub full of water. I had to wring them all out and wash them. While doing that, you went into the bathroom (after being put quickly and abruptly to bed by yours truly) and put soap suds all over yourself. I angrily, as my head pounded, washed you off in the sink and put you into bed again. Five minutes later, you screamed/cried down at me, "I pee the bed, Mom!"

December 4, 2019 – Maybe Not So Christmas-y

I've been pondering what may possibly be the least Christmas-y topic.

Death.

Not in a morbid or morose way. More from a philosophical viewpoint. Although, I'm sure at this point in my processing, the philosophical and the pragmatic are inextricably linked. Because of the mental, spiritual, emotional complexities of losing Chandler, I had an epiphany a couple of days ago.

Death is not an anomaly.

Other than birth, it is the one experience every human being who has ever existed will experience. We all have this in common. So why does it seem so surprising, so out-of-place when it happens?

Well, for one thing, if it's a child dying before his or her parent…
it just doesn't follow the proper order. If it's a young mom dying of
brain cancer, leaving her kids to grow up without her, it feels pre-
mature and unjust. If it's a marathon runner who has every health
advantage imaginable, it doesn't add up. The circumstances and the
timing and the manner and so many other details surrounding this
universal experience of death cause many of us to wrestle with it, to
question our faith, to pound the ground and scream in anger.

I'm trying to wrap my mind around the fact that either before me
or after me, Chandler would have died. So what I most disagree with
is the timing. Too young. And before his parents. That's something
I'll have to take up with the Lord someday. Or, more than likely,
once I get there, it will become a completely moot point.

I'm not attempting to simplify, minimize, or deny the absolute
shittiness of losing my son. I'm just beginning to realize that learning to accept death as a universal, natural part of life—as much a
part of life as birth—has the potential to transform the way I live
the rest of my days. I'm not sure what that looks like. But I'm a
willing student.

Honestly, I don't like the idea of death, certainly for people I care
about, and also for myself. I love my life. I don't want to think of
it ever ending…of someday leaving my family and friends. Of no
longer being able to explore this beautiful world and pursue new
goals and do meaningful work.

However, I do have the promise of a life after this one that is
beyond anything I could imagine. And…

I will see Chandler.

Today's Chandler-ness:

6/3/98—You asked, "What kind of Cindy is that?" Translated—
What's her last name? Or what does she look like? Or which Cindy
is that?

December 5, 2019—I Knew Him

Tonight I put some multi-colored Christmas lights on the bike. I
wish a picture could capture all the vibrant colors.

As I was taking the picture, a lady was walking her dog and

stopped so as not to walk between me and the bike. I said, "Thank you," and took a couple steps back to let her pass. She asked, "Did you know him?"

How do you answer that?

I used my whole hand to push his tiny heel out of my ribs and watched the impression of his pointy little elbow gliding across my belly. I saw my belly twitch when he got the hiccups. I held him in my arms for the first time and fell in love as I beheld those big brown eyes that would take in every adventure life would present. I held him when he got stitches, scolded him when he refused to embrace a consistent relationship with the toilet, kissed his chubby cheeks as he drifted off to sleep, rode all over Irvine with him in his George Jetson helmet on the back of my bike, then years later drove him all over Southern California so he could ride his own bike off of ramps and dirt jumps. I talked with him about theology, philosophy, fitness, food, and everything in between. I stroked his hands and kissed his forehead and sang to him and prayed he would open his eyes, look at me, and say, "Mom, when do I get out of here?" I watched him take his last breath.

I simply answered, "He was my son." And I cried.

She asked if she could give me a hug.

I am always appreciative of a heartfelt hug. Especially when it's from a fellow mom whose heart is hurting with mine even though she's never met me. Some moments of deep human connection are not contingent upon familiarity.

God, thank you for the privilege of knowing Chandler, of being with him for his first breath...and his last...though this is not at all how I would have planned it. Twenty-five years was not enough. I'm grateful I will someday be with him again where time will no longer impose its restraints. Amen.

Today's Chandler-ness:

1/5/99—Last night you prayed (as usual) for an extended period of time. It was precious. Among other things, you said, "Thank you God for dying on the cross because I really want to be forgiven...I really, really love you, God and Jesus. You're the best guy in the whole world!"

December 8, 2019 — Choices

But it is in our solitude that we are most affected by our loss. It is there, in our interplay with memory and our decisions about our energy and time, that we hold in our hands some control over the course of our grief...we are the best judges of when to stay in our grief and when to move on to something else.

~Martha W. Hickman

I've been making choices all my life. There have been some biggies, among them what to believe about God, who to marry, when to have kids and how to raise them. Then there are the mundane choices—which laundry soap to buy, where to find the best price on chicken breast this week, and what to take for the white elephant gift exchange at work.

I never dreamed that someday, my day-to-day choices would center on what to do with the intricacies of losing my son. Especially in moments of solitude.

Do I look through photos of Chandler? Sit in his room? Journal about how I'm feeling? Or do I focus my thoughts elsewhere, perhaps on pampering myself or being productive? There is no right or wrong answer, and if there were, it couldn't remain static because grief is not linear. Its margins are unclear, and it is unpredictable.

Today Aunt Cho and Ellen came down for lunch. We went to Board & Brew, and it just happened that the open table was right in front of Chandler's skate deck that's mounted on the wall, signed by friends and family. So good to see Brendan and our B&B clan. I know they are feeling a lot as we approach December 15.

Aunt Cho, Ellen, Charli and I talked a lot about Chandler, especially about his experience, and our experience, the last few days of his life. It was some brutal stuff (that's the sanitized version) we went through together. But most of all Chandler.

Today we made a choice to talk about the hard stuff.

On Thanksgiving, it seemed we had made an unspoken pact to focus on being together...on laughing and eating and appreciating our time together. There was no elephant in the room. We talked about Chandler. We all missed him. It didn't seem right for him not to be sitting shirtless at the table asking for third helpings. But we chose to keep it light and just appreciate our time together.

After lunch today, Aunt Cho suggested a movie, so we all went to see *Knives Out*. It was a good time. A very good choice.

My ability to make choices will end when I fall asleep tonight. I will get eight hours of respite. As soon as my eyes open tomorrow, the ball is once again in my court. I get to choose, to some extent, what direction I will go with my grief. My frequent trusty compass is often simply a glimpse down at my ring—WWHC (What Would Honor Chandler?).

God, I'm figuring this out a day at a time. Please guide me with your wisdom. Help me in this constant process of making choices about where my thoughts and moods will be centered. Help me come to a balanced, healthy interplay between the reality of my grief and the honoring of Chandler by being fully present in my life each day. Amen.

Today's Chandler-ness:

12/26/99—"The Bible is the best book to make your brain know about God."

December 11, 2019—Fear Not

I called on your name, Lord, from the depths of the pit. You heard my plea: "Do not close your ears to my cry for relief." You came near when I called you, and you said, "Do not fear."

~Lamentations 3:55-57

My friend and fellow grieving mom sent me this yesterday.

When I read the passage, my mind was immediately transported to a point in history when a young girl named Mary was told by an angel, "Fear not, Mary (Luke 1:30)." I picture myself, like that young girl, being confronted by a circumstance I never would have dreamed or imagined. Like her, my humanity begs an initial response of fear.

I admit I am afraid. Afraid of what it will feel like on December 15. Afraid of celebrating Christmas without the fourth Espinoza sibling. Afraid of waking up to the first day of the New Year, the last day I had with my sweet boy.

I wonder—is fear an unavoidable emotion given what I'm facing? Or is it possible to loosen fear's grip by simply accepting that I will feel sad, profoundly sad, that I will battle images that I wish were not imprinted in my brain, that I will so tangibly miss my son that my very insides will ache? By accepting this and knowing that it will not kill me, that I will move through it to the other side (whatever the other side is), can some measure of fear be allayed?

I don't know the answers to those questions. What I do know is I have a compassionate, loving Father who is WITH me in the questions, and He tenderly says, "Lisa, don't be afraid."

Today's Chandler-ness:

9/29/97—Today at church, I discovered you peeing on the tire of the van as Sharon, the music leader, passed by. Last week at church, you looked at the other kids and asked, "What the hell ith your problem?" I was teaching the class!

December 12, 2019 — Aftershocks

These days, as soon as sundown nears, everything in me vibrates at the frequency of what happened as the sun started to set almost a year ago to the day. If I had to name the feeling, it would be dread. As if by dreading I could somehow prevent what happened a year ago.

At the heart of dread is fear. I replay the words over in my head —"Do not fear."

I try to dissect my fear. Am I afraid Chandler will be hurt or die? That's already happened. So what am I afraid of? Quite simply, I am afraid of reliving last December's nightmare. Like I've written before, I know that pain will not kill me. I survived the earthquake, and I will survive its aftershocks.

Perhaps the best posture is to unclench my white knuckles and stand open-handed—offering every fear, every awful image, every heart stab, every endless pang of missing up to the God who is with me. And trust that He will see me through to the other side. Whatever that looks like.

Today's Chandler-ness:

4/2/98—We went to Green Meadows Farm today. It was so fun!!! (cold and muddy and foggy, but fun). You petted chickens, goats, sheep, cows (milked one too), chicks, ducklings, had a hayride and rode a pony. One time you yelled to Jeremy Sabo, "Hey, Jeremy, remember when you used to play with me?" Everyone laughed. Like you were thinking way back to the good old days.

On the way home, you said, "It was a good day, wasn't it Mom."

When Dad got home, you said, "Dad, we went to a fun place today."

December 13, 2019 — Surprised and Grateful

As difficult as today could have been, the emotions and thoughts that rise to the top this evening are centered on gratitude for the simple and yet overwhelming God-with-me encounters sprinkled throughout my day. That's what I want to focus on tonight. Immanuel. God is with me.

One of those God-with-me moments that left me in tears and almost speechless (there's not much that can rob me of all words) took place around noon at work. All of a sudden, I heard kids chanting, "We love Mrs. Espinoza…we love Mrs. Espinoza." I walked out of my office to see the Mission Hills Christian School 2nd and 3rd graders, grinning with the innocent, child-like anticipation that comes with knowing you're about to surprise someone and make them happy. They presented me with a beautifully arranged basket full of fruit, including a dragonfruit that looks almost too cool to crack open, or whatever it is you do with dragonfruit. The sweetest part of the basket—their precious hand-written notes. They told me they had prayed over my basket before delivering it and that they hoped I liked it.

Trying not to completely lose it, I told them, "You are God-with-me today." I reminded them that in this season when we celebrate baby Jesus in a manger, the meaning behind it all is that God is with us. That no matter what they go through in their lives, they are never alone. And I told them that God uses people, like them, to remind other people that God is with them.

I am so deeply grateful for the people who showed up in my life today as Immanuel—God is with me.

I pray that if you are reading this and are feeling the weight of grief or discouragement or fear or any of the myriad emotions that seem to magnify themselves during the holidays, that your heart will catch a glimpse of the reality—God is WITH you. Let someone know how you are feeling. Let them be Jesus with skin on for you.

Today's Chandler-ness:

(From The Gang section of my mom journal)

11/14/99—Today we went biking to the dirt jumps. We actually jumped three different places, then we went to Carl's Jr. and used coupons for two free orders of fries. Chandler's bike chain kept breaking which slowed us down on the way home, so we were riding in the dark almost. Chandler told me later that night, "Mom, this was a fun day." (Later that week, in his journal, Chandler wrote, "I like my mom. She's fun 'cuz she takes me to the dirt jumps.")

December 14, 2019—Wrestling

I find myself on the verge of tears quite often. I have to swallow, take a deep breath and remind myself that Chandler is more alive than ever, that he is not suffering or remembering his suffering.

But the anniversary of seeing my boy like…like he was…the imagining of the details of the accident, the day-to-day hoping against all hope that he would be OK—it is all alive and well in every cell, every firing neuron of my being. And unlike Chandler, who has moved on to a perfectly joyful, pain-free existence, my earth-bound humanity wrestles with what I saw…and what I didn't see.

Do I push away those thoughts, feelings, images? Do I replace them with an inner dialogue that goes something like:

It does not serve me well to speculate and ruminate over the details of what may have and what in fact did happen at Via Honesto and Antonio on Saturday evening, December 15, last year. Instead, remember all the good—his dimpled grin, his unquenchable thirst for life, his care for anyone who needed a friend, his inimitable Chandler-ness.

Or do I allow myself to go there? To relive the horror of the phone call while waiting in line at TJ Maxx, the rush to the hospital hoping this was like all the other ER visits that had turned out just fine, the devastating face-to-face news from the doctor…and so many more high-definition scenes and indelible sound bytes from that day. It is all embedded in my memory. Part of who I am, my story. Chandler's story. Our family's story. It seems that to relive it all is to heap on myself needless pain upon pain. But to forget? To ignore? That is also unacceptable.

I just don't know. For today, not knowing will have to be good enough.

One thing I do know is that God showed up for me tonight in the form of kind neighbors who stopped by with Chandler's favorite—Indian food.

This is how I get through it. How we get through it. This is God's highest plan—for people to love one another and help carry one another through hard times.

Today's Chandler-ness:

7/31/98—"Mom, I love how your heart loves God."

December 15, 2019 – December 15

8:00 a.m.—And so it begins. As I lay in bed, I tell myself that I need a game plan for the day, to know which t-shirt to wear. The t-shirt that says LIFE—that conjures sweet memories of Chandler and the time each of us had with him and the impact he made in so many lives. Or the t-shirt that says DEATH—that reflects the reality that this day will never again be simply December 15. This is the day that our lives were changed forever. The day that ultimately led to Chandler's last breath.

I cannot decide which t-shirt a grief expert would recommend, so I just choose to brush my teeth and get dressed. WWHC?

9:00 a.m.—Our family and some friends are meeting at Chandler's bike memorial. I'm grateful for every person who has graced that bike with lights, golf balls, flowers, and other symbols of love for Chandler, from the day it was placed there until now. It truly does my heart good to see that Chandler is being remembered.

It is really too much for my mind to comprehend and too painful for my heart to contemplate what happened at the site of the bike memorial a year ago today. And yet, the temptation is to try and fill in the blanks, to ask, "Was he afraid? Was he in horrific pain or maybe in shock? Was he aware of what had happened to him?" I go there, shed some tears, then return to, "No, it does not serve me or anyone else to think about those things."

3:20 p.m.—This time last year I yelled out to Chandler from my room as he ran down the stairs, "Can you go look at Christmas lights with us tonight?" He replied, "I've got to get to work." "OK, love you, son." "Love you, Mom." That is the last time I heard my son's voice.

I could recount a million details about what transpired after that. If I were so inclined, I could look back at my phone records and see the exact minute the unknown number appeared on my phone, a call I almost didn't answer because I figured it was probably a sales call. In the back of every parent's mind is that question, "But what if it's about one of my kids?" and you answer the unknown caller. Thankfully, it's rarely ever about one of your kids. This time it was.

6:53 p.m.—Looking back at the hours that made up this day, I think I've come to realize that most of the time, you can't choose one t-shirt over the other. I cannot pretend to only be grateful when I'm also feeling sad and wishing Chandler were here and remembering. And if I only focus on the heart-breaking events of last December 15, I will miss every opportunity to see God showing up in the form of my kids, my family, my friends. And sometimes in waves of hope and light that wash over me just after a bout of tears.

It is not either/or. It's both/and.

Like my friend Heidi said today, "It's the yin and yang of life." It is impossible to separate the pain from the joy. They must co-exist. Like the deep joy of having my family together this morning commingled with the awful reason for our being there.

In the evening, last December 15, our family gathered in an ER waiting room with no idea what news we would hear from the surgeon when he walked through the door. I said to them, "No matter what happens, we are going to be OK. We have each other. And we have the Lord. And we are going to get through this." I could not have imagined at that time what "no matter what happens" would look like.

Among the unimaginable scenes from that night, there are many that continue to strengthen my heart. Although I did not witness this myself because I was already in Chandler's room, I was told that when the time came that Chandler's siblings were allowed to go in, they joined hands and walked through the ICU doors together, down the hall, to see their brother. There is no greater blessing than seeing your children united in love and declaring, "We are in this together."

As the waiting room filled to capacity throughout the evening, to the point that security told me they would need to start asking people to leave, I was overwhelmed. This was Chandler's village, our village. We would get through this…whatever was to come.

A year later, I can say that we are OK, although now I'm not sure exactly what OK means. It certainly does not mean we are hurting less or remembering less or missing Chandler less. In fact, it's worse in the sense that every day takes us further from our last time seeing Chandler.

Maybe "OK" means we have chosen to continue living, not allowing ourselves to be overtaken by inertia, bitterness, or isolation. We have, I think, allowed one another the space to grieve in our own ways. We talk about Chandler and how much we hate that he's not here. We have an even deeper appreciation for our family than before. Perhaps the definition of "OK" will evolve as we move through our grief process.

Tonight, I am grateful for the shoulders I've cried on today. Well, maybe not shoulders…. I'm too short to reach that high. I am grateful for every single demonstration of care today—every act that said, "You are not alone."

God, there are no words. It's just so hard, too much. My heart hurts. I miss my boy. And in the middle of the sheer weight of this horrific anniversary, there has been genuine laughter. Community. A sense of peace. Thank you for showing up…over and over and over. Amen.

December 16, 2019—Relief After the Virus

It felt very different waking up today than it did yesterday. When I opened my eyes, a sense of relief washed over me as I realized I did not have to live through yesterday again. I had ridden the waves and did not get stuck in the undertow. Today was a new day.

The weight was less today. It was easier to swing my feet onto the floor this morning and walk to my toothbrush. Instead of dreading the next hours and fearing how it would be to stand at the bike memorial the 365th day after the day, my mood was guided by the mundane question, "What do I need to get done at work today?" I welcomed the mundane.

Today versus yesterday is like when you have the stomach flu and are wiped out from throwing up for two days, and then the virus passes. You take a deep breath and realize you are not nauseous for the first time in 48 hours. Relief.

Today, I'm allowing myself to savor the relief after the virus...the calm after the storm.

Today's Chandler-ness:

12/24/99—Last night we were reading the Christmas story and you grinned really big at the picture of baby Jesus and said, "He's got a fat face." Then you wiped off your grin and added, "But don't make fun 'cuz he's the baby Jesus."

December 18, 2019 – The Greatest Gift

The virgin will conceive and give birth to a son, and they will call him Immanuel—which means "God with us."

~Matthew 1:23

This scripture was read so beautifully today during my *Pray as You Go* Advent devotional. The narrator had a soothing voice and a Scottish accent. So to be honest, he could have read the phone book or the menu at Taco Bell, and I would have been lulled into a state of complete and utter relaxation.

Today when he said, "Immanuel—God with us," it struck a familiar cord in my soul.

This time last year, I found myself praying frequently and fervently some version of, "God, we cannot do this without you. We need you." And then rehearsing what I hoped desperately to be true, what I had believed all my life—"Thank you that you are with us." I was in the same company, am still in the same company, as the father in scripture who asked Jesus to heal his tormented son—"I do believe; help my unbelief" (Mark 9:24).

As the days in the ICU wore on, it became more and more clear to me—this is why Christmas matters. If God isn't with us, we're sunk. If He is, everything is different. It became my mantra—God is with me.

I always knew what the Christmas story was about, that it was more than the tale of a young mom who gave birth in a stable to a baby who was visited by some wise men and shepherds. I knew this was the story of God touching earth, intersecting with humanity, in a way that changed everything.

Last Christmas, I experienced personally the necessity of this all being real. It had to be more than a timeless story that has provided a venue for budding child actors and actresses everywhere in oversized robes who pick their noses and forget their lines and drop the baby Jesus while fiddling around with the swaddling clothes falling off the borrowed baby doll. I had nothing if not the hope of a God who cared so much that He would be WITH me in the ICU and at Chandler's memorial, and every day this year that I've tried my best to grieve and live in a way that would honor my son—WWHC.

Today when I heard the "God with us" scripture, I flashed back to the days in the hospital when this Christmas story I'd heard and believed all my life began to grip my heart, to settle into new places in my soul, and to serve as a central truth that would hold me together, no matter what.

A year later, I am more sure than ever—the reality of "God with us" is the greatest gift of all.

Today's Chandler-ness:

7/3/99—Tonight your brother got in trouble for trash mouth and it turns out you had been saying bad words too. So when we did our prayers at bedtime, you prayed, "Jesus, help me not say bad things anymore because You know I love You, and I don't want to have foul language anymore." It was precious.

December 22, 2019—One Stocking

For the past few years, I have hung our stockings, not on the chimney with care, but on the staircase bannister. We use the fireplace so often during the weeks leading up to Christmas, I don't want the stockings to catch on fire or to have to keep moving them on and off each night.

After dinner last night, we decided to switch it up and open gifts by the fire instead of in the room where the Christmas tree stands. We always do stockings before opening the regular gifts, so Charli grabbed the stockings from the staircase and brought them to each of us.

So it wasn't until late last night after everyone had left or gone to bed that I walked into the room where the stockings had been hanging, and I saw it. One stocking left.

Chandler's hand will never reach into that stocking again to grab a sleeve of his favorite golf balls, or socks, or a gas card. The finality. It is breathtaking. I can't think too deeply about it right now. I have to leave some of the sinking in, some of the "never again" for later.

It should have taken longer to unpack our stockings.

Today's Chandler-ness:

11/1/98—You saw me unloading a link sausage from the store, the kind that's tied together at the end and makes a circle—"Mom, you bought a ring of ding."

December 24, 2019—Near-Perfect

It was a near-perfect Christmas Eve.

After a relaxing day enjoying the sights and tastes around the beautiful Christmas-y Santa Fe Plaza, we went to dinner at El

Paragua in Española where Chip was born. Second night in a row of the most off-the-charts food on the planet. Christmas style (half red, half green chile) enchiladas with sopaipillas and homemade apricot jam.

When in New Mexico, we (mostly) unapologetically tempt the limits of our gastrointestinal capacities. On my bedside table at the hotel are Pepcid, Gaviscon, Nexium, and Gas-X. It's worth it.

I did well at dinner. I even held it together during the prayer when Chip choked up. "God, I pray that Chandler knows how much we love him…whatever he's doing right now."

It was good for my heart to look around the table throughout dinner and take in the smiling faces, the laughter, the stories, the deep sense of connection and knowing.

Then it hit me. I went to the restroom, buried my head in my hands, and sobbed. I walked out the front door of the restaurant. Chip caught up with me. I fell into his arms and cried, "I want Chandler here so bad." I didn't even need to say it. We take turns losing it. It was my turn.

It started snowing on our drive back to Santa Fe. Though it was obviously freezing cold, we couldn't let the Christmas Eve snow

go to waste. We parked back at the hotel and decided to take the hotel shuttle to the Christmas Eve Farolito walk on Canyon Road.

We had asked the front desk for the shuttle, and they told us it had arrived. We all rushed out front and saw a tiny purple hotel vehicle. Chip poked his head in the back and said, "This isn't it... there's no back seat." Then he noticed fold-down seats, and we all piled in, as many as could fit in the back. The driver hadn't yet arrived. Chase opened the front door and climbed in. Bent over at a right angle, he said, "There's no passenger seat. I guess I'll just have to crouch over." After waiting for a few minutes, I called the front desk and told them we were in the shuttle waiting for the driver. She replied, "Oh, no, that's not the shuttle!" About that time, the real shuttle pulled up behind us. It was what you would expect from a real shuttle—full-sized seats for plenty of passengers AND a driver. We piled out of the tiny car like a bunch of circus clowns, laughing all the way to the shuttle.

The walk down Canyon Road was magical. Farolitos (candles glowing inside paper bags) line this historic route marked by world-class art galleries and twinkling lights decorating adobe courtyards and gardens. The snow, the lights, and the smell of burning piñon wood conspired to create the quintessential winter wonderland. My heart was full...I was with my people, my amazing people I like and love so much, on this near-perfect Christmas Eve.

My sweet Chandler, having you here would have made it perfect. But I believe, I have to believe, that on this Christmas Eve, you are existing in a realm of sheer perfection, nothing lacking...no tears, no missing, no restrictions on the gravity-defying feats you can do to celebrate this special day. You are experiencing the absolute reality of Immanuel—God with us.

The last line of today's Chandler-ness is as true this Christmas Eve as it was 22 years ago.

Today's Chandler-ness:

(From The Gang section of my mom journal)

12/24/97—Tonight is Christmas Eve. We had a candlelight dinner of posole, chicken noodle soup, and chicken nuggets. We're still working on a Christmas Eve traditional dinner, but since Chip wants posole and the boys hate it and almost can't agree on something they all like, it's still in experimental stages. They played Nintendo (Diddy Kong Racing which they got from Russ, Pat and Tammi) and then we sat around the fire we made in the fireplace and read the Christmas story. Then we acted it out—Chip and I were Mary and Joseph; Chase was the angel who appeared to the shepherds; Chandler was the shepherd; and Chance was baby Jesus. We did great until, as we concluded with "Oh, Come Let Us Adore Him," Chandler started chasing Chile the dog (who was a sheep) with his staff (a cardboard wrapping paper roll) saying, "Bad sheep! Bad sheep!" We also sang and signed "Away in a Manger." The attention span was just about ended, so we wrapped it up. Later we watched the video called *The Nativity*. Then bedtime. I'm hoping even though it's Christmas morning tomorrow you guys will allow us eight hours sleep. Somehow I just feel better knowing I've gotten my eight hours. Thank you, God, for our family and a wonderful Christmas Eve. Help us honor you as we celebrate.

December 25, 2019 – Christmas Day – The First

We made it through the first Christmas.

Last Christmas was its own story...a first in its own rights. But this year, the first without Chandler living and breathing with us... it was beautiful and meaningful and joyous and heartbreaking and incomplete and incomprehensible and so full of missing, there aren't words for it.

Once again, we ate lots of the best food on the planet. At Casa de Chimayo, Chance and I split a plantain mole enchilada and a calabacitos tamale and then ate some of Charli's green chile chicken enchilada. I tried a green chile beer but gave half of it away when I realized the nuances of green chile in the beer disappeared in the bold green chile flavor of the enchilada.

We went to Aunt Val's house after lunch for a white elephant gift exchange game. All parties were happy with their gifts the first time around (or forgot that you could steal another person's gift), so none of the usual stealing, bartering, or begging took place. Well, maybe there was a bit of conflict surrounding the Señor Murphy's piñon fudge that Chip brought—with every intention of not giving it up.

In the end, he stole it back from his mom, Grandma Shari, but out of the goodness of his heart (or maybe due to guilt over setting his bed on fire as a child) agreed to share with her.

We drove back to our hotel and went for a walk around Santa Fe Plaza, then on to the Drury Hotel where the most beautiful views awaited us on the fifth floor. The Santa Fe sunset coupled with traditional luminarias atop adobe buildings set the Santa Fe horizon aglow. The staff at the rooftop bar lit the fire pit for us, a welcome opportunity to warm up while taking in the view before our trek back to the hotel.

Standing around the fire, Chance gave words to what lies deepest in each of our hearts. "The only thing that would make this better… is Chandler."

Today's Chandler-ness:

(From The Gang section of my mom journal)

7/29/96—I must document the messes which have begun to pervade everyday life around here. In a period of two weeks, here's what's transpired. Chandler you poured marshmallows out, poured Rice Krispies out (on the carpet); in one day three glasses of pink lemonade were spilled on the carpet in various places. You attempted to water my silk flower arrangement—with apple juice. Too many juice spills to recall. You colored your scalp magenta with a marker (I guess since you have a buzz cut, you needed to take advantage of it); Chase, you fell asleep with gum in your mouth and you and Chance woke up screaming because you were all sticky. It was everywhere! Chandler, you caked chocolate syrup on the kitchen chairs and table and various places on the carpet. I'm sick of messes!

December 28, 2019—Prayer

I don't pretend to understand the concept of prayer. Maybe I would be presumptuous if I said I did. Communicating with the divine being who created the universe, believing He hears my prayers—the ones shaped into words and otherwise? Hmmm. Understanding, really grasping the breadth and depth and implications and complexities of this interaction, appears to me to be beyond the human pay grade. At least beyond this human's.

I don't understand why some prayers seem to get answered and others don't. Why is it that millions of people can join in prayer for a particular outcome only to see the antithesis of what they had prayed for come to pass? Does this mean there's no reason for people to form armies of prayer for an individual's healing or a nation's reconciliation or any other noble cause? Apparently, the number of people praying doesn't necessarily shape the outcome.

When I was little, I was supposed to have surgery on my eyes because they didn't focus correctly. Mae Walker, the amazing woman who took care of me while my mom worked, said she just couldn't stand to see "her baby" have eye surgery. She hit her knees and prayed up a storm like only Mae could do. She was the person you wanted praying for you. There was no Facebook or Instagram or internet for Mae to summon others into the prayer circle. She just prayed fervently for God to heal my eyes. He did. I never even needed glasses until about age 46 when I noticed they started making the writing on medicine bottles so much smaller!

I've heard before that God always answers prayer. It's either yes, no, or not yet. This is one way we can try to fit the actions, or seeming lack thereof, of God into some understandable framework. In the middle of deep trauma or loss or chronic pain or depression, distilling the responses of God into three discreet categories serves only to bruise a heart that needs to know God is bigger than limits and categories. That His goodness and wisdom transcends our comprehension, and therefore our categories.

A year ago, the ladies at Newport Mesa Church quilted a beautiful blanket for Chandler, reminding him, and us, that with every knot, a prayer had been prayed for him. If the sole meaning behind those prayers was a desired end—Chandler healthy and whole and remaining with us here on earth— they were for nothing. I believe there is more to it than that, and I covet every single prayer that went up for Chandler last December by these kind ladies.

Years ago, I read a book that changed my perspective on prayer—*Toward God* by Michael Casey. His words blew my mind:

"Prayer is larger than any of us. It is less a question of bringing prayer into our hearts than of bringing our hearts into prayer; not drawing water from the sea to fill a bath, but being immersed in an immense ocean and becoming one with it…Prayer is nothing more or less than the interior action of the Trinity at the level of being. This we cannot control. We can only reverently submit."

I will be the first to admit, I like it best when God does what I want Him to do. I'm not pleased that He chose not to answer our prayers to heal Chandler and let him stay here. But still, I will pray. My heart will not allow me to do otherwise. I have prayed with unwavering faith for outcomes that did not happen, and I have prayed with barely the faith of a grain of sand and seen the result I asked for come to pass. In the end, I think the prayer itself was of greater significance than the outcome. The prayer was the action of Father, Son, and Holy Spirit in my heart and soul.

As I said, I don't understand the idea of prayer. What I do know for certain is that every time someone says, "I'm praying for you and your family," I am strengthened and comforted, and I know I'm not alone…we are not alone. And I believe that when I pray, I become immersed in a reality far greater than me.

God, always move my heart toward prayer. When I'm convinced of the absolute power of prayer and when I struggle to believe prayer even matters, move me to pray just the same. Amen.

Today's Chandler-ness:

3/5/99—Chandler, you and I went to Houston last week together to visit Aunt Pat, Russ, and Tammi. One time you said, "I can hold my peepee for eight hours!" We went ice skating, and you'd never been before. I was worried you'd get frustrated and not have fun. Instead, you hit the ice and never looked back. You stopped, did six turns in place, 180s, anything you saw other people do. You told me, "That guy asked me to teach his girlfriend to ice skate, so I teached her." It was a blast watching you.

December 31, 2019–Day Before

We are here. The day before the day.

My heart feels heavy. Really, everything feels heavy. A heaviness unconfined to the space beneath my skin. An external heaviness imposed by a world that is missing Chandler with me. It's in the air, the missing. It slows my steps and suffocates my words. There's a lump in my throat. I have to remember to breathe…to breathe deeply.

I hate the dark, a reminder of the last dark before I kissed Chandler's warm cheek one final time.

Yesterday my dear friend gave me a card with this scripture hand-written inside:

Do not be anxious about anything, but in every situation, by prayer and petition, with thanksgiving, present your requests to God. And the peace of God, which transcends all understanding, will guard your hearts and your minds in Christ Jesus.

~Philippians 4:6, 7 (NIV)

Throughout this year, many have shared this scripture with me, and it has been a great source of comfort. Today I am leaning into it with every bit of strength and resolve I possess. My heart still aches. Maybe I'm doing it wrong. Maybe the key is not strength and resolve but surrender. Or maybe, the peace that guards my heart in Christ Jesus is not so much a feeling or instant healing from a broken heart. Maybe it is the assurance that despite the pain, all is well…with Chandler and with my soul.

January 1, 2020—Imagine

What do you write on the first anniversary of watching your son take his last breath?

It's just too much. Too much anguish and sorrow and crying and missing and hurting and grieving and…just too much.

In some ways, it seems so long ago. But mostly, it seems like it's all right here, right now…like I've just relived the events of last December 15 through January 1. Maybe I want it to stay near. I don't want to acknowledge the distance between the last day with Chandler and now.

When I woke up today, I prayed, "God, give me peace today. Help me do this." You know in your head you will still be standing at the end of the day. But your heart isn't convinced.

Today, I allowed myself to cry…to just feel what I needed to feel. And I also said to myself, "Enough. You can cry more tomorrow." I had to allow myself some space to step away from the intense, profound pain. This is a marathon, not a sprint. I can't keep the same pace of grieving all day, every day. Especially today. It has been a long, difficult holiday season, starting with Thanksgiving followed by December 15 then Christmas and, of course, today…New Year's Day. It makes sense that I would feel all the pain on this day. But I just couldn't do it. I have wept and ached. And I have joked and laughed. I could not let the events of January 1, 2019, completely possess me today. It would have been too much heaped on top of too much.

As is so often the case in life, today was the best and the worst. The best because I was surrounded by family. The best because friends and long-distance family members checked in and sent prayers and words of encouragement. The best because Chandler's friend RJ dropped by to give me a hug and bring flowers to cheer me up. The best because another of Chandler's friends came by and told us he has been clean and sober for six months and is now living authentically into who he was meant to be. I can't think of a better way to honor Chandler today.

Given what Chandler went through a year ago today, was it the worst day of his life? Or was it the best?

If everything I've built my life on is true, every bit of suffering

Chandler endured on January 1, 2019, was instantaneously erased from his memory, and everything dark was enveloped in the brightest, purest light the instant he transitioned from this life to the next.

I imagine his heart finding its true home as he entered a new living reality of perfect—absolutely perfect—love. I imagine him discovering that gravity was no longer an obstacle. I imagine him being greeted by all those who were waiting for him there. Grandparents he never got to meet and those he knew in this life like Grandpa Bill and Grandma Trinnie. Friends he lost too soon. And Uncle Brett, who probably grabbed him straightaway and took him to ride the craziest celestial waves ever.

I imagine Chandler meeting Phillip and Lisa and Jojo and Brandon and Tanya and Kenzie and Haley and others because maybe when moms inducted into this shitty club find friendship and strength with one another, the Lord allows their children to find each other as well.

And I imagine one day when I take my last breath as Chandler did, I will see him again. I will run to him first. My sweet, dimpled boy who asked me to marry him. My strong, compassionate, thoughtful son who impacted so many because he chose to listen, to be present, to accept people unconditionally. My Chandler Man will give me one of those special hugs reserved only for his mom.

Today, 365 days later…I can only imagine.

Today's Chandler-ness:

10/5/98—Seeing an old picture of Chip in a toga for a dress-up party—"Why was Dad dressed up like that guy that lives up in the sky with God?"

January 2, 2020—Year Two—A New Thing

And so begins year two.

After January 1, 2019, I made a commitment to write every single day for a year. My purpose was threefold:

1. to honor Chandler—his life and his desire to become a writer
2. to work through my grief
3. and to encourage, inspire, or in some way help others.

It has not been easy, but I did it. Most of the time, I wrote at night, my way of processing the day's thoughts, feelings, and events. Some nights, the words flew onto the keyboard rapid fire, my fingers striving to keep up with my heart's expedient need to express itself. Some nights, I was exhausted, and the last thing I wanted to do was sit down and write. Most of the time, my writing was cathartic. Other times, my compulsory appointment with my laptop yanked me back into the reality of my loss and pain after some daytime hours of almost blissful distraction.

It is time for a change. It is bittersweet for me. I've grown accustomed to my routine. Even when it has required all that was left, or more, of a day's emotional and physical reserves, it has been like a security blanket for me. And, quite frankly, I've grown accustomed to the daily responses that have encouraged my heart and reminded me continuously that I'm not alone. Perhaps most of all, this has been a project Chandler and I have done together—I have felt he was with me and cheering me on. When I was about to fall asleep and couldn't fathom arranging my thoughts into a halfway coherent message, I would remind myself, "You are doing this for Chandler—one year, every single day."

This year has reminded me how much I love to write and how much I desire to make a difference through my writing. So I must continue to write. But now my blog post will happen weekly rather than daily. I have wondered these past few months how this will feel. Will some of the weight be lifted without a nightly appointment to sit down and stare straight into the face of this new uninvited reality?

Tomorrow will be the first day in over 365 days that I will not write a blog post. The thought is freeing and frightening.

Yesterday, someone sent Chip and me the same scripture that was in the first reading in the devotional I've chosen for 2020.

Forget the former things; do not dwell on the past. See, I am doing a new thing! Now it springs up; do you not perceive it? I am making a way in the wilderness and streams in the wasteland.
~Isaiah 43:18, 19 (NIV)

Standing at the threshold of a new year, I am ready for a new thing.

My primary goal for this year is to publish the *First, Brush Your Teeth* blogs from 2018-2019. I want something I can hold in my hands and say, "This is a gift to my son, inspired by his life." And I want it in a form that can be easily shared with others. Some of my greatest inspiration and strength this year has come through a daily reader written by a woman who was clearly familiar with grief and loss. Her honest emotions and thoughts closely mirrored mine, and I knew if she made it, I could too. Nothing would bring me greater satisfaction and joy than knowing I was able to come alongside others in this same way and be a companion to them in their loss.

The search for a new normal continues. There is still nothing normal about telling the waiter there are six of us instead of seven. Nothing normal about starting a group family text and making sure I don't inadvertently add Chandler. I've done it, and the sinking feeling in the gut…it's horrible. Nothing normal about holidays and special days without a shirtless Chandler strolling into the kitchen a few minutes late and heading straight toward the stove for food.

We will see what year two holds.

God, thank You for Your constant presence, especially demonstrated through people—such good, caring people—this past year. In year two, help me follow Your lead and welcome the new with open heart and open arms. It is all only by Your grace. Amen.

Today's Chandler-ness:

11/14/99—When people get married, they don't do a French kiss. They just do an American kiss and make it last for a long time.

Here and Now

As I write this, we are just a few weeks away from Chandler's birthday, our third without him. For most writing projects, I have

Chandler Willis Espinoza
July 2, 1993 – January 1, 2019
Unafraid, you always went first.

been able to dive in, work until midnight, get up and do it again until the project is finished. I've never missed a writing deadline. Not so with this labor of love and anguish. I've had to take long breaks, to come up for air. It has been a heavy, emotionally draining process. Although the publishing of this book marks the fulfillment of a deep desire, I have found myself engaging in some major avoidant behavior because it's just been so damn hard re-living everything over and over, starting with December 15, 2018, the day everything changed. Instead of sitting down at my computer, I would mop the floor, search for tasty new recipes, walk the puppies, get back on work emails, do some online shopping, or obsess over pretty much anything that seemed like a valid (or even semi-valid) distraction from the work at hand.

How does it feel now?

From the earliest days of grief, I wanted to know from others who have walked this path—what is it like in a week, a month, a year? I still want to know. What is it like after five years? Ten years?

Here are my own personal feelings after two and a half years without Chandler.

I still find it incredibly difficult to write or utter the phrase "after Chandler died." It just feels too final. Too real. I tend to dance around the words and land on something lighter like "after Chandler passed" or "after Chandler's accident" or even "after Chandler..." trailing off so as not to have to fill in the blank.

It still feels close in many ways. When I say that Chandler has been gone for two and a half years, parts of me don't believe it. Some things in my life that happened that long ago have exited my mind. Others are there but rarely surface. Losing Chandler...it still feels as close as my breath.

I realize I don't glance over at Chandler's memorial bench on the way home from work every single day and have thoughts of what happened at that intersection on December 15, 2018. But I do most days.

These days, the 1st or the 15th of the month rolls around, and often I don't even realize it. For so long, those dates were red letter for me. It's like I may as well have put them as recurring events with an alarm on my calendar. They were on my radar big time.

It still doesn't seem possible that I had four kids here. And now I only have three. How does that happen? It feels like it shouldn't.

What have I learned?

Family is everything. Within our family, we have varying political, social, and religious viewpoints. But we have chosen to focus on the one thing that is most important. We are a family, and we love and support one another in the best ways we know how.

Whether your family is related by blood or is a family forged simply through navigating life together, it is a gift. Forgive, listen, suspend judgement, appreciate, encourage, and hug. Please, don't forget to hug.

I have learned at a depth I never could have imagined that God is WITH me. He is WITH us. And He is WITH us mostly through other PEOPLE.

I have learned that people want to help. If someone offers a hand, we deprive them of a blessing if we refuse. And here's the thing. When you are grieving, you don't feel like writing thank you cards. The people who show up for you for the right reasons don't expect them.

I have learned that God's character and presence is not constrained by my right actions. He doesn't wait for me to pray enough, read my Bible enough, or go to church enough to show up for me. In fact, I have engaged in every one of those actions at times throughout my life because I was afraid if I didn't, God would not be there for me. I believe now more than ever that God is loving, gracious, merciful, good, generous, and kind. Those attributes are not contingent upon my actions. This is key to remember when you can barely take a breath much less engage in worship or read your Bible or do any of the other things that purport to put us in good standing with the Creator of the universe.

I have learned that you can make it through the worst of nightmares one minute, one hour, one day at a time.

When the sun rises and you struggle to find the strength to face the morning, don't think too far ahead or try to tackle all the hours at once. First, just brush your teeth.

From Chandler's India Journal

Even when times are seemingly unbearable, take a minute to acknowledge all of the circumstances/conditions that had to come together to land your two feet right where they are. You'll be shocked at how much better you feel.

~

Studying is to smart as observing is to wise.

~

In the West, the distance between point A and point B is merely a distance. In the East, the distance between point A and B is an experience.

~

I love nature. Something in me tells me I'm an old soul because the architecture of the grandest buildings does not match at all the intricacies of a single blade of grass, let alone the tree rooted in it.

~

In my past, I have encountered people who say doing charitable acts without pure intentions is worse than doing nothing at all. But I say the person with selfish intentions of helping others is still helping others, and you're doing nothing by judging the value of someone else's efforts. Plus, if you practice giving as a habit, selfish or selfless intentions aside, those actions and lifestyle will materialize into a pure intention. If it doesn't, nobody's happiness is at jeopardy but your own. After all, you are still helping others.

I have been told that I must hold onto what I know to be true. If I carefully analyze that command, what it really requests of me is to remain arrogant and static in my spiritual journey for truth.

Jesus was enlightened. He saw his enemies as his brothers and sisters that were only poisoned by their own ignorance. This is true love and compassion. We miss the objective of following His example because we're so caught up in what belief in Him gets us—into heaven.

We should pay attention to the miracles that are right in front of us.

More Chandler-ness

April 1, 1998

You came to me at bedtime and said, "Mom, I'm going to brush my teeth 'cuz I love you, and I don't want to get holes in my teeth before I marry you."

October 5, 1998

Chandler: I saw a guy on TV, and his hemorrhoids made him strong.

Mom: My hemorrhoids don't make me strong.

Chandler: But they made him strong.

It finally dawned on me.

Mom: You mean steroids?

Chandler: Yeah, steroids.

April 22, 1998

The other day you had circles under your eyes from lack of sleep, and I told you it was bedtime. The next day, you said, "Jesus can do anything He wants, and He's so powerful. But when He gets circles under his eyes, He has to go to bed."

August 13, 1999

"You know what I like most about Jesus and God? It's that they love us so much. And we love them back. I like lots of stuff about Jesus and God."

November 14, 1999

"When people get married, they don't do a French kiss. They just do an American kiss and make it last for a long time."

February 8, 2001

Yesterday you came home from school and (as you peed in the bathroom with the door open) you nonchalantly said, "Mom, you know what seems to be a problem? There's this kid that sits next to me in class, and he smells like boogers."

OCTOBER 15, 1998

Mom: "Who are some important people in your life?"
Chandler: "Everybody, cuz God made them."

About the Author

Lisa is a voracious, life-long learner and will happily engage in conversations with anyone anytime about her latest topics of interest—currently the enneagram, raising puppies, gluten-free cooking (or better yet, *not* cooking), or anything related to health and fitness. With honesty, humor, and wisdom born of some tough life lessons, Lisa encourages and inspires others through her music, her writing, and her speaking. Among her favorite pastimes—swinging in her egg chair with a book and a kombucha, hiking, having all her family in the same room, and trying pretty much anything new.

Connect with Lisa online at:

www.lisaespinoza.com

Also Available From

WordCrafts Press

An Introspective Journey
by Paula Sarver

I Wish Someone Had Told Me
by Barbie Loflin

Pressing Forward
by April Poynter

An Unlikely Evangelist
by Paula K. Parker

A Scarlet Cord of Hope
by Sheryl Griffin

The Power of Hope
by Patty Mason

www.wordcrafts.net